Protecting
the
Homeland
2006/2007

Protecting
the
Homeland
2006/2007

Michael d'Arcy

Michael O'Hanlon

Peter Orszag

Jeremy Shapiro

James Steinberg

BROOKINGS INSTITUTION PRESS
Washington, D.C.

Library of Congress Cataloging-in-Publication data

Protecting the homeland 2006/2007 / Michael d'Arcy . . . [et al.].
    p.   cm.
  Includes index.
  ISBN-13: 978-0-8157-6459-5 (paper ed. : alk. paper)
  ISBN-10: 0-8157-6459-6 (paper ed. : alk. paper)
1. Terrorism—United States—Prevention. 2. National security—United States.
3. Internal security—United States. 4. War on Terrorism, 2001– I. D'Arcy, Michael
II. Brookings Institution. III. Title.
  HV6432.P77 2006
  363.325'70973—dc22   2006002107

9 8 7 6 5 4 3 2 1

Typeset in Minion

Composition by Cynthia Stock
Silver Spring, Maryland

Printed by R. R. Donnelley
Harrisonburg, Virginia

CONTENTS

Foreword   vii

Preface   xi

1   Introduction   1
MICHAEL O'HANLON AND JEREMY SHAPIRO

2   Intelligence Reform   17
JAMES STEINBERG

3   International Cooperation on Homeland Security   47
JEREMY SHAPIRO

4   Protecting Infrastructure and Providing Incentives
for the Private Sector to Protect Itself   73
PETER ORSZAG AND MICHAEL O'HANLON

5   Border Protection   96
MICHAEL O'HANLON

6   The Roles of DoD and First Responders   113
MICHAEL O'HANLON

7   Technology Development and
Transportation Security   129
MICHAEL D'ARCY

8 Countermeasures against Specific Weapons   155
       MICHAEL D'ARCY

9 Conclusion   184
       MICHAEL D'ARCY

       Appendix   193
       Figures
       A-1. Doses of Inhalation Anthrax Antibiotics Stockpiled   194
       A-2. Doses of Smallpox Vaccine Stockpiled   194
       A-3. Number of U.S. Border Patrol Agents   195
       A-4. Number of First Responders Trained   195
       A-5. Percentage of Shipping Containers Inspected   196
       A-6. Number of Foreign Students Enrolled in U.S. Institutions
            of Higher Education   197

       Tables
       A-1. Homeland Security Budget Authority, by Agency   198
       A-2. Homeland Security Funding, by Budget Function   200
       A-3. Department of Homeland Security Spending and
            Credit Activity   201

       Index   203

FOREWORD

Brookings prides itself on combining the ability to think about the big picture over the long term while being alert to the broader implications of issues that, sometimes literally, explode in our face. Homeland security is a perfect example. We were fast off the mark after 9/11, largely because our scholars had been focused on terrorism and its causes for a long time. Within six months, we produced *Protecting the American Homeland.* The entire volume now in your hands is not just a sequel or an update to that earlier one; it is an entirely fresh look at the ongoing challenge. Like its predecessor, it relies on Brookings's defining strength—our ability to bring together a multidisciplinary team of experts in science, economics, defense, intelligence, and international affairs to offer an integrated analysis that is both broad and deep in an effort to address the new challenges facing our nation.

The team of authors responsible for this book includes Jim Steinberg, the dean of the Lyndon Johnson School of Public Affairs at the University of Texas and former director of our Foreign Policy Studies program, whose government experiences, culminating in the post of deputy national security adviser and work for the Markle Foundation, give him great insight into intelligence work in the counterterrorism effort; Michael d'Arcy, a physicist with a very good feel for how technology can help in the homeland security effort as well as a good recognition of its limits; Jeremy Shapiro, from the Europe Center at Brookings, who has studied European counterterrorism policy extensively; Mike O'Hanlon, our main defense analyst, who also has worked on homeland security for half a decade; and Peter Orszag, one of the country's best economists, who has been coming to grips with the critical question of how the private sector might better protect itself against possible terrorist strikes in an efficient and affordable way. (The authors are extremely grateful to Richard Falkenrath, John Gannon, and Admiral James Loy for their very helpful suggestions, although their help, of course, implies no responsibility for the contents of this book. And while the book's five authors share responsibility for its contents, each chapter was drafted by one or two people who shaped the chapter's principal messages. Inquiries should, where possible, be directed accordingly.)

This book emphasizes that while progress has been made and despite the lack of recent attacks in this country, Americans must maintain a national sense of urgency. Much remains to be done. The creation of the Department of Homeland Security, the new mega-agency, was an important step toward the institution building required to organize against new threats, but no one should confuse the creation of DHS with the solution of the homeland security problem. Hurricane Katrina revealed that FEMA, one part of the new DHS, clearly had not benefited from consolidation and may even have been weakened—something that several of the authors and other Brookings colleagues warned against in 2002 when the DHS was first proposed.

The authors present a number of analyses and recommendations on topics as disparate as how to defend against the surface-to-air-missile threat to airplanes, how to use biometrics more effectively in passports and visas, how many additional border inspectors to add to existing ranks, and how to further reorganize the intelligence community to cope with the terrorist threat. They also flag the important point that this is not a federal government project alone. The federal government must both integrate its efforts more fully with those of state and local governments and step up coordination with other nations on critical issues such as terrorist watch lists, border control activities, cargo inspections, and preparations against biological attack. Most important, the authors focus their analysis and prescriptions on ensuring that we not only "fight the last war"—prepare for events that the country already has experienced—but also address a number of vulnerabilities that terrorists could seek to exploit in the future (such as those of chemical plants and the hazardous cargo transportation industry).

Homeland security efforts will remain a tough struggle in the trenches, requiring continual adaptation in government organizational efforts, international cooperation, border defense, and preventive law enforcement. We at Brookings hope this volume will help flesh out both the broad strokes and the specific policies needed to ensure success in this critically important field.

STROBE TALBOTT
President

Washington, D.C.
February 2006

Preface

The Bush Administration's 2007 Budget Request

Just as this book was going to press, the Bush administration released its budget proposal and accompanying conceptual framework for homeland security for the fiscal year beginning on October 1, 2006. (More quantitative details of the proposal are found in the appendix.)

The broad contours of the plan are as follows. First, the overall homeland security budget would be 8 percent larger than it was in 2006, or more than 5 percent in inflation-adjusted dollars. Second, substantial increases would occur in the area of Customs and Border Protection as well as Immigration and Customs Enforcement, funding, among other things, an increase of 12 percent (1,500 people) in the number of Border Patrol agents. Third, according to the Office of Management and Budget, for the first time more than half of all funds flowing to state and local partners would be distributed on the basis of an assessment of the risks that they face.

To be more specific, the administration is requesting $58.3 billion in total budget authority for homeland security for 2007. Just under half of that amount, or about $28 billion, is for the Department of Homeland Security (DHS). More than one-quarter, or almost $17 billion, is for the Department of Defense (DoD), which, because of an accounting change, is now credited with roughly twice as much homeland security spending as it used to be. Other major recipients are the Department of Health and Human Services ($4.6 billion in homeland security funding, largely for vaccines and other bioterrorism-related preparations); the Department of Justice ($3.3 billion, for the FBI and other entities); the Department of Energy ($1.7 billion); the Department of State ($1.2 billion); and the Department of Agriculture ($650 million).

To get a sense of how much has changed over the years—after first deducting DoD's share of the budget to eliminate the vagaries of accounting changes and to focus on domestic-oriented agencies—the 2007 request is just under $42 billion. The amount has grown fairly slowly since 2004, but it is far greater than the pre-9/11 total of about $15 billion and the mid-1990s level of less than $10 billion.

In one final detail, not all of that $42 billion is to be provided through annual appropriations bills. About $2.5 billion is so-called mandatory funding, which is not subject to the annual appropriations process. Roughly $6 billion is not provided by taxpayers at all; it comes to the government through user fees instead.

The administration's 2007 budget proposal for homeland security devotes much of its justification to the related but distinct issues of immigration reform and Hurricane Katrina relief. In other words, homeland security programs are now being justified in large part for reasons other than counterterrorism. This change of emphasis is politically as well as substantively significant. It also underscores one of the main arguments made here—that homeland security activities overlap a great deal with other functions of government. That reality may muddy the waters for those interested in counterterrorism; on the other hand, it may also create opportunities. Policies that are designed to protect the country from attack may also be designed to help achieve other desirable purposes. That fact can help policymakers decide which new homeland security functions are worthy of funding, since not all possible protective measures can or should be supported.

Turning from broad numbers to more specific concepts and initiatives, the 2007 budget request features, as noted, an increase of 1,500 Border Patrol agents—implying an overall increase in their numbers of about 40 percent since 9/11, according to the government. Such an increase would go some distance toward satisfying a recommendation made in O'Hanlon's chapter on border protection. Nearly $1 billion in Coast Guard procurement has been requested, consistent with some of the arguments in this book and previous Brookings efforts. The Federal Emergency Management Agency would receive a budget increase that would restore funding to the 2005 level of just over $3 billion. Some $200 million would be added to the DHS budget for the Domestic Nuclear Detection Office, including important R&D activities that Michael d'Arcy examines here in some detail. The proposed several tens of millions of dollars in increased funding to improve airport security would continue to allow deployment of technologies such as the explosive "sniffers" that many American travelers have begun to get acquainted with.

Some initiatives seem quite modest in scope relative to the scale of the underlying problem or challenge. The budget would provide $60 million for efforts to improve the interoperability of the U.S.-VISIT program's database and other terrorist databases. That is an important objective, as discussed in Steinberg's chapter and elsewhere, but linking watch lists is only one of many that should be pursued within the broader information technology arena. The proposed increase in funding for vaccines and medications of more than $100 million is generous on one level, but it does not directly address the potential need for a more fundamental change in how the nation plans to quickly produce (and distribute) vaccines once research is completed (especially in the event of an acute crisis in which speedy response was important, as d'Arcy describes). A mere $10 million is allotted to helping improve chemical plant security through an information clearinghouse, even though, as Orszag and O'Hanlon argue in chapter 4, this and other private sector vulnerabilities remain quite serious and largely unaddressed. No additional initiative appears to be in the works for cargo security (though the chapters in this book are not in complete accord about the feasibility of convincing America's overseas partners to drastically increase the number of containers receiving focused inspections, as Shapiro's chapter in particular makes clear).

In other cases the administration's relatively restrained budget plan would seem to make very good sense, as with its more focused and streamlined effort to help state and local governments improve their responsiveness to terrorist actions. We agree with the need to establish priorities in homeland security as well as the desirability of placing a greater emphasis on prevention than on consequence management, and this budget proposal is consistent with both of those goals.

In short, the 2007 budget generally reflects more continuity than change after the major upheavals of the earlier part of the decade. The manner in which it is presented also hints at the waning public support for homeland security activities unless they are tied, wherever possible, to other national priorities.

MICHAEL O'HANLON
February 2006

Protecting
the
Homeland
2006/2007

1

INTRODUCTION

MICHAEL O'HANLON AND JEREMY SHAPIRO

How good have America's defenses against terrorism become in the years since September 11, 2001? The absence of any further attacks on American soil suggests that the country's security has improved. That fact is likely due to a combination of offensive military and law enforcement operations that have left al Qaeda and associated jihadist groups at least temporarily unable to attempt major strikes in the United States, and perhaps to some extent good luck as well. The subject of homeland security is so new that it is difficult to assess progress at the analytical level. And in Washington, it has also become a politically charged question in a country that is increasingly polarized along partisan lines.

Four years into the war on terrorism, homeland security is becoming not just an issue of immediate urgency but one of enduring importance. With that in mind, the authors of this book review the progress made in defending the U.S. homeland in the last four years, assess the country's remaining vulnerabilities, and introduce some new policy initiatives to improve U.S. security.

It is difficult to offer any firm judgment about the net effect of U.S. efforts to date. On one level, an extraordinary amount has been done. A multitude of specific initiatives, to protect everything from cargo to infrastructure, have gone from being mere ideas to being operational programs—at, by bureaucratic standards, astonishing speed. At the same time, entire new bureaucracies, such as the

Department of Homeland Security (DHS) and the Transportation Security Administration, have emerged into large functioning organizations. Even in the face of tragedies like September 11, governments are rarely capable of reacting so rapidly and so radically to newly perceived challenges.

But clearly much remains to be done. The quiescence of the last four years cannot obscure the fact that determined and ruthless enemies, inspired by the ideology of al Qaeda and the example of September 11, remain intent on carrying out major strikes against American targets. Moreover, for all of the federal government's activity, there remain pockets of puzzling inactivity and many glaring deficiencies in the efforts undertaken to date. State and local governments, widely acknowledged to be critical to both prevention of attacks and management of the consequences, have not been sufficiently integrated into federal efforts. Similarly, the private sector has only begun to contribute to homeland security. As a result, targets that ultimately need to be protected at the local level—skyscrapers and chemical plants, for example—have inconsistent protection or none. Terrorists continue to slip across international borders because no permanent regime has been created for gathering and sharing information, even with some of America's closest allies.

Even within the federal government, obvious problems remain. The Department of Homeland Security was created in large part to address a key pre-9/11 government failure—the so-called "connect-the-dots" problem. That image is meant to imply, of course, that the information necessary to prevent terrorist attacks often exists in pieces throughout the government but is never integrated in a way that reveals its significance. However, creating the Department of Homeland Security has proven a more daunting task than initially imagined. Although its accomplishments to date have actually been reasonable by normal standards of institution building, they leave much to be desired and much to be done. Hurricane Katrina, for example, revealed that whatever else the creation of DHS might have done, it certainly did not improve the Federal Emergency Management Agency's near-term response capacity for disasters, despite a budget increase.

The key challenge at this juncture is clearly not just to eliminate remaining vulnerabilities but also to establish priorities. This book attempts to do that. It is written in the form of individual chapters by different authors; taken together, the chapters compose not so much an alternative strategy as an agenda for change in terms of a number of specific proposals.

Where We Are Today

Since the attacks of September 11, 2001, a good deal has been done to improve the safety of Americans. Much of that improvement has come from offensive operations abroad—the military overthrow of the Taliban and associated attacks against al Qaeda, as well as the intelligence and covert operations conducted by the United States in conjunction with key allies such as Pakistan. These steps have reduced the threat of the kind of attacks the country suffered so tragically more than four years ago.

Homeland security efforts have improved too. Now aware of the harm that terrorists that can inflict, Americans are more alert, providing a first, crucial line of defense. Air travel is much safer, following measures such as screening all passenger luggage, installing hardened cockpit doors on all large American commercial aircraft, employing thousands of air marshals, and arming some pilots on commercial and cargo flights.

Intelligence sharing has improved, especially concerning information about specific individuals suspected of terrorist ties, through increased integration of databases and greater collaboration between the FBI and the intelligence community—the Central Intelligence Agency (CIA), National Security Agency (NSA), and so forth. These initial efforts have now been reinforced by the passage of the Intelligence Reform and Terrorism Prevention Act of 2004. Such database linkages can enable offensive operations abroad; they can also assist greatly in the more defensive, but equally critical, domain of homeland security operations.

The share of FBI resources devoted to counterterrorism has doubled, and the combined total of CIA and FBI personnel working on terrorist financing alone has increased from less than a dozen to more than 300 since September 2001.[1] International cooperation in sharing information on suspected terrorists has improved, extending beyond countries that have been helpful over many years, such as France and Britain, to include many other states, such as Pakistan and Saudi Arabia, that now take the threat more seriously.

Additional efforts have also been initiated, a number in response to the 2001 anthrax attacks and others in response to information gained in prisoner interrogations and other intelligence efforts. Suspicious ships entering U.S. waters are now screened more frequently. The country's exposure to biological attacks has been lessened by stockpiling of hundreds of millions of doses of antibiotics and enough smallpox vaccine for every man, woman, and child in the United States.[2] Oversight rules have been tightened on labs working with biological materials, though actual implementation of those rules, including completion of background checks on lab employees, has lagged.[3] Terrorism insurance is now backstopped by a new federal program. Certain types of major infrastructure, such as well-known bridges and tunnels, are protected by police and National Guard forces during terrorism alerts. Nuclear reactors have better protection than before.[4] Federal agencies are required to have security programs for their information technology networks, and many private firms have backed up their headquarters and their databanks so that operations could continue after the catastrophic loss of a main site.[5]

The United States has prepared fairly well to fight the last war—that is, to stop the kinds of attacks that it has already experienced. However, much less has been done to thwart other kinds of plausible strikes. It made sense to move quickly to prevent al Qaeda, with its long-standing interest in airplanes, from easily repeating the 9/11 attacks. But it is time to do a more comprehensive and forward-looking job of protecting the American people.

Al Qaeda may not be as capable as before of "spectacular" attacks in coming years. But it is certainly still capable of using explosives and small arms, with considerable lethality. It may be able to use surface-to-air missiles and other methods of attack as well.[6] There have not been more attacks on the American homeland since 9/11, but according to an October 2005 speech by President Bush, the United States has disrupted three attempted al Qaeda strikes inside the United States and intercepted at least five more terrorist efforts to case targets or infiltrate the country.[7] Moreover, the years 2002, 2003, and 2004 have been among the most lethal in the history of global terrorism, with attacks afflicting a wide swath of countries, from Spain to Morocco, Tunisia, Saudi Arabia, Pakistan, and Indonesia—and, of course, Iraq.[8] The pattern continued in 2005, and the July 7 attacks in London that year reminded Americans of their continued vulnerability and demonstrated to America's enemies the potentially dramatic effects of even small-scale attacks.[9]

A UN study in early 2005 argued that al Qaeda continues to have easy access to financial resources and bomb-making materials.[10] There were serious worries that al Qaeda would use truck bombs to destroy key financial institutions in New York, Newark, and Washington in 2004.[11] The "shoe bomber," Richard Reid, attempted to destroy an airplane headed to the United States in 2002.[12] U.S. intelligence reports in early 2005 suggested the possibility of attacks using private aircraft or helicopters.[13] Al Qaeda prisoner interviewers and confiscated documents suggested other possible attacks, ranging from blowing up gas stations to poisoning water supplies, using crop dusters to spread biological weapons, and detonating radioactive "dirty bombs."[14] And according to Richard Falkenrath, former homeland security deputy adviser, the country's chemical industry, as well as much of its ground transportation infrastructure, remains quite vulnerable.[15]

Although al Qaeda has been weakened at the top, it remains extremely dangerous.[16] It is now less a vertical organization and more a symbol of an ideology uniting loosely affiliated local groups that share similar goals—and that, like terrorist groups in general, watch and learn from each other.[17] Former CIA director George Tenet put it succinctly in 2004: "Successive blows to al Qaeda's central leadership have transformed the organization into a loose collection of regional networks that operate more autonomously."[18] There are benefits from this dispersal of al Qaeda; for example, the near-term risk of sophisticated catastrophic attacks has probably declined as a result. But the risk of smaller and sometimes quite deadly strikes clearly has not—and the possibility of further catastrophic attacks may well increase in the future.

The benefits gained by depriving al Qaeda of its sanctuary in Afghanistan may not be permanent. Over the years, al Qaeda has shown enormous adaptability. It may ultimately learn to reconstitute itself with a less formal and more virtual, horizontal network. It may also learn how to avoid terrorist watch lists with some effectiveness by using new recruits—possibly including women, non-Arabs, and European passport holders—to conduct future attacks against Western countries.[19] The United States is fortunate not to have, as far as it can determine, many al Qaeda cells presently on its soil, as several European countries do. It will be challenging, however, to keep things that way.[20]

In response to a question about whether he was surprised that there had not been another attack on U.S. soil since 9/11, Tom Ridge, then the secretary of homeland security said, "I'm grateful. That's a better way to put it . . . many things have been done that have altered their [the terrorists'] environment. . . . But maybe they just weren't ready. They are strategic thinkers. Even if we've altered their environment and our environment here, they aren't going to go away. They're just going to think of another way to go at the same target or look for another target."[21] CIA director Porter Goss told Congress in February 2005: "It may be only a matter of time before al Qaeda or another group attempts to use chemical, biological, radiological, and nuclear weapons."[22] DHS has conducted "red cell" exercises involving a diverse range of creative outside thinkers to contemplate new ways that al Qaeda might attack, but policy responses to such possibilities have typically been limited in scope and scale.[23]

The Iraq war, whatever its merits, appears not to have alleviated the global terrorism problem. In fact, it is quite possible that it has made it worse by aiding al Qaeda's recruiting efforts and providing an opportunity for a core of hardened terrorists to hone their skills and tighten their organizational networks. To quote Goss again, "Islamic extremists are exploiting the Iraqi conflict to recruit new anti-U.S. jihadists. These jihadists who survive will leave Iraq experienced and focused on acts of urban terrorism."[24] The National Intelligence Council reached a similar conclusion in its 2004 report.[25]

It is simply not possible to defend a large, open, advanced society from all possible types of terrorism. The United States contains more than a half-million bridges, 500 skyscrapers, nearly 200,000 miles of natural gas pipelines, more than 2,800 power plants—the list of critical infrastructure alone is far too long to protect everything, to say nothing of subways, restaurants, movie theaters, schools, and malls.[26] Certain special measures, such as providing tight security and even electronic jamming (against the possibility of global positioning system–guided munitions attack) around the nation's 104 nuclear power plants, clearly cannot, at reasonable cost, be extended to all possible targets.[27]

But to say that the nation cannot do everything is not to argue for inaction. There is a strong case for taking additional steps to reduce the risk of catastrophic attack. Al Qaeda's leadership seems to prefer such attacks for their symbolic effect and potential political consequences; it is also such tragedies that most jeopardize the country's overall well-being.

Catastrophic attacks include, of course, those that cause large numbers of direct casualties. They also include strikes causing few casualties but serious ripple effects, especially in the economic domain. If a shoulder-launched surface-to-air missile took down an airplane, casualties might be modest—depending on the plane, only a few dozen people might be killed—but the effects on the nation's air travel could be devastating and longer lasting than those of September 11, 2001. Similarly, the use in an urban area of a weapon that uses a conventional explosive to disperse radioactive material would be unlikely to kill many people, but it could cause mass panic and would probably require a very costly and time-consuming cleanup and spur the adoption of disruptive security measures throughout the country.[28]

Even in areas where homeland security has improved, deficiencies often remain. For example, while antibiotic stocks for addressing an anthrax attack are now fairly robust, means of quickly delivering the antibiotics appear still to be lacking.[29] In the domain of air travel, passengers are not generally screened for explosives, cargo carried on commercial jets is generally not inspected, and private aircraft face minimal security scrutiny. Perhaps most of all, whatever the security improvements made by U.S. carriers, fewer have been made by many foreign carriers that transport large numbers of Americans to and from the United States. Moreover, longer-term worries about biological attacks remain acute, since there could be many types of infectious agents for which antidotes and vaccines would prove unavailable (or nonexistent) when they were most needed. And as noted, the private sector has, for the most part, done very little to protect itself.[30]

It would be a mistake to assume that the creation of the Department of Homeland Security will automatically lead to better protection against such threats. Such institutional reorganizations can distract attention from efforts to identify remaining key U.S. vulnerabilities and mitigate them.[31] These problems were, of course, witnessed during and after Hurricane Katrina in 2005, despite the substantial increase in resources that FEMA received after 9/11.

Carrying out a major overhaul of government when the threat to the nation is so acute is a risky proposition—and it is not the way that the country has typically responded to national crises. The Department of Defense was not created during World War II, when military leaders had more immediate tasks at hand, but afterward. Even the much more modest Goldwater-Nichols reorganization in 1986 was carried out during a time of relative international peace. By contrast, the DHS was created in what amounts to a wartime environment—just when its constituent agencies need to focus on their actual jobs rather than bureaucratic reorganization. Now that the decision has been made and the third-largest department in the government created, it is imperative not to confuse its mere existence with a successful strategy for protecting the country. A department that lives up to the promise of its creators will clearly take years to develop.

And while Congress has improved its ability to address homeland security issues by creating dedicated authorization committees and appropriations subcommittees in both houses, it has not gone far enough. Those committees and subcommittees must share jurisdiction with many others that insist on their share of the decisionmaking power.[32] This approach is extraordinarily inefficient for the executive branch officials who must work with Congress; in addition, it breeds parochialism among the individual committees and subcommittees about the particular dimensions of homeland security that they address, and it reinforces the tendency for members of Congress to allocate precious homeland security dollars to their districts rather than to areas where they might do the most good.[33] Congress needs to establish the principle that homeland security committees and dedicated appropriations subcommittees have exclusive jurisdiction over funding within the homeland security realm. A requirement for cross-jurisdictional input—that is, the need to gain approval for any initiative from more than one authorizing or appropriating body per house of Congress—may in rare instances be good policy, but it should not be the norm.

The Way Ahead

Today the way ahead is more complicated than it was in 2002, when Brookings published its first post-9/11 book on homeland security. Then the policy backdrop was largely a tabula rasa, and making a first-blush assessment of where the country was vulnerable to terrorism and laying out a broad conceptual architecture for protecting it was a natural task for a think tank. Four years later, much has been done to improve the nation's security. Where progress is lacking, it is sometimes because of conceptual blinders or bureaucratic obstacles, but at other times it is because ongoing efforts simply take a very long time to bear fruit. Developing a clear alternative to existing policy in such circumstances is more complicated.

To guide the nation's efforts and to avoid making proposals for improving homeland security that include—at exorbitant prices—everything but the kitchen sink, the authors of this book have sought to prioritize. We argue that future efforts should focus on stopping catastrophic threats and that they should emphasize early prevention rather than later response. These guideposts can help organize the country's efforts. But most of our analysis requires a much more detailed and specific form of investigation that theory and conceptual frameworks can only do so much to inform.

There are several areas in which our findings show considerable consensus, but there are also a number in which the analytical findings and prescriptions evidence some tension or even disagree. Moreover, we cannot claim to have covered the waterfront of possible homeland security initiatives, and we are left with many unanswered questions about where to go from here. Beyond an assessment of the security of the nation at present, the book's main analytical findings can be divided into three categories: areas of accord that imply clear priorities, areas of tension or disagreement where hard choices will need to be made, and areas requiring further analysis and study.

Points of Consensus and Firm Recommendations

Because of the importance of preventing rather than responding to terrorist attacks, it is crucial that the United States take seriously the need to track and find terrorists before they strike. The need for prevention, the theme of several of the book's chapters, leads Jim Steinberg in particular to recommend a set of fairly strong measures in the realm of intelligence. They include reauthorization of the Patriot Act, establishment of a new agency separate from the FBI to carry out domestic intelligence operations, and implementation of federal standards for drivers' licenses.

O'Hanlon and Steinberg converge in arguing for an intensified effort on the information gathering side of homeland security efforts. It is critically important that agencies do more than maintain databases that connect terrorist watch lists; they must also share information within and among themselves about possible patterns of terrorist activity. To prevent abuse and protect civil liberties, relevant agencies should create independent "data czars" to adjudicate requests for information and keep records of how and when it is accessed. While integration of databases for terrorist watch lists proceeds, more needs to be done. In some cases, financing is lacking, and plans will take two to three more years to complete. For example, the country remains a considerable distance away from tracking when individuals leave the United States.

Another important analytical theme in the book is the need to make government more efficient by breaking down barriers between different layers of government and between the U.S. government and non-U.S. actors. One critical element in this area is simplifying the organization of the federal government so that outsiders can understand how it works and with whom they should coordinate their efforts. The natural response to September 11 was to create a plethora of new organizations, but the time has come to recognize that there is a cost to such complexity. That recognition leads Steinberg to advocate dissolution of the Homeland Security Council and assigning its functions in part to the National Security Council and in part to the Department of Homeland Security. It leads Shapiro to argue for recentralization of U.S. embassies abroad so that various U.S. departments do not work at cross-purposes.

As for organization of the government's major departments, at least three major changes are in order. First, Congress needs to create a separate domestic intelligence agency outside the FBI. The four years since 9/11 have proven, if any proof were necessary, that the culture of the FBI, as valuable as it is for many important tasks, is simply not conducive to intelligence work. Second, DHS needs a directorate for planning to set the overall direction for the department and for federal government efforts on homeland security in general. Third, the Department of Defense (DoD) needs more small units dedicated to disaster and terror response, as well as better planning for major catastrophes. Hurricane Katrina revealed how limited DoD's capacity for truly rapid action is at present; this is less an issue of physical resources than of proper planning and bureaucratic culture. There has been a barrier between FEMA and DoD in preparing for quick disaster response, with DoD commonly wishing to defer to FEMA, eschewing any large role or even any major planning effort to prepare for a possible role. But that paradigm should have been demolished by Katrina, and artificial barriers between these government agencies should be broken down as a result.

International cooperation in homeland security may sound oxymoronic, but in fact it is imperative, as Jeremy Shapiro's chapter in particular underscores. The United States has made some progress, for example, through its container security initiative, which stations U.S. inspectors in overseas ports. But much remains to be done. Many of the European databases that could potentially be most beneficial for U.S. homeland security, for example Eurodac, remain inaccessible to American officials. Europe's plan to use fingerprints on future passports as the biometric indicator is wiser than America's continued preference for photographs, as Michael d'Arcy's chapters emphasize. By contrast, the U.S. effort to digitize and biometrically secure passports quickly is better than the more leisurely efforts of some European countries. Each side needs to emulate the other's best practices. In another key example, while Europeans are now placing air marshals on at least some flights to the United States, they still have not achieved the same standards of security (such as reinforced cockpit doors) required for American carriers. The point here is not that either the Americans or the Europeans have found the correct balance between security and expense or between security and liberty. Rather, the continued divergence in their practices breeds distrust and invites political conflict. Standardization of practices is a foundation on which closer cooperation could be built.

The United States also needs to do much more to protect the private sector. The best approach, as Peter Orszag explains, is not through the heavy hand of government regulation—except to ensure a basic level of protection for especially dangerous facilities such as toxic chemical plants. Rather, the private insurance market should be used to encourage the private sector to adopt best practices, with the government stepping in only far enough to require large firms to carry terrorism insurance. And even though robust protection is infeasible for all large buildings as well as major transportation networks such as railroads and subway systems, the frequency with which al Qaeda uses truck bombs and suicide bombers demands greater vigilance against this challenge than the United States is currently displaying. For transportation, substantially greater federal resources are appropriate; for large buildings such as skyscrapers, again the private insurance market is the key—for example, to encourage use of better air filters as a defense against biological attack.

Points of Analytical Tension

While all the authors support the concept of bridging divides between differ-ent levels of government, determining exactly how that should be done and the priority that should be given to particular cases can be a difficult and con-tentious process. For example, it remains apparent that better cooperation between the U.S. federal government and its state and local counterparts is imperative. The latter already receive some help from Washington, through the FBI-led joint terrorism task forces. But as counterterrorism responsibili-ties get pushed to the local level—including, for example, an intelligence unit within the New York City police department—the problem of liaison, partic-ularly with foreign partners, becomes more difficult.

There are further important differences over the allocation of federal resources to first responders, and this issue requires further policy innova-tion. More money is now going to higher-threat areas, as it should. But there is still too little guidance about what types of local capacities should be cre-ated—and this book's authors were not all of the same view on that question. For example, rather than await the day in which all of the nation's 3 million first responders have interoperable radios, O'Hanlon recommends that municipalities purchase mobile interoperability centers that would allow liai-son between existing radios at whatever site they needed to be intercon-nected. But that recommendation was not reinforced in other chapters.

One area in which the authors were unable to reach consensus concerns U.S. border security. We agree that it is significantly better than before, and it may be the primary area where the creation of DHS has led to efficiencies and improvements. We also agree that there are still big problems. However, it is difficult to determine what to do about those problems. O'Hanlon and d'Arcy recommend that the country move toward "smart containers" with tamper-proof seals and transponders that indicate their position at all times. This type of approach would allow inspectors to concentrate efforts on ship-ments lacking appropriate security safeguards and hence requiring special scrutiny. But the authors diverge somewhat on how much to increase cargo inspection capacity at the border. O'Hanlon notes that today only about 5 percent of containers entering the country are inspected, while a better goal would be 10 percent or more. However, that particular quantitative goal is admittedly somewhat arbitrary—and contentious.

As for land borders, while the Border Patrol has doubled in size in the last decade, with some apparent reduction in illegal flows into the United States, the borders are far from airtight and represent a major vulnerability in the effort to prevent terrorist infiltration. Continued gradual but significant expansion of the Border Patrol is appropriate. It is difficult to be precise about the endpoint. O'Hanlon would sustain the pace of increases of the recent past—roughly 1,000 additional agents a year, along with adoption of technological innovations such as multispectral sensors set on land or carried by UAVs (unmanned aerial vehicles). But, again, not all of the authors would consider the added expense worthwhile—and Shapiro's chapter makes it clear that many U.S. allies would balk at such expanded efforts on their own borders.

Unresolved Questions and the Future Research Agenda

For all that should still be done, it is worth noting a few examples of efforts that we deem too expensive, too ineffective, or too marginal to the country's core security to warrant major initiatives at this time. They require further research and study—or further developments in the counterterrorism situation—before it would be appropriate to make decisions.

For example, the United States should not create huge quarantine facilities for the population. The scenario of an epidemic caused by an extremely lethal and contagious virus, such as smallpox—or even something worse, such as a genetically engineered cross between smallpox and a flu virus—seems unlikely to be within a weakened al Qaeda's reach anytime soon. (Avian flu may be a greater worry, but it is still not great enough to warrant such an extreme measure given its cost and the availability of better alternatives.) In the near term, the United States should instead be able to isolate some parts of existing hospitals to treat extremely contagious patients rather than invest in hugely expensive new bed capacity for a most unlikely scenario.

Similarly, as the Orszag-O'Hanlon chapter shows and as the book's broader conceptual framework would also argue, the nation's tens of thousands of chemical facilities do not all require top-tier protection. Only a few thousand pose the highest threat, combining lethal chemicals and proximity to large population centers.

As for two final and related examples, the authors do not now advocate taking major steps to deal with two types of missiles that pose a threat to the United States: surface-to-air missiles (SAMs), which could be used against airplanes, and cruise missiles, which could be launched from the sea (or over a land border) against an American city. The threat is undeniable. Indeed, a sting operation in 2005 that stopped a plot by arms merchants to bring anti-aircraft missiles into the United States was a sobering reminder of it, as was the 2002 incident in which two SAMs were fired at an Israeli passenger jet in Kenya.[34] But as Michael d'Arcy shows, the cost to address the threat is high and the effectiveness of any presently feasible efforts is questionable. Were a SAM to bring down a U.S. airliner, the estimated current cost for the imperfect technology needed to address such a possibility—$10 billion to $20 billion—might quickly seem justifiable. But at present, we support instead robust research and development to pursue less expensive and more effective technologies.

Cruise missiles launched at American territory are also a credible threat to the homeland. If they carried weapons of mass destruction, they could kill far more people than a shoulder-launched SAM. But the types of command-and-control arrangements needed to reliably find such threats—and activate the quick response needed to shoot them down without running a substantial risk of destroying manned aircraft by accident—remain elusive. The better course of action for now is to pursue effective cruise missile defense for military assets first, a task that is more limited in geographic and technical scope. The United States might then consider the nationwide defense option, as a function of cost, likely effectiveness, and estimated threat.

Several points are worth making about the state of the country's scientific research efforts regarding homeland security. As Michael d'Arcy explains, the field of biometrics is improving fast and can help greatly with reliable identification, through not only fingerprint technology but also iris identification and other methods. However, sensors for finding dangerous materials are improving relatively slowly, and they will remain limited in capacity into the indefinite future, necessitating labor-intensive efforts to search for weapons of mass destruction and other threats. In terms of the development of biological countermeasures, a fundamentally new approach is needed to encourage development of vaccines and antidotes. Either the private sector should be subsidized to perform the necessary research and development (R&D), especially in the early developmental stages, or the government should create dedicated R&D capacity of its own. The free market alone will not solve this problem.

Conclusion

The overall thrust of this book suggests that while discrimination and selectivity are always in order, much more needs to be done to improve the nation's defenses against terrorism. That does not require bank-busting activities—or, to put it differently, the authors generally do not find enormously expensive measures to be necessary or appropriate at this time. Even if all of our recommendations were adopted, federal financing for homeland security would wind up in the range of $50 billion to $60 billion a year, in contrast to today's $40 billion—and private sector expenses would probably increase by a roughly comparable amount. But while Americans can feel somewhat safer than they were four years ago, falling into any national sense of complacency would be a huge mistake.

Notes

1. Vicky O'Hara, "Terrorist Funding," National Public Radio, Morning Edition, November 20, 2003; speech of George W. Bush at the FBI Academy, Quantico, Virginia, September 10, 2003; and Philip Shenon, "U.S. Reaches Deal to Limit Transfers of Portable Missiles," *New York Times*, October 21, 2003, p. A1.

2. Tom Ridge, "Since That Day," *Washington Post*, September 11, 2003, p. 23.

3. Martin Enserink, "Facing a Security Deadline, Labs Get a 'Provisional' Pass," *Science*, November 7, 2003, p. 962.

4. There may be some gaps in these types of protective measures to date, but the overall level of security is generally good. See the statement of Jim Wells, General Accounting Office, "Nuclear Regulatory Commission: Preliminary Observations on Efforts to Improve Security at Nuclear Power Plants," GAO-04-1064T (September 14, 2004).

5. John Moteff, "Computer Security: A Summary of Selected Federal Laws, Executive Orders, and Presidential Directives" (Washington: Congressional Research Service, April 16, 2004), p. 2.

6. David Johnston and Andrew C. Revkin, "Officials Say Their Focus Is on Car and Truck Bombs," *New York Times*, August 2, 2004, p. A13.

7. President George W. Bush, speech on terrorism at the National Endowment for Democracy, October 6, 2005 (www.whitehouse.gov [October 6, 2005]).

8. See Gilmore Commission (Advisory Panel to Assess Domestic Response Capabilities for Terrorism Involving Weapons of Mass Destruction), Fifth Annual Report, *Forging America's New Normalcy: Securing Our Homeland, Preserving Our Liberty* (Arlington, Va.: RAND, December 15, 2003), p. 1; Alan B. Krueger and David D. Laitin, "'Misunderestimating' Terrorism," *Foreign Affairs* 83 (September-October 2004): p. 9; and Susan B. Glasser, "U.S. Figures Show Sharp Global Rise in Terrorism," *Washington Post*, April 27, 2005, p. 1.

9. Richard Benedetto, "Americans Expect Attacks, Poll Finds," *USA Today*, July 12, 2005, p. 1.

10. Leyla Linton, "Al Qaeda, Taliban Can Still Launch Attacks, Report Says," *Philadelphia Inquirer*, February 16, 2005.

11. Eric Lichtblau, "Finance Centers Are Said to Be the Targets," *New York Times*, August 2, 2004, p. 1.

12. Shaun Waterman, "Al Qaeda Warns of Threat to Water Supply," *Washington Times*, May 29, 2003, p. 6; and Eric Lichtblau, "U.S. Cites al Qaeda in Plan to Destroy Brooklyn Bridge," *New York Times*, June 20, 2003, p. 1.

13. Eric Lichtblau, "Government Report on U.S. Aviation Warns of Security Holes," *New York Times*, March 14, 2005, p. A1.

14. Matthew Brzezinski, *Fortress America* (New York: Bantam Books, 2004), pp. 16–17.

15. Richard Falkenrath, statement before the Senate Committee on Homeland Security and Governmental Affairs, 109 Cong., 1 sess., January 26, 2005, pp. 12–14.

16. See Marc Sageman, *Understanding Terror Networks* (University of Pennsylvania Press, 2004).

17. Gilmore Commission, *Implementing the National Strategy* (December 2002), p. 11; and Douglas Farah and Peter Finn, "Terrorism, Inc.," *Washington Post*, November 21, 2003, p. 33. On the assertion that modern terrorist groups watch and learn from each other, see Bruce Hoffman, "Terrorism Trends and Prospects," in *Countering the New Terrorism*, Ian O. Lesser and others (Santa Monica, Calif.: RAND, 1999), pp. 8–28; and on the nature of al Qaeda and affiliated as well as sympathetic organizations, see Paul R. Pillar, *Terrorism and U.S. Foreign Policy* (Brookings, 2001), pp. 54–55.

18. Cited in Daniel L. Byman, "Homeland Security: We're Safer than You Think," *Slate*, August 2, 2004.

19. "Washington in Brief," *Washington Post*, July 17, 2004, p. A5.

20. Byman, "Homeland Security"; and ABC News, "No 'True' Al Qaeda Sleeper Agents Have Been Found in U.S.," abcnews.com, March 9, 2005.

21. "Ridge 'Grateful' U.S. Has Not Been Hit Again," *USA Today*, August 11, 2004, p. 11; and John Mintz and Sara Kehaulani Goo, "U.S. Officials Warn of New Tactics by al Qaeda," *Washington Post*, September 5, 2003, p. 2.

22. Bill Gertz, "Goss Fears WMD Attack in U.S. 'A Matter of Time,'" *Washington Times*, February 17, 2005, p. 3.

23. John Mintz, "Homeland Security Employs Imagination; Outsiders Help Devise Possible Terrorism Plots," *Washington Post*, June 18, 2004, p. A27.

24. Dana Priest and Josh White, "War Helps Recruit Terrorists, Hill Told," *Washington Post*, February 17, 2005, p. 1.

25. National Intelligence Council, *Mapping the Global Future* (December 2004), p. 94.

26. Richard K. Betts, "The Soft Underbelly of American Primacy: Tactical Advantages of Terror," *Political Science Quarterly* 117 (Spring 2002): 30.

27. On jamming, see "U.S. Homeland Defense Strategists," *Aviation Week and Space Technology*, September 6, 2004, p. 20.

28. Peter D. Zimmerman with Cheryl Loeb, "Dirty Bombs: The Threat Revisited," *Defense Horizons* 38 (January 2004).

29. Lawrence M. Wein and Edward H. Kaplan, "Unready for Anthrax," *Washington Post*, July 28, 2003, p. A21.

30. Falkenrath, statement before the Senate Committee on Homeland Security and Governmental Affairs, pp. 14–15.

31. Ibid., pp. 2, 7.

32. For a similar critique of Congress's role, see National Commission on Terrorist Attacks upon the United States [9/11 Commission], *The 9/11 Commission Report: Final Report of the National Commission on Terrorist Attacks upon the United States* (New York: W. W. Norton, 2004), pp. 420–22.

33. See Falkenrath, statement before the Senate Committee on Homeland Security and Governmental Affairs, p. 4.

34. Julia Preston, "Arms Network Is Broken Up, Officials Say," *New York Times*, March 16, 2005.

2

INTELLIGENCE REFORM

JAMES STEINBERG

Intelligence reform has deservedly been at the heart of America's new strategy on homeland security. Prior to the emergence of the al Qaeda threat in the mid-1990s, domestic "intelligence" activities, which had largely been abandoned following the Pike and Church Committee investigations in the mid-1970s, were focused almost exclusively on operations countering foreign governments' intelligence and espionage efforts in the United States (and to a limited degree against "domestic" extremist groups). Although some information related to national security was developed in the course of criminal investigations by law enforcement agencies, the information was rarely shared with the intelligence community because of an increasingly high "wall" between law enforcement and intelligence investigations.[1]

In addition to the U.S. government's virtually nonexistent domestic security capabilities, a high barrier had been erected between foreign and domestic intelligence activities, a barrier that had its roots in law, the culture of the relevant agencies, and the incompatibility of information storage and retrieval systems that made sharing difficult even when the will to share existed. Even among agencies with responsibility for foreign intelligence, sharing was grudging, as each sought to protect its most valuable assets—sources (both human and technical) and the intelligence they produced—from the risk of compromise or inadvertent disclosure.

Those deficiencies were at the heart of the critique of both the joint inquiry of the Senate Select Committee on Intelligence and the House Permanent Select Committee on Intelligence and the 9/11 Commission. Even before the commission completed its work, the Bush administration had begun to implement a number of measures both to strengthen domestic intelligence collection and to improve intelligence sharing across the full range of agencies. Some of the legal impediments to sharing between law enforcement and intelligence agencies were eliminated by the USA PATRIOT Act (Patriot Act) of 2001. The administration also established the Terrorist Threat Integration Center (TTIC) with the idea that it would permit sharing across agencies. As part of the legislation establishing the Department of Homeland Security (DHS), a new directorate was created within DHS to strengthen analysis and information sharing on terrorist threats and to address the vulnerabilities of critical infrastructure; DHS itself was charged with building new links between the national intelligence agencies and state and local governments.

But critics argued that a more thorough reform was necessary to break down the intelligence stovepipes and to foster a culture of "need to share" rather than "need to know." That perspective got a significant boost from the 9/11 Commission's report, which called for the creation of a director of national intelligence (DNI) with power over budgets and personnel through-out the intelligence community, including agencies that deal with foreign intelligence as well as those that deal with domestic intelligence. The report also called for establishment of a National Counterterrorism Center (NCTC), reporting directly to the new DNI, which would not only take on the task of further developing cross-agency intelligence sharing and analysis but would also be responsible for counterterrorism operational planning (though not operations themselves, which would remain with the existing agencies). The commission also proposed new rules and advocated the adoption of new technologies that would foster information sharing.

The commission's report spurred Congress to enact the Intelligence Reform and Terrorism Prevention Act of 2004 (Intelligence Reform Act). During the debate over adoption of the act, the most controversial issues revolved around the scope of the new DNI's authority over the disparate elements of the intel-ligence community. In particular, the Department of Defense and its allies in Congress sought to restrict the DNI's authority over "military" intelligence, including agencies such as the National Security Agency (NSA), which reports to the secretary of defense, even though as "national" intelligence agencies they had responsibility for collecting information for civilian as well as military agencies. There was a similar debate that got much less attention over the degree to which the DNI should control "domestic" intelligence activities, especially those of the Federal Bureau of Investigation (FBI). In both cases, the issues concerned authority over budgets, operations, and personnel.

The result of those struggles was legislation that gave the DNI significant authority over the intelligence community but left important ambiguities that will depend critically on how the act is interpreted by the president and the executive branch. The act designates the DNI to "serve as head of the intelligence community" and "principal adviser to the President, to the National Security Council (NSC), and the Homeland Security Council for intelligence matters related to the national security."[2] He or she is charged with providing national intelligence to the president, the heads of departments and agencies of the executive branch, the chairman of the Joint Chiefs of Staff, and Congress. The DNI has been given access to all national intelligence collected by federal units, as well as the authority to give the agencies that form part of the intelligence community guidance for developing their portions of the National Intelligence Program budget. The DNI, then, with the advice of the Joint Intelligence Community Council, can "develop and determine an annual consolidated National Intelligence Program budget" (as well as monitor its implementation and execution) and subsequently manage appropriations. However, the secretary of defense retains authority over the development of the "annual budgets for the Joint Military Intelligence Program and for Tactical Intelligence and Related Activities," with the DNI only "participating" in the process.[3] And while the DNI has been given tasking authority to "establish objectives, priorities, and guidance for the intelligence community to ensure timely and effective collection, processing, analysis, and dissemination . . . of national intelligence," that authority does not apply to areas where the secretary of defense exercises tasking authority.[4] The DNI has also been given the task of overseeing the NCTC and, in consultation with the heads of the other agencies of the intelligence community, prescribing personnel policies and programs.

Implementation is going to be crucial, considering the number of ambiguities that have been left in the legislation. Though it is too early to reach firm conclusions about the law's implementation—and earlier still to judge its efficacy—ten central challenges remain if the intelligence community is to make its needed contribution to protecting the homeland and to developing a more seamless structure that recognizes the multifaceted nature of the mission, tying together foreign countries, U.S. federal agencies (operating both internationally and domestically), state and local governments, and the private sector.

Further steps are needed to erase the seams between domestic and foreign intel-
ligence/counterterrorism operations and to clarify the roles and responsibilities
of the relevant agencies.

Even before the 9/11 attacks, the FBI had begun to expand substantially its
operations overseas as concerns about international criminal organizations
grew in the 1990s. Those activities were largely uncoordinated with the
Central Intelligence Agency (CIA), which felt the FBI was encroaching on its
"turf." Fierce disputes also emerged between the bureau and the State
Department, including in-country ambassadors who, supported by CIA station chiefs, claimed "chief of mission" authority to regulate all U.S. agencies
within a country.[5] Their concern was to minimize diplomatic gaffes and conflicting intelligence activities. Similarly, the CIA had continued its own activities within the territorial United States, based on its authority to take action
(including the recruitment of sources) with respect to non-U.S. residents and
to debrief returning U.S. citizens.[6]

Since 9/11, both the CIA and FBI have expanded their activities on the
other's turf.[7] In particular, the FBI has stepped up recruitment of foreigners
in the United States and sought to maintain control over those sources after
they return overseas. In the CIA's view, the FBI's efforts encroach on the CIA's
traditional responsibility for handling agents abroad and risk uncoordinated
and potentially conflicting operations. The dangers range from the risk of
false corroboration (both agencies receiving reports from a single source but
believing that the reports come from two different agents) to compromising
sensitive operations. There has also been concern over recent cases in which
FBI agents operating abroad have failed to inform the CIA of their operations. The FBI and CIA had been in negotiations to resolve these conflicts and
establish rules governing their respective roles.[8] They have jointly developed
a classified memorandum of understanding (MoU) to address this problem.
The DNI has approved that MoU.[9]

There is another dimension to the problem as well—a state and local one—
with actions such as those taken by the New York City Police Department
(NYPD), which has placed officers in seven different cities around the world
through its overseas liaison program to collect information, among other
activities. NYPD officials stated that one reason for this action was that they
were being kept out of the loop by the federal agencies and that if they had not
taken such a step, they would not have had access to information from those
sites; even if they did receive information, they said, it would take months to
get it. While their role is limited and does not include participating in

enforcement activities or investigations, their efforts are deeply resented by the FBI where, in a complaint that ironically mirrors that of the CIA about the FBI's activities abroad, the feeling is that they add to the confusion about who officially represents the U.S. government. To add to the problem, there is little coordination: for example, a NYPD officer stationed in Israel had little, if any, contact with the FBI agent working out of the embassy in Tel Aviv.[10]

Similar problems are beginning to emerge between the CIA and the Department of Defense, as the Pentagon begins to expand its use of human intelligence sources in terms of numbers, scope, and geographic reach. Difficulties occur in both the domestic and the foreign context (the problem of intelligence collection and operations by military personnel abroad will be addressed below). Some press reports suggest that the U.S. military has increased its unilateral development of sources in the United States as part of its force protection mission (to protect itself against attacks on military facilities in the United States as well as abroad), risking conflict with both the CIA and the FBI.[11] Congress is currently considering legislation that would potentially give agents of the Defense Intelligence Agency permission to approach a "United States person" as a source (without notifying the person of their affiliation) if the person is credible or suitable and if "such United States person possesses, or has access to, foreign intelligence information."[12] The Defense Department's new strategy regarding its homeland mission also calls for the development of a group of intelligence specialists on counterterrorism within the department, many of whom would be deployed to interagency centers within the United States to work with the FBI and other domestic law enforcement entities on counterterrorism and homeland defense issues.[13]

The creation of the DNI offers an opportunity to clarify the roles and missions of all the agencies with a potential role in foreign intelligence collection. Whenever possible, the rules should be designed to foster specialization and avoid the hazards of unnecessary duplication and conflict. The FBI should be responsible primarily for handling foreign intelligence collection in the United States as well as collection on civilians in support of protecting military facilities in the United States. (The FBI already collaborates with the Pentagon's counterintelligence field activity group, which is responsible for protecting military infrastructure from terrorist and foreign intelligence agencies' espionage activities). Sources developed by the FBI in the United States who move abroad should be transferred to CIA handlers. The Robb-Silberman Commission called for the formation within the CIA of the Human Intelligence Directorate, which would be responsible for coordinating the work of "all U.S. agencies conducting human intelligence operations overseas" (including the CIA's own Directorate of Operations).[14] They wanted this directorate to also develop a national HUMINT (human intelligence) strategy, and, as appropriate, to integrate collection and reporting systems. As part of its response to these recommendations, the Bush administration emphasized that the CIA's authority over overseas human intelligence operations would be strengthened. A national HUMINT manager—a senior CIA official—would coordinate human intelligence activities conducted by all agencies abroad.[15] More recently, the DNI and the director of the CIA announced the creation of a National Clandestine Service (NCS) within the CIA. The senior CIA official who would head the service would also coordinate, but not supervise or direct, the human intelligence operations of all the agencies collecting intelligence overseas.[16] While the office of the DNI "will establish policy related to clandestine HUMINT, the NCS will execute and implement that policy across the IC."[17] Implementing this initiative correctly is going to be important. The director of the NCS will have to ensure that all of the agencies, not just a few, consistently coordinate their operations. In the case of state and local agencies with foreign liaisons, the solution is to get the FBI and CIA to cooperate more and be more responsive to the needs of state and local authorities.

The relationship between military and civilian intelligence functions needs to be clarified, and the authority of the DNI (and the jurisdiction of congressional oversight committees) over these operations needs to be addressed.

Overseas, the Pentagon is contemplating a significant expansion of its intelligence gathering role, not only in connection with the battlefield (for example, in Iraq and Afghanistan) but also as part of the so-called global war on terror in virtually any part of the world where terrorists might operate. The Pentagon has increased its intelligence missions and personnel, raising concerns about overlap with other agencies' functions and questions about whether some of these related initiatives are appropriate for military personnel.[18] Press accounts have detailed the creation of the Strategic Support Branch, which "deploys small teams of case officers, linguists, interrogators and technical specialists alongside newly empowered special operations forces." The reports indicate that the unit, created to provide the secretary of defense with expanded independent human intelligence operational tools, had been operating in Iraq, Afghanistan, and "emerging target countries."[19] Thus in the overseas context, the contemplated military role would not be limited to intelligence collection but would extend to intelligence operations as well. This enhanced role was endorsed by the 9/11 Commission, which stated that "lead responsibility for directing and executing paramilitary operations, whether clandestine or covert, should shift to the Defense Department,"[20] and the Defense Science Board, which called for the establishment of "a more robust Defense human intelligence (HUMINT) capability than exists today."[21] There are a number of reasons to be concerned about this approach:[22]

—COORDINATION OF SENSITIVE OPERATIONS. Since military authorities operate independently of civilian agencies (the military chain of command runs through the secretary of defense to the president) and for operational security reasons the military rarely shares information on its operations with its civilian counterparts, covert military operations take place without the input or perspective of other key actors (ambassadors, senior State Department officials, and so forth) who have an important stake in U.S. relations with foreign countries and who have both expertise and a perspective frequently lacking in the military. On the other hand, both CIA operations and operatives are better linked to the civilian leadership than their military counterparts are, though the link is not perfect, through the CIA station chiefs. Moreover, under current practice, true covert operations must be approved by the president after review through the interagency process, which provides an opportunity for all perspectives to be heard and risks and benefits assessed. Military operations, even covert ones, receive no such scrutiny.

—OVERSIGHT. Congress has established explicit mechanisms for oversight of covert operations, both because of the sensitivity of the operations involved and because the tight secrecy associated with them has raised concerns about abuses of executive power. There is considerable debate over whether covert actions by the military fall under Title 50 of the U.S. Code (which requires Congress to be kept informed of all intelligence activities), with some Pentagon officials broadly interpreting the exemption for "traditional diplomatic or military activities or routine support to such activities" to exclude all such actions, arguing that Defense Department intelligence missions should not be subject to the same congressional oversight process as equivalent CIA operations. They argue that their actions fall under Title 10, which covers the military and has different authorization and notification requirements.

A narrow reading of the statute to exempt these actions from Title 50 would create an enormous loophole allowing the executive branch to conduct operations through the military without oversight. Conversely, a broad reading would risk inserting congressional intelligence committees into legitimate tactical battlefield intelligence collection, which could seriously impair the military's ability to fight wars. The best way to avoid the dilemma is to avoid the use of the military for covert operations away from the field of battle (defined in terms of tactical military operations).

—EXPERTISE. The U.S. Armed Forces are trained to fight wars. While the Special Forces are increasing their training in a broader set of skills (language, culture, history, politics), it is unlikely that they will develop the kind of expertise built of long experience found among Foreign Service and CIA personnel. At best, expanding the role of the military will duplicate existing capabilities (that could be augmented elsewhere); at worst, it will mean the deployment of personnel poorly trained for highly sensitive tasks.

—PRESENCE. The military currently does not have a presence in as many countries as the CIA does, nor does it have the CIA's established contacts with third-country nationals.

—LEGAL PROTECTION FOR MILITARY PERSONNEL. While in uniform, the military enjoys the protection of the Geneva Conventions. Operating covertly, U.S. military personnel risk being held and treated as spies if detained. That could have a long-term deleterious impact on military morale and could more broadly undermine respect for the Geneva Conventions themselves.

—FOREIGN POLICY IMPLICATIONS. Any exposed covert operation poses serious political risks for the United States, but the revelation that the United States is conducting covert "military" operations in friendly (or at least non-hostile) countries poses a risk that such actions will be seen and treated as acts of aggression, with far more damaging consequences for U.S. foreign policy.

The Intelligence Reform Act left uncertain whether the DNI had the authority to resolve the respective roles of the CIA and the military in covert intelligence collection and operations.[23] The office of the DNI and the Pentagon have been working toward resolving some of these issues. Recently, the CIA and the Pentagon also drafted a memorandum of understanding to "deconflict" and coordinate their operations, which is awaiting approval.[24] While the Robb-Silberman Commission suggested the creation of a Human Intelligence Directorate more generally, on covert action specifically its recommendations were classified. Reports indicate, however, that its suggestion to shift planning of covert operations out of the CIA's hands was rejected, with the administration stating clearly that the "CIA also will strengthen its management of covert action."[25] With the creation of the NCS, the CIA has been given authority to coordinate all human intelligence operations overseas and develop common rules and standards. Along with one deputy to oversee the HUMINT work of the CIA and another to oversee that of the intelligence community as a whole, the NCS will also have a "covert action executive" who will coordinate covert operations.[26] However, while the authority to coordinate (but not direct operations) has been assigned, it has not been clarified—for example, it is not quite clear who will resolve disputes between the agencies (and how) or whether that individual will have the ability and not just the authority to do so. It is also not clear which authority (Title 50 or Title 10) governs. The ambiguities need to be resolved and authorities need to be made clear. In cases of disagreement that cannot be resolved by the office of the NCS director, the DNI and the newly established Joint Intelligence Community Council should be given oversight responsibility. Even in cases in which the military is the most suitable instrument for conducting clandestine and covert operations, appropriate safeguards comparable to those in Title 50 should be applied.

The Homeland Security Council should be merged into the National Security Council to ensure full integration of the domestic and foreign aspects of counterterrorism operations.

In the immediate aftermath of the 9/11 attacks, the Bush administration created the Office of Homeland Security (OHS) in the Executive Office and an associated Homeland Security Council, with a "principals committee" consisting of the secretary of the treasury; the secretary of defense; the Attorney General; the secretary of health and human services; the secretary of transportation; the director of the Office of Management and Budget; the assistant to the president for homeland security (who serves as chair); the assistant to the president and chief of staff; the director of central intelligence; the director of the FBI; the director of the Federal Emergency Management Agency; and the assistant to the president and chief of staff to the vice president (the national security adviser would be invited to the meetings of the HSC/PC). This organizational response was understandable, given the urgent need to give focus to addressing the deficiencies revealed by the 9/11 attacks, particularly the critical need for coordination and systematic planning to address the threat of terrorism in the United States. Since the initial creation of the OHS, there has been an evolution, spurred on by experience and by the creation of DHS. Today, DHS has superseded most of the operational responsibilities of the OHS, which retains an advisory and coordinating role. The HSC membership now consists of the president, vice president, secretary of defense, secretary of health and human services, Attorney General, secretary of transportation, secretary of the treasury, director of the FBI, director of the

CIA, and secretary of homeland security, and it is staffed by, among others, the assistant to the president for homeland security. In addition, the DNI also acts as an adviser to the HSC.

From the beginning, the administration has struggled with how to ensure the linkages between "homeland security," under the aegis of the OHS, and the broader counterterrorism effort, which had been the province of the NSC. Shortly after 9/11, in October 2001, the administration created a new position within the NSC, the national director and deputy national security adviser for combating terrorism, who also served as a deputy to the homeland security adviser on "matters relating to global terrorism inside the United States." The dual-hatted deputy was responsible for the day-to-day coordination of the response to threat information and was intended to be "the President's principal advisor on matters related to combating global terrorism, including all efforts designed to detect, disrupt, and destroy global terrorist organizations and those who support them."[27] When Frances Townsend was elevated to homeland security adviser in 2004, for a time she kept the deputy national security adviser position at the NSC. In May 2005, with the appointment of Juan Carlos Zarate to the deputy national security adviser position, it reverted to being a dual-hatted one.

It seems increasingly clear that the separation of the HSC is at best artificial and at worst counterproductive. As the authors discuss throughout this volume, protecting the homeland requires a seamless connection of efforts abroad, across U.S. borders, and in the United States itself. Intelligence collaboration needs to relate information about terrorist cells collected by local officials in Buffalo with CIA information from Afghanistan. Public health officials must prepare for biological and chemical attacks planned and launched abroad. The U.S. military is enhancing its operations in and around the United States, both for homeland defense (for example, interdicting threats to U.S. territory) and to support domestic agencies (as, for example, with nuclear response teams to augment local officials' efforts in the event of an incident). The nature of the jihadist terrorist threat to United States interests at home and abroad does not neatly divide into a "homeland" and "external" problem.

The principal objections to merging the two coordinating bodies and their associated staffs have been the risk of overload on the national security adviser and the need to include agencies in NSC deliberations that have not traditionally participated. The first concern should not be treated lightly. But even today, the national security adviser is often involved in issues concerning the HSC, and given the priority on counterterrorism, it stands to reason that that should be an important focus of the adviser. The creation of the NCTC, which has responsibility for intelligence and operational planning across all agencies, foreign and domestic, is a further impetus, since according to the Intelligence Reform Act the NCTC reports to the president (and ideally this should be through the NSC). Some of the staffing burden can be moved to DHS, which should have a more prominent role in leading the interagency process on many operational aspects of homeland security and response.[28]

Problems associated with including agencies unfamiliar with the NSC seem overstated. In recent years many agencies that are primarily thought of as domestic agencies have joined NSC deliberations on appropriate issues—the inclusion of the Department of Health and Human Services and the Centers for Disease Control and Prevention on AIDS and bioterrorism before 9/11 are examples. So the idea of flexibility for NSC processes is nothing new.

Linkages between the United States and its foreign partners need to be strengthened.

It is widely accepted that the United States has a compelling need for international cooperation in fighting terrorism. President George Bush, for example, has emphasized that "the wars of the 21st century are going to require incredible international cooperation. . . . We need to cooperate."[29] Much of the threat emanates from abroad and, with limited exceptions, the United States cannot operate unilaterally either to collect the necessary intelligence or undertake the operations necessary to thwart or eliminate that threat. Prior to 9/11, the principal linkages between U.S. intelligence agencies and their foreign counterparts were almost exclusively "bilateral" in two important senses.[30] First, the sharing was largely between the United States and individual countries (there is some exception in the case of collaboration on technical intelligence between the United States, the United Kingdom, Canada, and Australia, and within NATO), and second, sharing was between homologous entities (SIGINT, or signals intelligence, agencies with other SIGINT agencies; human intelligence agencies with liaison services; law enforcement with law enforcement). These bilateral relations were largely a function of differing degrees of trust, a reflection of the prevailing cold war emphasis on information security rather than sharing.

While these special relationships have intensified in many cases since 9/11, sharing structures remain fragmented and stovepiped. There is a limited degree of sharing of cross-community assessments (for example, from the United Kingdom's Joint Intelligence Committee), but the barriers to sharing raw intelligence across the full range of analysts remain high. Moreover, in the transatlantic context, there are serious problems in sharing with Europe as a result of the fragmented nature of the European system itself. While the European Union (EU) as an entity and the European Council and Commission have important responsibilities and authorities that affect counterterrorism across the EU (for example, ports, the "Schengen" border information system), intra-European information sharing (apart from bilateral sharing) is weak, and the new EU institutions developed to address the deficiencies revealed by the Madrid bombing (such as the office of the "coordinator for the fight against terrorism") are understaffed and undersupported by the member states. Some intra-EU collaboration is possible on the strategic level through the EU's Joint Situation Centre (SitCen), which could provide an avenue of cooperation and exchange with the United States.

As with sharing among U.S. agencies and actors, there is a need to reassess the balance of risks and benefits from enhanced sharing with partners abroad. It is self-evident that in the face of the current jihadist terrorist threat, intelligence collected by foreign agencies is indispensable, a fact that was underscored by the crucial role of liaison agency intelligence in foiling the plots to attack U.S. embassies abroad in 1998 and 2001 as well as potential attacks associated with the millennium celebrations. Yet without adequate methods of sharing, it will be impossible to "connect the dots" between information held by the United States and by others.[31] Improved sharing is also needed to build a greater sense of reciprocity, which is critical to effective long-term intelligence relationships. While security remains a legitimate concern, many of the tools to protect the security of information in the U.S. context could be applied to international sharing.

There are a number of other aspects to this problem. One is the lack of clarity regarding which agency in the United States has responsibility for interaction with foreign partners. As mentioned above, in the case of intelligence the CIA, FBI, Department of Defense (DoD), and even some state and local agencies have a presence abroad. Add to that the Department of Homeland Security, which has a full-time attaché to the European Union, and the State Department, in its traditional role as diplomatic liaison, and the arena seems crowded. Their activities lack coordination, and that lack is likely to cause confusion in the minds of international partners and continued stovepiping of information. While there have been indications that the CIA and DoD have been working to resolve this issue, it is not clear that the FBI and DHS are coordinating their activities with the other agencies. The Intelligence Reform Act does give the DNI some coordinating authority, which some consider ambiguous, but the statute is being interpreted broadly, which might serve to alleviate the problem.

Problems associated with the lack of coordination extend to policy development as well. A recent example was the dispute over the Transportation Security Act of November 2001, which stated that airlines had to provide U.S. authorities with detailed information on all passengers before arrival at a U.S. port of entry through the passenger name record (PNR), which includes information on the passenger's name, date of birth, method of payment, and meal preferences. This announcement was seen as a unilateral imposition of rules, and European airlines found themselves in a difficult situation. Compliance with the rules would require them to provide what the European Union considers sensitive information on their passengers within fifteen minutes of departure to the United States and would require them to defy EU privacy protection laws. There were concerns in the EU about the kind of information that was required, retention periods, and the resistance of U.S. authorities to limiting the use of data collected to the counterterrorism realm.

European airlines were stuck in the middle. Noncompliance with the U.S. law would likely result in fines, delays, and possible flight cancellations. In March 2003, the EU and the United States reached an interim agreement that allowed the kind of access that the act required while a more permanent agreement could be reached. In December 2003, they finally reached an agreement, formalized in May 2004, that is to be in effect for three and a half years, at which point it is to be renegotiated. Under the agreement airlines can legally transfer PNR data on the basis of the DHS's promise to implement protections for the use, sharing, security, correction, and oversight of data that are sufficient to guard passenger privacy.[32]

The uproar and objections that met the U.S. demand for passenger information could have been avoided or at least reduced had there been an integrated strategy—one that included a diplomatic element before, not after, the fact—that had taken into account broader transatlantic interests in counterterrorism cooperation. Similar problems have arisen from U.S. requirements concerning armed sky marshals, though there are indications that the problems were not as bad because both sides have learned some lessons since the PNR case.

It is apparent that the United States needs to integrate its diplomatic strategy with its homeland security strategy—and not leave diplomacy to post facto efforts to gain support for domestic decisions reached without regard for the consequences to international cooperation. Coordination needs to take place both at the national level and in the field. This is a powerful argument for integrating the responsibilities of the HSC into the NSC, as well as for enhancing the chief of mission's role in embassies with regard to the full spectrum of U.S. counterterrorism agencies.

The role of the National Counterterrorism Center and its relation to the DNI and the National Security Council need to be clarified.

One of the most significant features of the Intelligence Reform and Terrorism Prevention Act is the creation of the NCTC. The center has two key missions: coordination of all foreign counterterrorism analysis and preparation of "operational strategic plans." The first mission builds on the work of the Terrorist Threat Integration Center, and much of the progress to date has focused on this role. The second is a new function (although it has some roots in the interagency Counterterrorism Security Group created by President Clinton under PDD-62 in 1998). The statute creates a bifurcated reporting requirement for the director of the NCTC: to the DNI for the intelligence coordination and analysis function and to the president for the operational planning activities. This bifurcation reflects two quite legitimate imperatives: that the intelligence analysis remain independent of the policymaking function and, equally, that the policy-laden dimensions of operational planning be subject to review by the appropriate policy officials. This division rectifies a shortcoming in the 9/11 Commission's report, which had the NCTC overseen only by the DNI. But in order for it to work, the director of the NCTC should report to the president through the NSC, which will need to set up its own structures to provide the appropriate oversight, perhaps drawing on the experience of the Clinton era's national coordinator for counterterrorism, lodged in the NSC.[33]

The line dividing the analysis and the operations functions is not a bright one. Where does intelligence collection, including tasking, fit? It is certainly an element of any operational plan, yet traditionally these decisions are determined by the intelligence community, and the Intelligence Reform Act clearly gives the DNI authority in this respect—even over the domestic intelligence collection activities of the FBI.

Even more difficult is the linkage between planning and operations. In the military context, the authorities primarily responsible for developing operational plans—the combatant commanders (formerly CINCs, the commanders in chief of the regional commands)—are also responsible for (and have authority over) executing them. Under the current model for the NCTC, the operational agencies will be involved in the planning process, but there is no equivalent of the combatant commander to oversee execution (other than the NSC itself) and the director's role is limited to "monitor[ing] the implementation of strategic operational plans."[34]

This problem, which has plagued interagency implementation of policy across the board, could be particularly problematic in the fast-moving world of counterterrorism operations.[35] In that extraordinarily time-sensitive world, complex interagency procedures are poorly structured to ensure prompt response, yet without some centralized authorities to resolve conflicts and eliminate gaps, operations will remain suboptimal, with extraordinary risks for national security. To resolve this difficulty, the director of the NCTC will need greater operational authority and resources, subject to the oversight of the NSC, which provides a forum for appeal for agencies that disagree with the NCTC director's decisions. The director will also have to develop an appropriate governance structure for joint interagency planning that can overcome the difficulties that have characterized such attempts in the past.

The FBI's domestic security operations need to be substantially strengthened and to be given significant independence from its criminal investigative functions (if a U.S. equivalent of MI5, the United Kingdom's domestic intelligence agency, is not created).

Since 9/11 the director of the FBI, Robert Mueller, has sought to transform the bureau from an agency focused on traditional law enforcement and criminal prosecution toward one that plays a more proactive intelligence collection and assessment role. The bureau and its supporters have fought hard to maintain the FBI as the lead agency for intelligence activities in the United States, in the face of calls for a greater role for DHS and the CIA or the creation of a new domestic intelligence agency along the lines of the United Kingdom's MI5. They argue that creating a new agency would be too disruptive at a time when the threat is immediate and would put at risk important synergies between law enforcement and intelligence activities.

The efforts to date to transform the FBI into an effective counterterrorism intelligence organization reflect strong commitment from the top, but the results have been limited. Key terrorism investigations were centralized at headquarters, buttressed by a national joint terrorism task force (JTTF) to collect terrorism information and intelligence. This information is then channeled to an increased number of JTTFs (they doubled in number after 9/11), which serve as a forum for information sharing and joint action by federal, state, and local agencies. A number of FBI agents were moved into counterterrorism missions.[36] The director oversaw the creation of a Directorate of Intelligence headed by an experienced senior intelligence official that is to be staffed by linguists, analysts, agents, and support staff who collect, analyze, and distribute intelligence. New concepts of operations were developed for key aspects of the intelligence/counterterrorism mission and field intelligence groups (FIGs) were set up in each of the bureau's local offices. The Robb-Silberman Commission had also suggested the creation of "a separate National Security Service within the FBI that includes the Bureau's Counterintelligence and Counterterrorism Divisions, as well as the Directorate of Intelligence."[37] In June 2005, the administration adopted the commission's recommendation and announced the creation of the National Security Branch (NSB), which would bring together the FBI's intelligence and counterterrorism assets and operations under one roof.

There has been an effort to adapt both technology and training to the new counterterrorism mission, but serious problems remain; some are inherent in the role and culture of the FBI, and changing mind-sets is far more difficult than changing organization charts. But many of the problems stem simply from failure to implement a well-considered vision, which would go much farther than adaptation at the margin.

Despite the creation of new roles and reporting relationships as well as new training and career tracks, the FBI still has limited intelligence capability in the field and limited analytical capabilities. The FIGs have run into both cultural and budgetary obstacles. Analysts at the FIGs lack the standing to task special agents to collect needed intelligence (or hold them accountable) as well as resources such as desktop Internet access.[38] While the number of intelligence reports emanating from the bureau has increased, the quality of intelligence still arouses skepticism, especially in the rest of the intelligence community. The reports emerging from analysts in the field still seem to be focused on tactical rather than strategic analysis. The overall functioning of the FBI is still highly decentralized, with special agents in charge (SACs) still in control. The focus still tends to be on building cases rather than identifying and assessing potential threats, and there is still a reluctance to work with other agencies, with only marginal linkages in practice. The attempt at upgrading the computer systems proved a disastrous failure, with the result that technology is still a major barrier to sharing. The bureau has hired new personnel and retrained old personnel, but retention has proved a problem both at the lower and higher levels (there were five chief intelligence officers over the period 2002–03, and the FBI's last head of the counterterrorism division was its sixth since 9/11).

A separate domestic intelligence agency is still the best option; in lieu of such an agency, the FBI needs to strengthen the sense of a separate intelligence service within the bureau. In implementing the recommendations of the Robb-Silberman Commission, the SACs could be like ambassadors with chief-of-mission responsibilities, but the intelligence side of the bureau should have clear and separate links to its own agents and analysts and the authority to supervise them. The new security branch will have to work hard to establish itself as an effective player in the intelligence community. In addition, the bureau should work harder to integrate its intelligence function with that of the rest of the intelligence community. A step in the right direction has been the administration's delegation to the DNI of coordination and budgetary authority over the FBI's new NSB.[39]

The implementation of the "information sharing environment" mandated by the Intelligence Reform Act needs to be accelerated with attention both to facilitating information sharing and to protecting privacy both within the government and across the boundary between the government and the private sector.

At the core of the recommendations of the House and Senate intelligence committees' joint inquiry report and the 9/11 Commission's report was the need to establish a new culture of sharing, backed up by a set of policies and technologies to facilitate information exchange and collaboration. In a 2003 report, the Markle Task Force on National Security in the Information Age recommended the creation of a decentralized network, trusted by users to be secure and effective, that through a combination of policies and technologies would permit information sharing across the full range of potential contributors to the counterterrorism mission: federal, state, and local governments, the private sector, and possibly even foreign partners, while protecting privacy and liberties. Based on the Markle task force's recommendations, the Intelligence Reform and Terrorism Prevention Act explicitly called for the president to create an information sharing environment (ISE) "for the sharing of terrorism information in a manner consistent with national security and with applicable legal standards relating to privacy and civil liberties."[40] This proposal amplified and codified steps already taken by President Bush in August 2004. In response to it, the president issued executive order 13356 to implement the ISE.[41] The following are the key elements in creating that environment:

—Putting an end to the culture of restricting access to information ("need to know") in favor of "need to share," including by reducing or eliminating the right of an agency that produces intelligence to control its dissemination (ORCON, or originator control). The act encourages federal agencies and departments to reduce "over-classification of information and unnecessary requirements for originator approval" as far as possible since they are considered to be barriers to information sharing.

—Increasing the commitment to developing unclassified or less restrictively classified versions of intelligence reports. To "maximize the dissemination of intelligence," the act charges the DNI with establishing and implementing guidelines for the intelligence community to prepare reports in a way that would "allow for dissemination at the lowest level of classification possible or in unclassified form to the extent practicable," for example, by removing information on sources. As part of the ISE, the president is also required to issue guidelines that would ensure that information is "in its most shareable form," again possibly by using "tear lines" to detach the data from the sources and methods through which it was acquired.

—Making information available to those who need it. For information to be useful, those who need it, who often will be unknown to those who collect it, must be able to find it. The Intelligence Reform Act sought to facilitate the task by requiring the ISE to provide "electronic directory services, or the functional equivalent, to assist in locating in the Federal Government intelligence and terrorism information and people with relevant knowledge about intelligence and terrorism information." The program manager responsible for information sharing across the federal government was given 180 days to establish at least the initial capacity to provide such services.

—A system based on a "network of networks" rather than a single all-encompassing network. Creating an entirely new network to facilitate sharing is neither achievable nor desirable. Massive infrastructure projects have a poor track record. They often are out of date even before being completed, and creating a new network would create an unacceptable time lag in the urgent task of improving sharing. Creating massive consolidated databases also poses serious security and privacy risks, as well as problems of data quality assurance. Therefore the act envisions an approach based on linking existing and new systems and databases through the adoption of protocols and standards that would facilitate sharing across diverse networks.

—Building security and privacy protections into the design. In order for the new information sharing environment to be "trusted" and thereby to gain the acceptance necessary to reap the benefits of wider sharing, there must be adequate assurances to protect the security of sensitive information and the legitimate privacy and civil liberties interests of the public. The Markle report and the Intelligence Reform Act seek to achieve that goal by encouraging the use of technologies that protect privacy, such as anonymization and permissioning, along with the adoption of policies governing the appropriate collection, dissemination, and use of data, supplemented by strong audit and oversight features to ensure compliance.[42] Although some trade-offs between security and privacy are inevitable, many of the features that protect privacy (such as strong audit capabilities and procedures, and avoiding the centralization of data) will also contribute to protecting the security of information.

Although these principles have gained wide assent, there is much to do to ensure their implementation. Such a system will have to try to encompass what has been estimated as fifteen different intelligence components among federal government agencies and potentially 17,784 state and local law enforcement agencies, 30,020 fire departments, 5,801 hospitals, and numerous first responders.[43] It will have to ensure that intelligence access and sharing tools are available across the system to all the relevant actors; leverage existing networks; and integrate local, private, and foreign actors as well. It is an enormous challenge to get the various actors to trust the system and other actors, and to get the public to trust the system to protect its privacy and civil liberties as a whole. Recurring scandals involving lost and stolen personally identifiable data from the private sector and poorly conceived government efforts—such as the now abandoned Total/Terrorism Information Awareness (TIA) program and CAPPS II passenger screening program—have increased public wariness.[44] But building such trust is possible through clear and systemwide guidelines for the collection, handling, distribution, retention, and accuracy of information, with some guidelines needing special attention, such as those related to predicate-based searching, and the use of tools—technological and others—to ensure compliance with the guidelines. In addition, while new or improved tools and rules will go a long way in meeting the challenge, they are unlikely to prove effective if the *culture* of the agencies remains the same. Guidelines and technologies can help change the culture, but incentives, training, and leadership will also be needed.

Information sharing with state and local government agencies needs to be improved.

One of the most vexing problems in the post-9/11 environment has been coordination between the federal government and state and local authorities.

Coordination has proved particularly problematic in the intelligence context for a number of reasons. Few state and local law officials have security clearances or training in intelligence work. Most state and local units lack the technology, including IT systems and secure facilities, that would permit obtaining and retaining sensitive intelligence information. Yet state and local governments—especially law enforcement agencies—represent a potentially invaluable resource in the counterterrorism effort. They act as "force multipliers"— 87, 575 extra pairs of eyes and ears—and with their intimate knowledge of their own communities, they often may be better placed to recruit sources and spot anomalies than the FBI.[45]

To overcome these difficulties, the FBI has relied primarily on the JTTFs, which were first set up in 1980 but whose numbers increased after 9/11. Today there are 103 JTTFs, more than half of which were created after 9/11.[46] They bring together federal, state, and local officials and provide a forum for information sharing as well as coordination of operations. While the task forces are a welcome improvement, critical problems remain. The JTTFs are of uneven quality. There are repeated complaints that even in this improved context, little information is shared and the sharing is one-way (state and local governments give information to the federal government, which gives little in return). Another concern is that the task forces are heavily law-enforcement oriented and do not include the full spectrum of relevant state and local agencies that are essential to the counterterrorism effort and that need access to this kind of information. Furthermore, officials representing their agencies at the JTTFs often cannot pass on a lot of the information that they receive to their agencies because staff members there lack the requisite security clearances.[47]

In response, a number of major local law enforcement agencies have substantially expanded their own intelligence collection and analysis capability— including by forming liaison relationships (or other informal information networks) with other state and local governments and even foreign intelligence agencies, with little coordination with the federal government. Needless to say, this is hardly an ideal solution to the problem of coordination and sharing, which is so central to an effective counterterrorism strategy.

Effective implementation of the information sharing environment mandated by the Intelligence Reform Act can make a substantial contribution to ameliorating these problems. Elimination of ORCON and dramatically increased use of unclassified tear-line information will expand the scope of information that can be more widely shared with state and local governments. Implementation of directories will make federal information more accessible and usable in a timely manner by the cop on the beat or by a public health official, while minimizing the risk of disclosing sensitive intelligence sources and methods. Interoperable standards will enhance two-way information flows. And audit and oversight features could go some way in ensuring that the system is "trusted."

An effective relationship between the federal agencies and state and local authorities will require trust and sharing that operates both ways. Also crucial to implementing this solution is to create a locus of responsibility for facilitating sharing between levels of government. Today that responsibility is divided, with both the DHS and the FBI playing important roles. These roles will have to be clarified to avoid overlap and confusion. The principal strength of the FBI in this arena is its growing role in and increased focus on the domestic intelligence mission. Its weakness is its tendency to concentrate on relationships with other law enforcement entities rather than the broader spectrum of relevant actors. With the implementation of the NCTC (with its responsibility for intelligence coordination and analysis), it will be both possible and necessary to create linkages with state and local governments and the private sector. The Intelligence Reform Act provides that the NCTC "shall . . . support the Department of Justice and the Department of Homeland Security, and other appropriate agencies in fulfillment of their responsibilities to disseminate terrorism information . . . to State and local government officials and other entities."[48] The FBI and its associated JTTFs can and should be one conduit for these exchanges, but they should not be the exclusive channel.

Effective exchanges will also require better training. To enhance capabilities while encouraging cooperation and sharing at the state and local level, as recommended by the Markle task force, the secretary for homeland security, paralleling the work of the DNI at the federal level and collaborating with the Department of Justice, should take the lead in providing training guidelines for the agencies.[49] The secretary of homeland security has already created an Office of Intelligence and Analysis within the department to improve information sharing with state and local partners.[50]

The DNI needs to implement personnel strategies that enhance the sense of community across the broad array of intelligence and counterterrorism agencies.

As much of the preceding discussion shows, the barriers to collaboration and sharing in the intelligence and counterterrorism communities are as much about organizational culture as organizational arrangements. Even strong

centralized authority in the DNI is unlikely to achieve the kind of cooperation necessary if individuals see their mission in terms of their individual
agency's responsibilities rather than the collective good. At the same time,
diversity in the intelligence community also has value in that it can broaden
the range of expertise available and help avoid groupthink.

All of the major post-9/11 reviews have urged attention to the need to
develop a sense of "jointness" in the intelligence community, drawing on the
experience of the military under the Goldwater-Nichols Act of 1986, which
sought to reduce the traditional tension between military services that
impeded effective war fighting.[51] Elements of the strategy include career
incentives to participate in joint assignments, training, and education, and to
accept assignment to billets in other services. The Intelligence Reform Act
specifically mandated steps along these lines by requiring incentives for service in joint positions such as on the staff of the DNI and the NCTC, and
mechanisms for rotating personnel among intelligence agencies and establishing training and education requirements across the community. However,
the statute largely exempts military personnel from these provisions.

Following up on the Robb-Silberman Commission's recommendations,
the administration directed the DNI (to be assisted by a chief human capital
officer) to develop "creative performance incentives and a 'joint' personnel
rotation system" and stated that a National Intelligence University system
would be established, which could facilitate joint training. A senior training
and education officer in the office of the DNI would oversee its establishment and management.[52] To overcome cultural differences that inhibit joint
efforts and to foster a collaborative work ethic and common practices, the
Markle task force has recommended that the DNI should also develop a
common federal government curriculum for intelligence analysts across at
least all the agencies involved in counterterrorism; an entry-level core curriculum that would establish a basic standard of training for the intelligence
community; and a system of details and exchange assignments that would be
required for promotion.[53]

The experience under the Goldwater-Nichols Act suggests that effective
implementation of these provisions could play a crucial role in changing cultures and breaking down stovepipes, but the barriers to doing so are daunting.
Unlike in the military, the concept of rotation is not ingrained in most civilian agencies, which have highly vertical structures, and the ability of the DNI
to oversee the personnel policies of highly diverse agencies will prove challenging at a time when other more time-sensitive concerns associated with
establishing the new position compete for attention. To date the penalties for

inappropriate disclosure of sensitive information are clear and substantial, the rewards for sharing minimal at best. It is vital that the DNI move quickly to adopt procedures to implement these aspects of the Intelligence Reform Act and the recommendations mentioned above to give a strong signal, even to those not serving in a cross-agency appointment, that collaboration and cooperation are the norm for career advancement.[54]

Congressional oversight needs to be enhanced.

The 9/11 Commission identified as a major problem the lack of power and capability of the House and Senate intelligence committees to undertake effective oversight of intelligence activities. It went as far as calling congressional oversight "dysfunctional" and stated that it was one area in need of "substantial" change. The commission suggested that Congress create a joint intelligence committee or separate committees that had both "authorizing and appropriations powers." The members of this committee or committees would be encouraged to develop the necessary expertise in the subject and would be held accountable for their work. It further suggested that committee staff be nonpartisan and work for the committee or committees as a whole. It suggested that the committee(s) should have the following:

—a subcommittee solely devoted to oversight

—subpoena authority

—majority party representation that never exceeds that of the minority party by more than one

—in order to incorporate other related interests, at least four members who also serve on one of the following: Armed Services, Judiciary, or Foreign Affairs Committee or the Defense Appropriations Subcommittee

—members who serve indefinitely in order to allow them to "accumulate expertise"

—a smaller number of members than on other committees in order to encourage "a greater sense of responsibility, and accountability, for the quality of the committee's work."[55]

The Intelligence Reform Act of 2004 did not include reform of the congressional oversight process. In March 2005, the Robb-Silberman Commission also urged reform of congressional oversight. It recommended that "the House and Senate intelligence committees create focused oversight subcommittees, that the Congress create an intelligence appropriations subcommittee and reduce the Intelligence Community's reliance on supplemental funding, and that the Senate intelligence committee be given the same authority over joint military intelligence programs and tactical intelligence programs that the House intelligence committee now exercises."[56]

While the House Permanent Select Committee on Intelligence has set up an oversight subcommittee, much remains to be done. The Senate Intelligence Committee has yet to appoint such a subcommittee. Furthermore, while the House and Senate appropriations committees now have homeland security subcommittees, there are still no such subcommittees on intelligence. The defense subcommittees that handle appropriations for intelligence consider that budget to be "just a blip" and therefore do not devote much time or attention to it. Senate efforts to create an intelligence subcommittee stalled even after its creation was approved because of concerns about making the classified intelligence budget public.[57]

In April 2005, one of the 9/11 commissioners reiterated that congressional oversight remained a problem, stating that while Congress had done a lot on its recommendations, "What the Congress did not do is deal effectively with the question of the robust oversight of the intelligence community." While recognizing that it was unlikely that one committee each would be created in the House and Senate and given appropriations and authorizing power, he said that a solution had to be found, adding: "The key factor here is that the intelligence community doesn't pay that much attention to the authorizing committees because they don't have to. They get their money from the appropriating committees."[58]

Reform is not going to be easy—especially since committees are likely to resist any potential loss of jurisdiction and the structure of the intelligence community that is being overseen is itself evolving. Nevertheless, it is necessary. Before it is pursued, however, there needs to be a debate about what the roles and responsibilities of the committees overseeing the intelligence community should be. Without clarification, any reform is likely to be scattered and probably short-sighted.

Notes

1. The intelligence community consists of fifteen agencies: Air Force Intelligence, Army Intelligence, the Central Intelligence Agency, Coast Guard Intelligence, the Defense Intelligence Agency, the Department of Energy's Office of Intelligence, the Department of Homeland Security's planned Office of Intelligence and Analysis, the Department of State's Bureau of Intelligence and Research, the Department of the Treasury's Office of Terrorism and Finance Intelligence, the Federal Bureau of Investigation's Directorate of Intelligence, Marine Corps Intelligence, the National

Geospatial-Intelligence Agency, the National Reconnaissance Office, the National Security Agency, and Navy Intelligence.

2. See sec. 102b (1) and (2) of the Intelligence Reform and Terrorism Prevention Act of December 17, 2004 (Public Law 108-458).

3. See sec. 102A(c)(3) of the Intelligence Reform and Terrorism Prevention Act of December 17, 2004 (Public Law 108-458).

4. Nor does it apply to the direct dissemination of information to state and local government officials and private sector entities.

5. The lack of cooperation was evident in the investigation of the Cole bombing, when the Department of Justice sent a team to investigate, the Pentagon sent an intelligence cell, and the State Department dispatched its ambassador to oversee the investigation. Christopher Whitcomb, "Fixing a Dysfunctional U.S. Spy Network," *International Herald Tribune*, May 17, 2004, p. 8.

6. Dana Priest, "CIA Is Expanding Domestic Operations; More Offices, More Agents with FBI," *Washington Post*, October 23, 2002, p. A2.

7. As the report of the Commission on the Intelligence Capabilities of the United States Regarding Weapons of Mass Destruction (referred to in the rest of this chapter as the Robb-Silberman Commission) states: "The expansion of the FBI's intelligence collection and reporting activities over the past few years has engendered turf battles between the CIA and the FBI that have already caused counterproductive conflicts both within and outside of the United States. In particular, the two agencies have clashed over the domestic collection of foreign intelligence—an area in which they have long shared responsibilities." See Commission on the Intelligence Capabilities of the United States Regarding Weapons of Mass Destruction [Robb-Silberman Commission], *Report to the President of the United States* (March 31, 2005), p. 32.

8. Mark Sherman, "FBI, CIA Seek Ground Rules on Intelligence," Associated Press, January 28, 2005; Robb-Silberman Commission, *Report to the President of the United States*, pp. 468–71.

9. "CIA, FBI Agree Intelligence Roles, Officials Say," Reuters, June 12, 2005; see "Bush Administration Actions to Implement WMD Commission Recommendations," June 29, 2005 (www.whitehouse.gov/news/releases/2005/06/20050629-5.html [July 6, 2005]).

10. Judith Miller, "A New York Cop in Israel, Stepping a Bit on the FBI's Toes," *New York Times*, May 15, 2005, p. 37.

11. Michael Isikoff, "Intelligence: The Pentagon—Spying in America?" *Newsweek*, June 21, 2004, p. 6; Robert Block and Gary Fields, "Is Military Creeping into Domestic Spying and Enforcement?" *Wall Street Journal*, March 9, 2004, p. B1.

12. U.S. Senate Select Committee on Intelligence, *A Bill to Authorize Appropriations for Fiscal Year 2006 for Intelligence-Related Activities of the United States Government, the Intelligence Community Management Account, and the Central Intelligence Agency Retirement and Disability System, and for Other Purposes* (S. 1803) (http://intelligence.senate.gov/arm05j35_lc.pdf [November 2, 2005]), p. 80.

13. Department of Defense, *Strategy for Homeland Defense and Civil Support* (June 2005).

14. Robb-Silberman Commission, *Report to the President of the United States*, p. 22.

15. Walter Pincus, "CIA, Pentagon Seek to Avoid Overlap," *Washington Post,* July 4, 2005, p. A2.

16. See "DNI and D/CIA Announce Establishment of the National Clandestine Service," October 13, 2005 (www.cia.gov/cia/public_affairs/press_release/2005/pr10132005.html [October 27, 2005]).

17. See "Fact Sheet: Creation of the National Humint Manager," October 13, 2005 (www.cia.gov/cia/public_affairs/press_release/2005/fs10132005.html [October 27, 2005]).

18. Pincus, "CIA, Pentagon Seek to Avoid Overlap."

19. Barton Gellman, "Secret Unit Expands Rumsfeld's Domain," *Washington Post,* January 23, 2005, p. A1.

20. National Commission on Terrorist Attacks upon the United States [9/11 Commission], *The 9/11 Commission Report: Final Report of the National Commission on Terrorist Attacks upon the United States* (New York: W. W. Norton , 2004), p. 415.

21. Defense Science Board, *Report of the Defense Science Board 2003 Summer Study on DoD Roles and Missions in Homeland Security,* vol. 1 (November 2003), p. 20. The DSB also stated that the secretary of defense "should accelerate the ongoing transformation of the Defense HUMINT Service, with particular attention to ensuring that the nation has the global coverage and sustained foreign presence that is needed in regions ripe and important" in its *2004 Summer Study on Transition to and from Hostilities,* released in December 2004.

22. A detailed look at these reasons can be found in Jennifer D. Kibbe, "A Loophole for Covert Operations," *Fort Worth Star-Telegram*, August 8, 2004.

23. The act merely says, "The Director of National Intelligence, in consultation with the Secretary of Defense and the Director of the Central Intelligence Agency, shall develop joint procedures to be used by the Department of Defense and the Central Intelligence Agency to improve the coordination and deconfliction of operations that involve elements of both the Armed Forces and the Central Intelligence Agency consistent with national security and the protection of human intelligence sources and methods."

24. Pincus, "CIA, Pentagon Seek to Avoid Overlap."

25. See "Bush Administration Actions to Implement WMD Commission Recommendations," June 29, 2005 (www.whitehouse.gov/news/releases/2005/06/20050629-5.html [July 6, 2005]). On rejection of the recommendation, see Douglas Jiehl, "Bush to Create New Unit in F.B.I. for Intelligence," *New York Times,* June 30, 2005, p. 1.

26. Bill Gertz, "Covert Action Operations to Remain in CIA's Control: 9/11 Panel's Suggestion of Pentagon Role Rejected," *Washington Times*, October 14, 2005, A13.

27. See "Fact Sheet: Bush Names Terrorism, Cyberspace Security Advisors," October 9, 2001 (www.usembassyjakarta.org/Factsheet_bush.html [July 6, 2005]).

28. The CSIS–Heritage Foundation report *DHS 2.0: Rethinking the Department of Homeland Security* (December 2004) suggested "strengthening the Secretary of Homeland Security's policymaking function by creating an Undersecretary for Policy" (p. 5).

29. George W. Bush, "Moment of Truth for World in Iraq," press conference with President Bush, Prime Minister Tony Blair, President Jose Maria Aznar, and Prime Minister Jose Manuel Durao Barroso, Azores, Portugal, March 16, 2003.

30. Occasionally in the 1990s, information was shared with multilateral organizations, but this was often ad hoc, for very specific assignments.

31. See "Written Statement for the Record of the Director of Central Intelligence before the National Commission on Terrorist Attacks upon the United States," March 24, 2004 (www.9-11commission.gov/hearings/hearing8/tenet_statement.pdf [July 6, 2005]). See also Samuel L. Berger, "Testimony before the National Commission on Terrorist Attacks upon the United States," March 24, 2004 (www.9-11commission. gov/hearings/hearing8/berger_statement.pdf [July 6, 2005]).

32. There is a detailed discussion of this case in chapter 3 of this book.

33. In this respect, the PDD-62 model differed from the Office of National Drug Control Policy (ONDCP), which does not lead any formal interagency processes.

34. "The Director of the National Counterterrorism Center may not direct the execution of counterterrorism operations." See sec. 119(g) of the Intelligence Reform and Terrorism Prevention Act of December 17, 2004 (Public Law 108–458).

35. This problem was addressed in a Center for Strategic and International Studies report, *Beyond Goldwater-Nichols: Phase 1* (March 2004). It states that "there is little capacity on the National Security Council staff dedicated to integrating agency strategies and plans or monitoring their execution, even though both functions are critical to achieving unity of effort across the U.S. government and success on the ground. . . . While it remains true that lead responsibility for the planning and conduct of operations should rest with individual agencies, it also is true that the NSC staff has a critical role to play in leading an interagency process to develop an integrated strategy and a coherent U.S. game plan" (p. 61). Furthermore, "another source of poor U.S. performance in complex operations is the lack of rapidly deployable experts and capabilities in most civilian agencies. Most civilian agencies do not focus on the conduct of operations and therefore lack an operational culture" (p. 62).

36. According to the FBI's report to the 9/11 Commission in April 2004, the number of special agents working on "terrorism matters" had increased since 9/11 from 1,351 to 2,398 and the number of intelligence analysts from 1,023 to 1,197; in addition, 700 new translators had been hired.

37. Robb-Silberman Commission, *Report to the President of the United States*, p. 31.

38. See Alfred Cumming and Todd Masse, "Intelligence Reform Implementation at the Federal Bureau of Investigation: Issues and Options for Congress" (Washington:

Congressional Research Service, August 16, 2005) (www.fas.org/sgp/crs/intel/ RL33033.pdf [September 16, 2005]). See also Siobhan Gorman, "FBI Might Lack Tools to Analyze Terrorism; New Field Units Short of Equipment, Authority, Government Study Says," *Baltimore Sun,* September 14, 2005, p. 1A.

39. See "Bush Administration Actions to Implement WMD Commission Recommendations," June 29, 2005 (www.whitehouse.gov/news/releases/2005/06/20050629-5.html [July 6, 2005]). The administration has also directed a reorganization of the Justice Department so that its intelligence and counterterrorism assets would be brought together under a new assistant attorney general for national security.

40. See sec. 1016b (1) of the Intelligence Reform and Terrorism Prevention Act of December 17, 2004 (Public Law 108–458).

41. See "Executive Order: Further Strengthening the Sharing of Terrorism Information to Protect Americans," October 25, 2005 (www.whitehouse.gov/news/releases/2005/10/20051025-5.html [November 1, 2005]). It replaced the executive order of August 27, 2004 ("Executive Order: Strengthening the Sharing of Terrorism Information to Protect Americans").

42. See the Markle Task Force on National Security in the Information Age, second report, *Creating a Trusted Network for Homeland Security* (December 2003). On anonymization: "Technologies are being developed for anonymization of the data that would enable the enforcement of privacy policies without encumbering intelligence analysis" (p. 134). Anonymization is the "ability to convert actual data values to anonymous values before the data is shared between parties" (p. 144). In terms of permissioning, the Markle report states that "the network also needs to have strong data protection, including the ability to restrict access privileges so that data can be used only for a particular purpose, for a finite period of time, and by people with the necessary permissions . . . a variety of new technologies has increased the capacity for online identification and authentication, which are prerequisites for providing permission to the right people to use the network for the right reasons" (p. 17).

43. Ibid., p. 14.

44. The *New York Times* described the TIA system as one that "will rely on a set of computer-based pattern recognition techniques known as 'data mining,' a set of statistical techniques used by scientists as well as by marketers searching for potential customers. The system would permit a team of intelligence analysts to gather and view information from databases, pursue links between individuals and groups, respond to automatic alerts, and share information efficiently, all from their individual computers." John Markoff, "Pentagon Plans a Computer System That Would Peek at Personal Data of Americans," *New York Times,* November 9, 2002, p. 12. DHS describes the computer-assisted passenger prescreening system (CAPPS II) as "a limited, automated prescreening system authorized by Congress in the wake of the Sept. 11, 2001, terrorist attacks. The system, developed with the utmost concern for individual privacy rights, modernizes the prescreening system currently implemented by the airlines. It will seek to authenticate travelers' identities and perform risk assessments to detect

individuals who may pose a terrorist-related threat or who have outstanding Federal or state warrants for crimes of violence." See "Fact Sheet: CAPPS II at a Glance" (www.dhs.gov/dhspublic/display?content=3162 [July 6, 2005]).

45. The U.S. Census Bureau in December 2002 estimated that "there were 87,576 governmental units in the United States as of June 30, 2002. In addition to the federal government and the 50 state governments, there were 87,525 units of local government." U.S. Census Bureau, *2002 Census of Governments* (December 2002), p. V.

46. See "A Closer Look at the FBI's Joint Terrorism Task Forces" (www.fbi.gov/page2/dec04/jttf120114.htm [July 6, 2005]).

47. David Thacher, "The Local Role in Homeland Security," *Law and Society Review* 39 (September 2005).

48. See sec. 119(f)(1)(E) of the Intelligence Reform and Terrorism Prevention Act of December 17, 2004 (Public Law 108–458).

49. See Markle Task Force on National Security in the Information Age, *Networked Analytic Methods and Tools* (December 15, 2005).

50. Jim McKay, "The Security Shuffle," *Government Technology*, November 4, 2005 (www.govtech.net/magazine/channel_story.php/97157 [November 10, 2005]).

51. The congressional joint inquiry on the intelligence community stated that "Congress should consider enacting legislation, modeled on the Goldwater-Nichols Act of 1986, to instill the concept of 'jointness' throughout the Intelligence Community. By emphasizing such things as joint education, a joint career specialty, increased authority for regional commanders, and joint exercises, that Act greatly enhanced the joint warfighting capabilities of the individual military services. Legislation to instill similar concepts throughout the Intelligence Community could help improve management of Community resources and priorities and insure a far more effective 'team' effort by all the intelligence agencies. The Director of National Intelligence should require more extensive use of 'joint tours' for intelligence and appropriate law enforcement personnel to broaden their experience and help bridge existing organizational and cultural divides through service in other agencies. These joint tours should include not only service at Intelligence Community agencies, but also service in those agencies that are users or consumers of intelligence products. Serious incentives for joint service should be established throughout the Intelligence Community and personnel should be rewarded for joint service with career advancement credit at individual agencies. The Director of National Intelligence should also require Intelligence Community agencies to participate in joint exercises." See the report of the U.S. Senate Select Committee on Intelligence and U.S. House Permanent Select Committee on Intelligence, *Joint Inquiry into Intelligence Community Activities before and after the Terrorist Attacks of September 11, 2001* (December 2002).

52. See "Bush Administration Actions to Implement WMD Commission Recommendations," June 29, 2005 (www.whitehouse.gov/news/releases/2005/06/20050629-5.html [July 6, 2005]).

53. See Markle Task Force, *Networked Analytic Methods and Tools*.

54. The Intelligence Reform Act states that the DNI should "provide incentives for personnel of elements of the intelligence community" to serve on his or her own staff, the national intelligence centers, the National Counterterrorism Center, and "in other positions in support of the intelligence community management functions of the Director." Incentives could be financial or whatever the DNI considered appropriate; promotions would depend on what had been assigned or detailed; and the DNI would have to "prescribe mechanisms to facilitate the rotation of personnel of the intelligence community through various elements of the intelligence community in the course of their careers." It furthermore states, "It is the sense of Congress that the mechanisms prescribed under this subsection should, to the extent practical, seek to duplicate for civilian personnel within the intelligence community the joint officer management policies established by chapter 38 of title 10, United States Code, and the other amendments made by title IV of the Goldwater-Nichols Department of Defense Reorganization Act of 1986 (Public Law 99–433)." See Intelligence Reform and Terrorism Prevention Act of December 17, 2004 (Public Law 108–458).

55. 9/11 Commission, *The 9/11 Commission Report*, pp. 419–21.

56. Robb-Silberman Commission, *Report to the President of the United States* (March 31, 2005), p. 20.

57. Walter Pincus, "Plans to Create Senate Intelligence Oversight Panel Run into Snag," *Washington Post,* February 10, 2005, p. A21.

58. Megan King, "Hamilton Continues Push for 9/11 Recommendations," *Roll Call,* April 25, 2005.

3

International Cooperation on Homeland Security

Jeremy Shapiro

Homeland security, as the name implies, often is thought of as primarily a domestic task. Borders and oceans traditionally have been seen as walls that separate and secure the homeland from the unknowns that lurk beyond. Despite the nomenclature, however, the task of defending the borders and the integrity of the U.S. homeland is not purely or perhaps even primarily a domestic activity. As the introduction emphasized, policymakers cannot consider domestic and external counterterrorism measures as even conceptually distinct from one another. Homeland security requires, in the words of former Secretary of Homeland Security Tom Ridge, "more than just the integration of a nation . . . but the integration of nations."[1] Accordingly, the *National Strategy for Homeland Security* asserts that "America must pursue a sustained, steadfast, and systematic international agenda to counter the global terrorist threat and improve our homeland security."[2]

While this agenda recognizes that the 9/11 attacks originated abroad and profited from porous U.S. borders, it also recognizes that the same borders allow the types of international exchange that underpin global prosperity. While border controls can be and have been improved since the attacks, the reality is that the volume, speed, and economic importance of cross-border connections makes the idea of walling off the United States self-evidently unworkable and undesirable. Moreover, international cooperation offers the United States opportunities to achieve many homeland security goals, such as countering the proliferation of weapons of mass destruction, more cheaply by attacking the problem before it spreads and with less need to infringe on civil liberties at home. Securing the United States without choking off the international connections that sustain it will require institutionalized cooperation with a wide variety of countries and international institutions in a number of different areas, from civil aviation to law enforcement to food safety. Many of these areas traditionally have not been thought of as subjects for international negotiation or at least have not been considered to have national security implications.

Large gaps persist in international efforts to ensure homeland security: in preventing the travel of dangerous persons; in monitoring international cargo, both on the sea and in the air; and in halting the proliferation of dangerous technologies such as nuclear devices and man-portable missile systems. The United States has many important international partners in homeland security, among them Canada and Mexico, with which it shares land borders, and various Middle Eastern countries that provide key intelligence. But for reasons that will be explained, it is the European countries that provide the most fruitful path for understanding how well international cooperation on homeland security is proceeding. This chapter will explore ways of closing those gaps through the lens of America's cooperation with its European partners.

The United States and the nations of Europe have accomplished a great deal together in homeland security since 9/11. In the process, there have been many disagreements and many difficult negotiations, but in almost all cases a way forward has been found. At the same time, the sense of urgency and importance that the United States has given to this issue in international negotiations has meant that its partners often have been willing to bend toward the U.S. position, even to the point of making agreements that may compromise cherished principles. As a result, the international homeland security agenda often is seen, particularly in Europe, as an externalization of American domestic needs. Most European leaders have made little effort to explain to their publics the importance of cooperating with the United States on homeland security issues.

Three years into the war on terrorism, homeland security is beginning to move from an issue of immediate urgency to one of enduring importance. At a similar juncture in the early days of the cold war, the challenge was to cement the ad-hoc alliances created under the pressure of war into an enduring institution—ultimately, NATO—that could rally support for a long struggle. Similarly, the next great challenge for international cooperation will be to institutionalize the various homeland security arrangements created in the wake of 9/11 and, in so doing, create a sense in U.S. partners that they have a similar stake in international cooperation on homeland security. International cooperation on this issue will never be complete; there are simply too many differences in interests—even given a common foe like Islamist terrorism—to achieve perfect cooperation. But it can be better. For the transatlantic partnership, part of the process of making it better will involve encouraging the European Union (EU), slowly but surely, to become America's key partner, alongside individual EU countries, on issues of homeland security.

The Challenges of International Cooperation

Achieving the necessary level of cooperation and coordination among the myriad different public and private actors involved in homeland security within the United States is hard enough. Taking cooperation to the international level presents yet another layer of complexity. In essence, this further complexity results from the need to negotiate among sovereign bodies with different cultural values, institutions, and histories. Moreover, even when cultural, institutional, and historical differences are factored out, there are still disputes about the nature and extent of the threat terrorism presents and appropriate strategies for dealing with that threat.

Dealing with this complexity is an enormous task. One way of reducing it is to recognize that not all states play the same role in U.S. homeland security issues. The United States has a variety of different relationships with respect to homeland security with various international actors. Many states in the developing world, such as Pakistan and Indonesia, while of critical importance in the war on terror, have very little exchange of goods and people with the United States. Moreover, such states often lack the institutional or technical capacity to implement the types of homeland security measures—container security, biometric passports, or legal assistance—that top the international agenda.

More capable and economically integrated states, primarily in North America, Europe, and parts of Asia, have sufficient exchange with the United States that a lack of integration on issues of border and transportation security would create severe vulnerabilities for the United States. Canada and Mexico, because of their long land borders with the United States, present unique challenges, which are examined in chapter 6. Europe also is a particularly important partner for the United States. In the first instance, that is because the United States and Europe represent the two largest trading blocs and the largest bilateral trading and investment relationship in the world.[3] Most of the member countries of the EU are in the U.S. visa waiver program (VWP), through which their citizens enjoy visa-free travel for short-term visits to the United States. Partially as a result, Americans and Europeans made nearly 21 million trips across the Atlantic in 2003—the largest such exchange of people between the United States and another region.[4]

This vast exchange of goods and people is critical to the prosperity of the Atlantic community, but the numerous interconnections that it creates between the United States and Europe also make Europe an ideal location from which to launch terrorist attacks against the United States—a point demonstrated by the role of Europe as one of the staging grounds for the 9/11 attacks. Because of Europe's large Muslim population—and the reported priority of Islamist terrorist groups to recruit members with European passports, already demonstrated in the attempt of British citizen Richard Reid to bomb a transatlantic flight—Europe may continue to be a source of terrorist activity.[5] Since 9/11, there have been more than 1,000 arrests of terrorist suspects in Europe, including cells apparently intending to launch chemical weapons attacks in Europe, an attack on the U.S. embassy in Paris, and attacks on U.S. targets in New York, New Jersey, and Washington, D.C.[6] These trends have accelerated of late with a spate of terrorism-related arrests in Germany, Spain, and the Netherlands.

Even beyond the direct threats, however, Europe is important to U.S. homeland security because the nations of Europe tend to be the most capable partners, able and willing to implement a wide range of measures that most states lack the institutional infrastructure to even contemplate. Europeans also have tended to be the toughest negotiators among those states that participate in U.S. homeland security. Each of the countries of Europe has its own view of the terrorist threat, of how to fight terrorism, and of how to conduct homeland security operations; moreover, those countries have a semi-unified voice in the form of the European Union, which makes sure that their views are heard. Most of the advanced Asian states—Japan, South Korea, Singapore—have been much more accepting of U.S. initiatives. As a result, U.S.-European agreements on homeland security, though hard won, help establish that homeland security is not merely an American fixation but rather a legitimate concern for all states. Such agreements also increase the legitimacy of U.S. initiatives and provide leverage for encouraging other countries to follow along. As a result of all of these factors, Europe and the United States often set the standard for international cooperation in homeland security.

For example, once the European Union had agreed on the American-initiated container security initiative, the international community as a whole, under the auspices of the World Customs Organization, was able to build on that initiative to develop the Framework of Standards to Secure and Facilitate Global Trade, which sets minimum standards for global cargo security.[7] For all of these reasons, according to William Pope, formerly the U.S. State Department's counterterrorism coordinator, "The U.S.-European relationship is the critical relationship [for counterterrorism]. That view is widely shared within the U.S. government."[8]

This chapter, therefore, will concentrate on U.S.-European cooperation and especially U.S.-EU cooperation on homeland security. Of course, the U.S.-European relationship is far from the definitive word on international cooperation, and the United States has a wide variety of different relationships with the diverse countries of Europe. However, improving the U.S. relationships with Europe is the first and most important step in closing the gaps in U.S. homeland security caused by porous borders and incomplete international cooperation.

U.S.-European Homeland Security Cooperation

The United States and the countries of Europe have a long history of cooperation on what is now thought of as homeland security. U.S. and European intelligence agencies, for example, have long shared information on terrorist threats. From a U.S. perspective, the 9/11 attacks served to group much of that preexisting cooperation under the rubric of "homeland security," thus creating a new sense of urgency and importance and often involving new actors and new issues. The very term "homeland security" is an American invention, and the agenda of issues for international cooperation in homeland security has been set largely by the United States. Issues such as airplane passenger data sharing and container security have been brought up by the United States in response to American domestic security concerns. European-initiated measures have focused on internal security issues rather than on the transatlantic homeland security agenda.[9] That is not to say that all of Europe always accepts whatever the United States dictates—far from it. Europeans often have objected to specific U.S. proposals and the agreements reached all represent some degree of compromise on both sides.

Moreover, the United States and many of the nations of Europe have had a number of sharp philosophical and political divides over how to combat terrorism, even after the terrorist attacks in Madrid in March 2004 and London in July 2005. Many of these countries have a long experience with terrorism and have set ideas on the best strategies for dealing with the problem. Many Europeans therefore recoil at the use of the word "war" to describe the struggle against terrorism and question the emphasis that the United States has placed on military means for fighting terrorism.[10] European commentators have frequently condemned the U.S. use of extrajudicial detentions at Guantanamo Bay and elsewhere, and European politicians have expressed concern about the effects of U.S. actions on the privacy rights of their citizens.[11] Most prominently, European counterterrorism officials often have rejected the U.S. claim that the war in Iraq was part of the effort to destroy al Qaeda or part of the war on terrorism, seeing it at best as a distraction from the struggle against al Qaeda, at worst as a gift to al Qaeda recruiting efforts.[12]

The member states of the European Union themselves also have a wide variety of capabilities for combating terrorism and differing views on the importance of these issues. There is in fact no "European" view on most of these issues and certainly no centralized authority capable of imposing a single view. Countries that historically have not faced terrorist threats have less counterterrorism capacity and less willingness to expend scarce resources or to limit civil liberties for what they may see as a negligible threat to their own country.

Still, by and large, the governments of Europe clearly have—and understand that they have—an interest both in their own homeland security and in helping the United States to protect itself. Europe has its own Islamist terrorist threat, equal to or, by some lights, greater than that faced by the United States. Many European states have been coping with terrorist threats for many decades and have consequently developed sophisticated means of fighting terrorism, which, contrary to many stereotypes, are far from being "soft." French counterterrorism, for example, is based firmly on the principle that terrorism must be met with a swift and forceful response. Antiterrorist officials in France have and regularly exercise powers—placing wiretaps, issuing subpoenas, rounding up suspects as a preventative measure, and so forth— that are in many ways more far-reaching than any measures that the U.S. government has contemplated, even in the wake of September 11. Indeed, the principal French dispute with the United Kingdom during the late 1990s over terrorism stemmed from a British judge's decision not to allow the extradition of a terrorist suspect to France on the grounds that he might be tortured.[13]

Because of Europe's experience, the philosophical debates and political crises mentioned have only rarely intruded upon the relatively mundane agenda of homeland security cooperation. In most cases U.S. homeland security initiatives are not fundamentally at odds with European practices or goals. Moreover, efforts to deal with the day-to-day practical issues—the meetings between law enforcement officials, the sharing of threat information by intelligence agencies, or the daily grind of cargo inspection—are unobtrusive and proceed apace through the ups and downs of transatlantic political crises. Policy differences have often been finessed in the name of expediency, particularly since September 11. Thus, for example, France and Germany agreed to provide the United States with information on the alleged 9/11 conspirator, Zacarias Moussouai, although the fact that the U.S. government was seeking the death penalty against him would ordinarily have precluded such cooperation.[14]

The Role of the European Union

On the day-to-day level, most transatlantic cooperation on homeland security and on the broader issue of counterterrorism remains bilateral; that is to say, it occurs between the United States and a specific European country rather than between the United States and the European Union.[15] That is particularly true when it comes to the most sensitive issues, such as intelligence sharing and joint operations. The United States has developed a variety of different close and effective bilateral relationships with specific intelligence and law enforcement agencies, relationships that were built up during the cold war and have intensified since 9/11. These relationships show a great deal of individual variation, ranging from a close, intense collaboration with the British secret services to almost nonexistent relationships with some services of the new eastern Europe member states.[16] In December 2003, for example, when American intelligence suspected that specific transatlantic flights originating from London and Paris might be targets of hijackers, they approached their counterparts in Britain and France to cancel the flights rather than go to any European Union agency.[17]

Indeed, even within Europe, most operational cooperation remains bilateral, or in any case it takes place within small, ad-hoc groups with an interest in a particular issue. In one example of many, in 2003 the interior ministers of the United Kingdom, France, Germany, Spain, and Italy set up an informal group outside the EU framework to develop closer cooperation on security and policing, and they continue to meet regularly for that purpose. Part of the reason for these groupings is that national agencies fear that too much liaison with other countries, particularly with countries with less-developed security services, presents a risk that sensitive information will be leaked or used inappropriately. More prosaically, however, national authorities often feel that involving the EU machinery or even involving other EU member states that have different capabilities or different levels of threat perception would simply impede the process of cooperation. In general, national government officials, particularly in the large countries of Europe, feel that the European Union has neither the bureaucratic competence nor the sense of urgency required to take on such tasks.

Even within EU structures themselves, cooperation remains difficult. Homeland security is a new issue that crosses many of the traditional boundaries set up within the European Union. Important parts of the authority necessary for homeland security remain distributed among statutorily independent organizations that cannot be compelled to cooperate. Thus, for example, the European Commission, the EU's executive body, claims the authority to regulate border and transport security by virtue of its role in ensuring the EU's internal market and in representing the EU in external commercial relations. But the European Council, essentially committees of the twenty-five member states, remains primarily responsible for issues of justice and home affairs (for example, policing, standard of criminal codes, and so forth) and for foreign and defense policy. Finally, the European Parliament regards itself as having an important role in these issues, particularly as the guardian of citizens' privacy rights against government encroachment. To help resolve the competition, the new EU counterterrorism coordinator, a position established with much fanfare after the 2004 Madrid bombings, has focused principally on rationalizing EU institutions' own efforts rather than on the even more daunting task of coordinating counterterrorism policy across the member states.[18]

As a result of these impediments, Europe is simply not capable of taking a centralized approach to homeland security. Despite the real progress in European integration, the core elements of sovereignty—including policing, criminal justice, and intelligence—remain firmly in the hands of national governments. At the same time, the European Union has taken on many of the functional characteristics of a nation-state, which include, significantly, the lack of internal borders. This mismatch between functionality and sovereignty means that areas of government action critical to post-9/11 homeland security have not been unified or even standardized across Europe.

That mismatch has real consequences for homeland security and international cooperation. Most directly, it means that Europe has a very strong potential to encounter "connect-the-dots" problems, identified by the 9/11 Commission and others as a key factor in the failure to prevent the attacks in New York City and Washington. In the complex, decentralized European governance system, there is a high risk that pieces of information necessary to prevent attacks are known somewhere but that they are not appropriately combined or put in the hands of an organization that can use the information. That may have been the case in the Madrid train bombings, which killed nearly 200 people. As in the case of 9/11, it is impossible to say with certainty that more efficient cooperation could have prevented the bombings, but it does seem that information from French, German, and Norwegian authorities that might have led to the arrest of key individuals involved in planning the attack did not reach the relevant Spanish authorities.[19] More important, it remains clear that little has been done in the wake of that attack to ensure that such problems do not recur in Europe.

The mismatch also means that the intra-European borders that have disappeared for ordinary citizens and criminals alike still limit security services. In one example, two IRA terrorist suspects under surveillance in France crossed the unguarded, and indeed often unmarked, border into Belgium and then the Netherlands. Because of the different definitions of law enforcement and intelligence in Belgium and the Netherlands, continuing the surveillance required French authorities to work with the Belgian police on one hand and Dutch intelligence on the other, greatly complicating the task of coordination. Worse, Dutch intelligence apparently has no nighttime surveillance capability and thus lost the trail of the IRA suspects. They were able to return to France unobserved, where they were suspected of attempting to buy and hide weapons.[20] Given the ready access to the United States from Europe, this is also a problem for U.S. homeland security.

The decentralized nature of homeland security efforts in Europe also hampers international cooperation, including with the United States. In the first instance, that is because coordinating and negotiating with twenty-five individual member states creates a greater burden on scarce U.S. resources than is necessary and may slow implementation of urgent agreements. Therefore, for example, when the United States decided in the wake of the perceived threats against transatlantic flights in December 2003 to insist that certain countries provide sky marshals on flights to the United States, they encountered little resistance in France but a great deal in the United

Kingdom, whose airlines did not want to allow guns in the cabin, and yet different issues in the smaller European countries that often did not have sufficient staff or expertise to provide sky marshals. A single interlocutor would have helped speed handling of what was seen as an urgent issue and would have made sense given the ability of potential hijackers to move effortlessly across European borders.

More subtly, the complicated structure of European governance means that the appropriate interlocutor is not always obvious, even to the Europeans. In the case of the sky marshals, the European Commission did not further complicate the issue by asserting that it had the authority to negotiate for the EU, but that outcome was not preordained because the commission does have jurisdiction over transport regulations. The problem of the appropriate interlocutor has caused difficulties in implementing homeland security initiatives, including, for example, the container security initiative.

Cooperation and Conflict

Despite these issues, since 9/11 the United States and Europe have developed a number of effective mechanisms for cooperation on homeland security. A few specific areas are highlighted below. They hardly do justice to the many homeland security–related exchanges happening at all levels of the transatlantic relationship, but they encompass many issues, both those on which the greatest progress has been made and those on which the most remains to be done, and they illustrate many of the key difficulties that remain.

Liaison with EU Organizations

Since 9/11, the United States and the European Union have adopted a number of formal and informal mechanisms for liaison between U.S. agencies and various EU institutions and for coordinating policy. In order to avoid surprising each other with new initiatives, they have launched permanent U.S.-EU policy dialogues on border and transport security (begun in April 2004) and terrorist finance (in September 2004). The Department of Homeland Security has sent an attaché to the U.S. mission to the EU to complement the exchange of attachés with national law enforcement agencies and with the relatively new pan-European police organization, Europol.

Nonetheless, the relationship with Europol indicates some of the difficulties. Europol, and its analogue for coordinating judicial authorities within

Europe, Eurojust, have no operational role in police investigations or criminal prosecutions. They serve simply as clearinghouses for information coming from national agencies and sometimes help to coordinate investigations with cross-border aspects and to conduct analysis on cross-border networks and emerging trends. Another new agency along these lines, the European Border Agency, which is intended to facilitate greater cooperation between national border guards, began operations in May 2005.

In theory, these agencies' broad databases covering criminal activity and immigration data within Europe should allow them to cross-reference reports from a wide variety of national sources and identify emerging trends in terrorism that others cannot see. This effort was interrupted when, after the initial rush of enthusiasm after 9/11, Europol's counterterrorism unit withered away for lack of support from the national organizations and when the FBI liaison to Europol was withdrawn in 2002, apparently because the FBI felt the relationship with Europol was not productive. After the Madrid bombings, EU leaders reestablished the unit with a specific mandate to conduct analysis on terrorism, and in late 2004, the U.S. Justice Department announced that the liaison with Europol would be reestablished. There is no liaison at Eurojust, although Eurojust does have a contact point within the U.S. government and the first high-level meeting between Eurojust and U.S. officials took place in February 2005.

From the perspective of the United States, these organizations have the potential to greatly simplify the difficult problem of liaison with the myriad law enforcement organizations within Europe. At the moment, however, there is considerable doubt as to the quality and quantity of information that European national agencies are in fact sharing with European Union agencies. There also is no parallel structure for coordinating the national intelligence agencies. Although most of the European intelligence agencies do meet regularly in an informal organization known as the Club of Berne, it is outside the European Union framework and has no clearinghouse role or permanent staff. Proposals by Austria and Belgium in the wake of the Madrid bombings to form a European intelligence agency, perhaps along the lines of Europol and Eurojust, were firmly rejected by the larger countries.[21] Given the lack of EU capacity for intelligence gathering and the unwillingness of established agencies to share sensitive information in such large forums, an EU intelligence organization probably was not a good idea in any case. Still, the proposal does indicate recognition that the current level of coordination of intelligence within Europe is inadequate.

Mutual Legal Assistance and Extradition Treaties

In June 2003, the United States and the European Union signed treaties on mutual legal assistance and extradition, the first treaties between the United States and the EU on criminal matters.[22] Although proposed by the United States and concluded in response to 9/11, they apply not only to terrorism but also to all serious criminal matters from tax evasion to organized crime. Perhaps the most significant feature of the treaties is that they obligate the European Union to ensure that every member state implements treaties of equal or greater quality with the United States and demand that new member states accede to such treaties. At the time of the agreement, a number of states, including Germany, did not have mutual legal assistance treaties (MLATs) with the United States and a number of the existing extradition treaties provided for more cumbersome procedures and fewer extraditable offenses than the EU treaty.[23]

The extradition treaty is intended to reduce delays in the handling of requests for extradition, to facilitate direct contact between central authorities, and to provide mechanisms to determine the extent to which sensitive information in the extradition request can be protected by the extraditing state. It specifically allows for European states to deny extradition in cases in which the death penalty may be applied (article 13), but it also opens up the possibility that extradited suspects might be later tried for other offenses that could carry the death penalty.

The mutual legal assistance treaty is an even bigger advance for law enforcement officials, particularly because some states had no such bilateral treaty and because it allows for giving legal testimony via videoconferencing and even for creating joint investigative teams. Such teams will allow investigators to operate in each other's territory and give law enforcement authorities access to bank accounts and other sensitive information during investigations into serious crimes, including terrorism and financial crimes. Moreover, for the first time, it envisages using the information obtained to prevent an immediate and serious threat to public security—in other words, using it as actionable intelligence. The treaty does contain various grounds for refusal of legal assistance by the requested state, including simply when the request would "prejudice its sovereignty"; however, the treaty clearly shifts the burden of proof to the state refusing to give assistance.

In a broader sense, the treaties, when ratified by the United States and the EU member states, will be important milestones because they will represent an advance in what has been the most difficult area of cooperation between the United States and Europe: judicial cooperation. Judicial cooperation is difficult because it involves more formal and generally more publicly scrutinized procedures than do, for example, intelligence or law enforcement activities. Moreover, judicial procedures tend to vary greatly, not just across the Atlantic but also within Europe, particularly between countries adhering to common law and those adhering to civil law. Countries often are quite reluctant or even incapable of compromising on judicial procedures. In the case of Europe and the United States after September 11, this normally difficult situation has been greatly complicated by the long-running dispute over the death penalty and by the newer European legal objection to the American use of extrajudicial procedures in its war on terror.

However, those disputes have to a large extent been finessed and have not presented any serious practical problems in day-to-day cooperation. A more serious practical issue in judicial cooperation is the difficulty many legal systems have in accepting intelligence information as evidence in judicial procedures, in allowing interrogation of suspects for intelligence purposes once they are in judicial proceedings, and in protecting sensitive information from disclosure. Addressing the problems of homeland security today clearly requires careful integration of intelligence information and judicial procedures, but that integration does not now exist on either side of the Atlantic.

The result, particularly when it comes to international cooperation, is that intelligence and judicial authorities do not trust each other. Therefore, for example, the conviction of Mounir al-Motassadeq, the first person convicted anywhere in the world of complicity in the September 11 attacks, was dismissed by a German court in part because U.S. officials refused to allow the court access to intelligence information that he claimed would exculpate him.[24] (It should be noted that in this case the United States was able to grant the German court's request in Motassadeq's retrial and that the information provided was, in fact, exculpatory.) The extradition and mutual legal assistance treaties are an important step in rectifying this situation, but they contain a great deal of ambiguity about specific procedures, particularly when it comes to data protection, the death penalty issue, and the authority of the joint investigative teams. They can serve as starting points for specific negotiations, but particularly in time-sensitive investigations, they will need to be supplemented by measures on both sides of the Atlantic to create procedures that ensure timely exchange and that allow intelligence information to be admitted into evidence and protect it from disclosure.

Border Security

A principal focus of U.S. Department of Homeland Security efforts and transatlantic homeland security cooperation since 9/11 has been on border security: ensuring that persons and cargo entering the United States by sea, land, or air do not represent a threat to the United States. Three issues stand out on the transatlantic agenda: container security, air passenger data, and border control documents.

CONTAINER SECURITY. As noted elsewhere in this volume, the security of cargo containers is one of the main concerns of the U.S. Department of Homeland Security (DHS). Nearly 9 million containers are offloaded in U.S. ports every year, but only about 6 percent are opened and directly inspected.[25] To confront the possibility that those containers might be used to smuggle in terrorists or terrorist weapons, in January 2002 the United States began its container security initiative (CSI), which is designed to enlist the support of ports of origin. The CSI creates a procedure for the inspection of suspicious cargo in the presence of U.S. personnel before it leaves a foreign port. Screened containers then receive expedited passage through U.S. customs on arrival in the United States. As of December 2004, the CSI covered more than 70 percent of container movement to the United States from ports in which terrorists might be likely to attempt to smuggle in a weapon of mass destruction, according to Robert Bonner, commissioner of U.S. Customs and Border Protection (CBP), and the goal is to cover 95 percent of cargo from such ports.[26] Currently thirty-seven ports are in the program, twenty of them in the European Union.

In an effort to implement this initiative, in 2002 the United States negotiated agreements with a number of countries—including France, Germany, Belgium, and the Netherlands—to allow their key ports to participate in the CSI. However, in January 2003, the European Commission launched infringement procedures against those countries, asserting that the agreement constituted a preferential trading arrangement that must apply to all EU members and that cannot be negotiated by individual member states.[27] Eventually the commission and the member states agreed that the commission did indeed have negotiating authority on this issue, but the wrangling held up final implementation of the initiative for more than a year.

The CSI dispute demonstrates several important aspects of the transatlantic homeland security relationship. First of all, the dispute was not over the content of the initiative, which received the broad acceptance of all parties from the start; rather, it was over the appropriate parties to the negotiation.

But that was enough to delay implementation of what the United States considered an important initiative. Second, it demonstrated how the European Union is slowly becoming an important actor in homeland security. That is particularly true in areas that touch on international commerce, where the European Commission can claim jurisdiction from its role as Europe's trade representative. And of course, nearly any issue that affects the regulation of the border between the United States and Europe will have an important commercial component.

Finally, the CSI demonstrates the role that Europe can play as a catalyst for international cooperation in homeland security. The vast majority of the initial and most important ports are in Europe, and the agreement with Europe, as well as the success that the CSI has had in facilitating inspection while not disrupting trade, will make it far easier to negotiate with the other nations needed to reach the 95 percent goal. A follow-on program that builds on the CSI model, the Customs-Trade Partnership against Terrorism (C-TPAT) can expect to experience a similar evolution. This program encourages private companies to ensure that their supply chains meet certain higher standards of security by granting their shipments expedited processing when entering the United States. Currently 8,200 companies are certified members of this program, and they account for about 40 percent (by value) of the cargo brought to U.S. ports.

AIR PASSENGER DATA. The November 2001 Aviation and Transportation Security Act gave CBP the authority to require airlines to provide CBP with extensive information on all passengers before landing, the so-called passenger name record (PNR). The PNR includes a variety of data, ranging from the passenger's name and date of birth to ticket payment method and even meal preference. European airlines became concerned, however, that in supplying this information to U.S. authorities they would violate the 1995 EU Data Protection Directive. That directive creates standards for designating non-EU countries as "safe harbors" with respect to data protection, which is to say that European companies can transfer data to entities in these countries as if they were in Europe. Because the United States has not met the requirements of a safe harbor, transfers of data by private companies to U.S. entities are strictly regulated. The European airlines were thus caught between violating either European or American law and appealed to the European Commission for help out of their quandary.

The U.S. Department of Homeland Security and the European Commission, after long negotiation, were able to reach agreement on a compromise that allowed the airlines to provide the data—on a temporary basis beginning in February 2003 and later under a formal agreement reached in May 2004 for a period of three and half years.[28] There are many compromises in the agreement: only very carefully specified data are to be transferred, data are to be used only for counterterrorism purposes, and they can be kept only for a limited time. A channel also was established between the DHS and EU privacy offices to correct information found to be in error.

Nonetheless, it is clear that the United States achieved the majority of its demands. First and foremost, the agreement was reached relatively quickly. There was fear that the European Commission would insist that the agreement demanded new legislation, greatly slowing down the process. Even introducing that possibility would have, at the minimum, increased European leverage in the negotiation. Instead, the commission was willing to use a rather liberal interpretation of the current data protection directive to give the CBP special status in return for certain restrictions on the use of the data, including limiting the period of retention (to 3.5 years) and limiting the right to transfer the data within the U.S. government. Nonetheless, the CBP was granted the right to share the data with any government body that has a counterterrorism or law enforcement function, an ill-defined but certainly large set of organizations. Those organizations have made no promises about how they might use the data. Moreover, there is no right of legal redress for European citizens, a principal tenet of the data protection directive.

Most tellingly, the agreement failed to confront European disquiet over the way the data are used. It failed to guarantee that European data would not be used in any future passenger profiling systems that the U.S. might implement, a condition that originally was one of the EU's firm demands. One current use of the data is for comparison against a U.S.-maintained "no-fly" list. Flights carrying passengers on the list may be diverted to other airports or even turned away from U.S. airspace. The problem from the European standpoint is that the list is utterly opaque, an issue that the PNR agreement does not address. The U.S. refused to discuss even in generic terms the list's sources or the criteria used to place people on the list—or even to offer a process to discover or remove erroneous entries.[29] This lack of transparency encourages European officials to believe that the United States uses the list for selective enforcement—forcing European airlines to divert flights under conditions that would not apply to U.S. carriers.

These perceived deficiencies in the PNR agreement angered the European Parliament, which was not consulted. It has brought a case against the European Commission with the European Court of Justice alleging that the agreement with the United States violates the data protection directive. However, the court is not expected to rule for two or three years, and in the meantime, PNR data is flowing across the Atlantic according to the agreement—an agreement that has set the baseline for similar agreements with other countries.

As the controversy continues, events have conspired to expand the U.S. desire for passenger data. On April 8, 2005, Mexican authorities informed U.S. authorities that a KLM 747 scheduled to pass through U.S. airspace on the way to Mexico had two passengers aboard whose names appeared on the U.S. no-fly list. U.S. authorities denied the plane permission to enter U.S. airspace, and it had to return to Amsterdam. As a result of that incident, the United States is considering demanding passenger data for flights that would pass over U.S. airspace as it now does for flights bound for U.S. destinations.[30] From a data protection standpoint, this requirement would mean that passengers who never had any intention of entering the United States would nonetheless have their personal data forwarded to the U.S. government.

BORDER CONTROL DOCUMENTS. The USA PATRIOT Act (Patriot Act) also placed new requirements on passports that can be used to enter the United States. One example is that all countries that participate in the visa waiver program (twenty-seven countries in total, including fifteen EU member states) were required to issue machine-readable passports by October 2003 and to begin issuing passports with biometric identifiers by October 2005. Congress established that a country's failure to comply with these requirements would mean that its citizens would have to obtain visas to enter the United States. Nearly all of the affected countries failed to meet the deadlines, but Congress and the president authorized an extension of one year for the first deadline.[31] In the meantime, visitors to the United States without visas (essentially all short-term European visitors) are now required to be fingerprinted and photographed upon entry into the United States.

The European Commission has asked for an extension of the biometric deadline until August 2006, citing technical problems in implementing biometrics on passports. Congress has recently shown some willingness to finesse the deadline as long as progress is being made. But at the same time, the visa waiver program is coming under increasing fire as a critical vulnerability in U.S. border security, especially after the July 2005 attacks in London.[32] If Congress decides to strictly enforce the biometric deadline, most Europeans with passports issued after October 2005 will require a visa to enter the United States (those with passports issued before will not) and the EU may impose reciprocal visa requirements on American travelers. Business associations on both sides of the Atlantic have condemned such a "visa war," asserting that it would cause large economic losses, running into the tens of billions of dollars.[33] Even more perversely, the new requirement might have a negative effect on U.S. homeland security: requiring visas for the immense number of travelers from the VWP countries would strain the already over-burdened U.S. visa issuance system and inevitably reduce the care taken in making the decision to issue individual visas to citizens of VWP countries.[34]

There has been a great deal of grumbling from individual European travelers and civil liberties organizations about new border control measures, but European policymakers have not indicated much discomfort. EU policy-makers are not concentrating on the privacy or civil rights implications of changing passport requirements. Rather, the main problem has been technical feasibility and intra-European disputes over technologies and standards.[35] Given the progress that the EU has made in this regard and the negative effects of a "visa war" on U.S. security and commerce, strict enforcement of biometric requirements seems unlikely, but that decision is ultimately in the hands of the U.S. Congress.

Moving Forward

As this brief review indicates, the United States and Europe have achieved a great deal in homeland security since 9/11. There have been many disputes, and many more loom in the future—over the death penalty, over privacy issues, and over intelligence sharing. But the two partners appear to be working out mechanisms to deal with their disputes, many of which take advantage of the European Union's ability to strike Europe-wide bargains. The philosophical differences over the conduct of the war on terror and the dramatic political crises surrounding the Iraq War do not seem to have appreciably slowed progress in this area.

Of course, much remains to be done, particularly in the areas of information sharing and institutional liaison. The EU and the United States already collect a phenomenal amount of data in a huge variety of databases, both public and private. As other chapters in this volume have demonstrated, efforts within the United States to fuse these data sources to make them useful for homeland security purposes have encountered a number of technical and political obstacles. A similar, although perhaps even more dire situation, pertains within the European Union, where the existence of twenty-five different countries with distinct laws, varying technologies, and incompatible organizational schemata immensely complicates the process of fusion.

As a result, a host of data sources that might be useful for border protection are simply not used. For example, Interpol has a database of 1.7 million lost or stolen passports, which many countries, including the United States, simply do not update or use at border crossings because they lack the systems or procedures to do so.[36] Similarly, many potentially valuable European databases, such as Eurodac, a database that tracks asylum seekers, and the Schengen information system, a database meant to facilitate border checks (and soon the new visa information system), exist for specific purposes and are not available for many counterterrorism uses because of either technical or legal restrictions. In his 2004 annual report, EU data protection supervisor Peter Hustinx specifically termed efforts to widen access to the Schengen information system and other databases for counterterrorism purposes as "unacceptable" and vowed to use his authority to stop them.[37]

Most of these information sharing issues are in the first instance domestic issues that require new investments of political and financial capital if they are to serve domestic homeland security needs in the United States or Europe. Nonetheless, the lesson from the problems that the United States and Europe have already experienced is that these systems need to be designed from the ground up with international cooperation in mind. That means that controls must be put in place from the moment that data sharing begins in order to give potential partners some confidence that the systems can adequately and flexibly prevent inappropriate access to or use of the data. This means the incremental merging of databases using diverse technologies rather than any sort of grandiose vision of a single unified system. The SHARE network, presented in chapter 2, which uses current information technologies to flexibly and securely cross-reference information from a variety of information sources, is one way of applying this model to the international sphere.[38]

Another issue is the manner of institutional liaison between the United States and Europe. Even before 9/11, the number of agencies involved in international issues was proliferating to the point that major U.S. embassies abroad were becoming reflections in miniature of the entire U.S. government. Since 9/11, entire new agencies, such as the Department of Homeland Security, have emerged and demanded their place in U.S. diplomacy. Meanwhile, nearly every agency of the U.S. government has become involved in one way or another with the war on terror. Even the New York City Police Department has begun to deploy liaison officers abroad, in Europe and elsewhere.[39] Each agency has its own links back to Washington (or New York), and there is often little coordination of positions.[40]

On the European side, the increasingly complex division of labor between the European Union and its member states and the EU's outdated division of the economic, foreign policy, and domestic spheres means that often it is hard for even experienced observers to know where to go and how to coordinate responses. These issues already have complicated negotiations on such issues as container security and intelligence sharing. If both sides are serious about the need to cooperate in homeland security, they need to think more systematically about streamlining liaison, both for policy and operational purposes, so that both sides know where to go to get things done.

Related to this, the United States also needs to think more strategically about its views on the issue of Europeanization. Currently, the United States seems fairly agnostic about whether any particular issue is handled at the European or member state level. On a multilateral level, many U.S. officials, particularly in the Department of Defense, would prefer that NATO took the lead in European counterterrorism efforts rather than the European Union. U.S. intelligence officials clearly value their established relationships with many national security services, while other U.S. officials appreciate the type of one-stop shopping that the European Union can provide on issues such as container security.

Obviously, the issue of European governance is primarily a European domestic issue, but U.S. actions affect how European governance evolves. Frequently, European institutions are spun off in response to political problems that have acquired public salience. They are then left to sink or swim in the European policy process. Some mature into effective and powerful organizations; others wither away into irrelevance. The United States undoubtedly has the ability to affect this process, because an institution's relationship with its U.S. counterpart is often a valuable asset within the European policy process.

The question then becomes whether U.S. homeland security would profit from greater Europeanization of homeland security—for example, from having a stronger Europol or Eurojust lead EU counterterrorism efforts. The answer is a qualified yes. Since 9/11, the European Union has proven that it can be an effective partner of the United States on issues of homeland security. The EU is gradually acquiring more authority in areas such as law enforcement, judicial cooperation, and border security, which are critical to counterterrorism. Given the EU's bureaucratic ways and its lack of operational capacity on security issues, the transition will certainly be slow and difficult. But the fact that internal European borders no longer inhibit the movement of citizens but still limit the authority of security services makes the already difficult "connect the dots" problem essentially impossible to solve unless there is some movement toward Europeanization of security. NATO, with its primarily military orientation, could never hope to take the lead in assembling the critical domestic and law enforcement pieces of the counterterrorism puzzle. Only the European Union has the capacity and the political legitimacy within Europe to take actions across the numerous domestic and foreign policy areas involved in counterterrorism.

Beyond theses difficult issues, however, is the more conceptual problem of building a political foundation for U.S.-European homeland security cooperation. The United States government has established counterterrorism and homeland security as its main priorities. In Europe, only those countries that see a direct Islamist threat have made it a top priority. Given the lack of unanimous agreement among the member states, the European Union has not made counterterrorism and homeland security its top priorities. The EU's agenda to create the so-called "single area of security and justice" and of better regulating immigration is often consistent with a homeland security agenda, but that agenda often focuses on harmonizing diverse regulations rather than security policy, and it does not require much cooperation with the United States.

Because counterterrorism and homeland security are such high priorities in the United States, Americans place a much greater emphasis on homeland security issues and, as noted, the United States tends to set the transatlantic security agenda. The urgency with which the United States has pushed its agenda since 9/11 has also meant that negotiations often have been carried out in exceptional circumstances, avoiding the normal, cumbersome European process of involving parliamentarians, interest groups, nongovernmental organizations, and experts in the policy process. The result has usually been a successful negotiation from the U.S. point of view but also a settlement in which Europeans have little stake and which has little or no political support within Europe. The perception among many European officials is that American domestic security needs are being foisted upon Europeans with the connivance of the European Commission and at the cost of European privacy and civil liberties.

In the short term, this perception means that the implementation of agreed-upon homeland security measures in Europe, still largely the duty of member states, remains weak.[41] In December 2004, the European Council adopted yet another counterterrorism action plan, including a series of more than 150 measures to improve intra-European cooperation. But many of these measures, some of which were proposed in previous action plans, have not yet been implemented. Even the showpiece post-9/11 European counterterrorism initiative—the European arrest warrant—took more than three years to implement in all of the member states, and according to the European Commission, its implementation in at least nine countries is not complete.[42] Worse, in July 2005, the German Constitutional Court decided that the German implementation of the European arrest warrant did not conform to the German constitution and left some doubt whether any implementation could.[43] In so doing, the court effectively suspended Germany's acceptance of the warrant for the purpose of extraditing German citizens, occasioning retaliation in kind by Spain.

The 3/11 attack in Madrid created another spurt of activity, but it did not resolve the issue. On the first anniversary of the 3/11 attack, Josep Borrell, president of the European Parliament, expressed a common frustration with EU member states' implementation of terrorism directives when he asserted that "several of the measures agreed by the action plan against terrorism that the Council adopted after March 11 have not yet been put into place . . . the traditional forms of police and judicial cooperation are not enough."[44] The impetus was renewed once again after the July 2005 attacks in London, but judging by the early progress, there seems little reason to believe that Borrell's statement will not remain valid one year after the London bombings.

In the longer term, the perception that homeland security is a U.S. concern means that such measures have little political constituency and are vulnerable to political disruption if they acquire greater public visibility or if there are more scandals associated with the U.S. prosecution of the war on terror. If the EU does become a more important U.S. partner in homeland security, the representative and oversight bodies of the EU will begin to demand a say. In this sense, the European Parliament's rejection of the PNR agreement may be a harbinger of things to come, particularly if the data sharing regime the agreement established expands to cover, for example, flights passing through U.S. airspace. Already European monitoring organizations, such as the office of the data protection supervisor, are becoming more assertive in challenging EU agreements. For example, the joint supervisory board of Europol recently called into question the legality of data transfer under the 2002 U.S.-Europol agreement.[45] Even more troubling, the idea that European governments would extradite suspects that might eventually face the death penalty in the United States or that they might give legal assistance to death penalty cases in the United States such as the Moussaoui case has the potential to provoke a popular backlash in some European states.

There is no simple solution to this problem. At a minimum, the United States should recognize that real progress in international cooperation on homeland security requires not just the capacity to impose agreements on its partners but also an effort to create a sense in its partners that they have a similar stake in cooperation. As the urgency of the post-9/11 period fades, there may be an opportunity to create a broader negotiation that can move beyond quick-fix solutions to urgent vulnerabilities. Such a negotiation would seek to establish general rules, consistent with both European and American practice, for sensitive types of cooperation, particularly those involving data sharing, while protecting civil liberties. It also would indicate appreciation of the new type of security threat that terrorism poses for modern societies.

Notes

1. Tom Ridge, "Secure Borders, Open Doors: International Cooperation in the 21st Century," London School of Economics Public Lecture, London, January 14, 2005.

2. U.S. Office of Homeland Security, *The National Strategy for Homeland Security,* June 2002, p. 59.

3. World Trade Organization, *International Trade Statistics 2004* (www.wto.org/english/res_e/statis_e/statis_e.htm [December 8, 2005]; and U.S. Department of Commerce, Office of Trade and Industry Information. The United States and the EU accounted for $454.9 billion in two-way merchandise trade in 2004. The next largest relationship was that between the United States and Canada, at $446.1 billion. For comparison, the United States and China exchanged less than half as much, $231.4 billion worth of goods.

4. U.S. Department of Commerce, International Trade Administration, Office of Travel and Tourism Industries (http://tidev.ita.doc.gov).

5. On Islamist efforts to recruit European passport holders, see Robert Leiken, *Bearers of Global Jihad? Immigration and National Security after 9/11*, Nixon Center, Washington, March 2004.

6. See Daniel Keohane, *The EU and Counterterrorism*, Centre on European Reform Working Paper, London, May 2005, p. 5.

7. See World Customs Organization, *Framework of Standards to Secure and Facilitate Global Trade,* Brussels, June 2005. According to one analyst, "the WCO framework represents a significant policy achievement for Washington as it creates global standards built around U.S. principles." See Oxford Analytica, "Customs Framework Will Transform Trade," August 18, 2005 (www.oxanstore.com/itemlist.php?C=WTO [December 8, 2005]) .

8. William Pope, speech at conference entitled "Transatlantic Policies to Counter Global Challenges: Towards Effective Multilateral Strategies," SAIS Center for Transatlantic Relations, Washington, April 28, 2005.

9. Dirk Haubrich, "September 11, Anti-Terror Laws, and Civil Liberties: Britain, France, and Germany Compared," *Government and Opposition 2003* 38 (1): 3–28;

Adam Townsend, *Guarding Europe,* Center for European Reform, London, May 2003; Jonathan Stevenson, *Counterterrorism: Containment and Beyond,* Adelphi Paper 367 (London: International Institute for Strategic Studies, November 2004), pp. 51–55. The initiative to establish a database for lost and stolen passports is an exception to this rule.

10. For one prominent example, see Michael Howard, "What's in a Name? How to Fight Terrorism," *Foreign Affairs* 81 (January-February 2002): 8–13.

11. Ibid., p. 8; Jonathan Stevenson, "How Europe and America Defend Themselves," *Foreign Affairs* 82 (March-April 2002): 76–77.

12. This view is expressed by one of Europe's top antiterrorism officials in Jean-Louis Bruguière, "Terrorism after the War in Iraq," U.S.-France Analysis series, Brookings, May 2003. Also see Philippe Errera, "Three Circles of Threat," *Survival* (Spring 2005).

13. See Jeremy Shapiro and Bénédicte Suzan, "The French Experience with Counterterrorism," *Survival* 45 (Spring 2003): 47–98.

14. See Larry Margasak, "Germany, France Agree to Cooperate in Moussaoui Case," *Associated Press Worldstream,* November 28, 2002. France and Germany cooperated on the condition that the evidence given be used only in the guilt or innocence phase of the trial, not in the separate penalty phase, which might lead to execution. This type of agreement had never been reached before and would seem to violate the spirit of France and Germany's commitment not to aid in death penalty cases.

15. A third potential forum for transatlantic cooperation on homeland security is NATO. However, due to NATO's primarily military nature and the dispute between the United States and Europe over the appropriateness of using military means to combat terrorism, the organization has not played much of a role in homeland security. See Richard A. Clarke and Barry R. McCaffrey, *NATO's Role in Confronting Terrorism* (Washington: Atlantic Council, June 2004).

16. On the special U.S.-U.K. intelligence relationship, see Charles Grant, *Intimate Relations: Can Britain Play a Leading Role in European Defense and Keep Its Special Links to U.S. Intelligence?* (London: Center for European Reform, May 2000).

17. For more on intelligence sharing, see chapter 2 of this volume.

18. Author's interview with European Union official, March 2004.

19. See Richard Aldrich, "Transatlantic Intelligence and Security Cooperation," *International Affairs* 80, no. 4 (2004): 731–53; and Lawrence Wright, "The Terror Web," *New Yorker,* August 2, 2004.

20. Author's interview with a French official, April 2004.

21. The Joint Situation Centre, located within the European Council Secretariat, does serve to some degree as a locus for intelligence sharing, but it is intended primarily for strategic analysis and for crisis warning and monitoring in support of the European Common Foreign and Security Policy rather than for internal security. See Sigurd Hess, "Intelligence Cooperation in Europe: 1990 to Present," *Journal of Intelligence History* 3 (Summer 2003): 61–68.

22. For the text of the agreements, see Council of the European Union, "Agreements on Extradition and on Mutual Legal Assistance between the European Union and the United States of America," 9153/03, June 3, 2003 (http://register.consilium.eu.int/pdf/en/03/st09/st09153en03.pdf).

23. Bruce Zagaris, "US-EU Extradition and Mutual Assistance Agreements Are an Important Milestone," *International Enforcement Law Reporter* (November 2003).

24. See Craig Whitlock, "9/11 Cases Proving Difficult in Germany," *Washington Post*, December 13, 2004.

25. U.S. Customs and Border Protection, "Fact Sheet on the Container Security Initiative," January 7, 2005 (http://www.cbp.gov); interview, Michael d'Arcy with Todd Horton and Lisa Clark, Customs and Border Protection, February 14, 2005.

26. Robert C. Bonner, remarks at DHS Cargo Security Summit, Georgetown University, December 17, 2004; reported by the Federal News Service, December 17, 2004.

27. See Gregory Crouch, "Europe Acts against U.S. Efforts on Ports," *New York Times*, January 28, 2003.

28. For the text of the PNR agreement, see Bureau of Customs and Border Protection, "Undertakings of the Department of Homeland Security, Bureau of Customs and Border Protection," May 22, 2003 (www.dhs.gov/interweb/assetlibrary/CBP-DHS_PNRUndertakings5-25-04.pdf [November 23, 2005]). Data did flow to U.S. authorities even before this agreement.

29. Author's interviews with European and American officials, May and June 2005.

30. "US May Demand Passenger Lists from Flyover Planes," Agence France-Presse, April 22, 2005.

31. For a defense of this extension, see Colin Powell, "Secure Borders, Open Doors," *Wall Street Journal*, April 21, 2004.

32. See for example, Reuel Marc Gerecht, "Jihad Made in Europe," *Weekly Standard*, July 25, 2005. Senator Dianne Feinstein moots the possibility of a VWP moratorium in "Senator Feinstein Seeks Major Improvements to the Visa Waiver Program: Moratorium May Be Necessary if the Program's Failures Can't Be Remedied Quickly," May 13, 2004 (http://feinstein.senate.gov/04Releases/r-visawaiver.htm).

33. Andrew Ward, "CBI Chief Attacks New U.S. Passport Measures," *Financial Times*, April 6, 2005, p. 9; Roger Bray, "US Urged to Delay Visa Waiver Change," *Financial Times*, April 7, 2005, p. 12.

34. See GAO, "Border Security: Implications of Eliminating the Visa Waiver Program," November 2002 (http://www.gao.gov/new.items/d0338.pdf). This report estimates that eliminating the program would cost the State Department between $739 million and $1.28 billion to retool and annual recurring costs of $522 million to $810 million.

35. See chapter 9 of this book for more on the technology issues involved in biometric passports.

36. Craig S. Smith, "Few Nations Check to See if Passports Are Stolen, Interpol Says," *New York Times*, August 23, 2004.

37. "Free Police Access to Databases Unacceptable, Says Supervisor," *European Report*, April 2, 2005.

38. See chapter 2 in this volume and Zoë Baird and James Barksdale, "There Is Security in Sharing: Information Network Would Aid Terror Fight," *San Jose Mercury News*, August 16, 2004.

39. Judith Miller, "New York Cop in Israel, Stepping a Bit on F.B.I. Toes," *New York Times*, May 15, 2005.

40. For more on the issue of intelligence liaison, see chapter 2 in this volume.

41. On the implementation of European counterterrorism legislation in the member states, see European Commission, "Report from the Commission Based on Article 11 of the Council Framework Decision of 13 June 2002 on Combating Terrorism," COM(2004)409, June 8, 2004.

42. European Commission, "Report from the Commission Based on Article 34 of the Council Framework Decision of 13 June 2002 on the European Arrest Warrant and the Surrender Procedures between Member States," COM(2005)63 final, February 23, 2005. The report did not evaluate Italy's implementation, which did not occur until May 2005.

43. Bundesverfassungsgericht Press Office, "European Arrest Warrant Void," press release no. 64/2005, July 18, 2005 (www.bundesverfassungsgericht.de/bverfg_cgi/pressemitteilungen/text/bvg05-064e). The European arrest warrant faces a similar challenge from the Belgian courts.

44. "EU Rapped on Terrorism," *Euronews*, March 10, 2005.

45. "Europol Data Protection Watchdog Admits Problems with the United States," *European Report*, no. 2948, March 25, 2005.

4

Protecting Infrastructure and Providing Incentives for the Private Sector to Protect Itself

Peter Orszag and Michael O'Hanlon

Since the attacks of September 11, 2001, the private sector generally has not done nearly enough to improve its security against terrorist attack. For example, the Congressional Budget Office recently concluded that "there is relatively little evidence that firms have been making additional investments since September 11 to improve their security and avoid losses."[1] About 85 percent of the nation's critical infrastructure is owned by the private sector. Security typically had not been sufficient before the attacks, so the failure to materially improve security measures in many key industries represents one of the most glaring and dangerous shortcomings in the nation's response to terrorism.

Markets respond to incentives. It follows, therefore, that the key to improving security in the private sector is to structure incentives properly, but to date, the federal government has done little to do that. Most private sector infrastructure remains vulnerable. Apart from efforts to protect those types of infrastructure that already have been attacked, such as commercial airliners, the administration's policy has been very restrained. Part of its reluctance to intervene may be a reflection of the admittedly daunting nature of the task—and the impossibility of knowing exactly which types of infrastructure to protect, to what standards of robustness. Nonetheless, the administration's laissez-faire approach risks leaving undefended targets within the United States, and an attack on those targets could cause catastrophic harm.

The greatest concerns apply to key pieces of private infrastructure—chemical facilities, skyscrapers, other large buildings, many hospitals, and so on. Such infrastructure is predominantly owned by the private sector, but it is critical to the functioning of broader society. In such settings private incentives are not always consistent with protection of the public interest. Given existing incentives, economic logic suggests that from the standpoint of the broader public interest, owners of key infrastructure will underinvest in security precautions.[2] At present, many industries view counterterrorism protection as an expensive way to provide an uncertain degree of protection against an unlikely threat; they see few benefits and many costs. As Frank Cilluffo, former special assistant to the president for homeland security in the Bush administration, puts it: "We need to be able to spur [that] investment by providing incentives. Right now, the incentives are disincentives."[3]

Private markets by themselves do not generate sufficient incentives for ensuring homeland security, and government intervention therefore may be warranted, for several reasons. First, and most broadly, national security is a core constitutional responsibility of the federal government. Even if a given terrorist attack affects only private property, it can have broader ramifications for the country's sense of safety. In the terminology of economists, such an attack imposes a "negative externality." That means that private markets will undertake less investment in security than would be socially desirable. Individuals or firms deciding how best to protect themselves against terrorism are unlikely to take the external costs of an attack fully into account and therefore generally will provide an inefficiently low level of protection on their own.[4] Without government involvement, private markets therefore will typically underinvest in antiterrorism measures.[5]

Second, a more specific negative externality exists with regard to *inputs* into terrorist activity. For example, loose security at a chemical facility can provide terrorists with the materials they need for an attack. Similarly, poor security at a biological laboratory can provide terrorists with access to dangerous pathogens. The costs of allowing terrorists to obtain access to such materials generally are not borne by the facilities themselves; the attacks that use the materials could occur elsewhere. Such a specific negative externality provides a compelling rationale for government intervention to protect highly explosive materials, chemicals, and biological pathogens even if they are stored in private facilities. In particular, preventing access to such materials is likely to reduce the overall risk of catastrophic terrorism, as opposed to merely displacing it from one venue to another.

Third, a related type of externality involves "contamination effects." Contamination effects arise when a catastrophic risk faced by one firm is determined in part by the behavior of others, and the behavior of the others affects the incentives of the first firm to reduce its exposure to the risk. Such interdependent security problems can arise, for example, in network settings. The problem in these settings is that the risk to any member of a network depends not only on its own security precautions but also on those taken by others. Poor security at one establishment can affect security at others. Often, the result can be weakened incentives for taking security precautions.[6] For example, once a hacker or virus reaches one computer on a network, the remaining computers can be contaminated more easily. That possibility reduces the incentive for any individual computer operator to protect against hackers. Even stringent cybersecurity may not be particularly helpful if a hacker already has entered the network through a "weak link."

A fourth potential motivation for government intervention involves information—in particular, the cost and difficulty of accurately evaluating security measures. For example, one reason that governments promulgate building codes is that it would be too difficult for each individual entering a building to evaluate its structural soundness. Since it also would be difficult for an individual to evaluate how well a building's air intake system could filter out pathogens in a bioterrorist attack, the same logic would suggest that the government should set minimum antiterrorism standards for buildings for which a reasonable threat of terrorist attack exists. Similarly, it would be possible, but inefficient, for each individual to conduct extensive biological antiterrorism safety tests on the food that he or she was about to consume. The information costs associated with that method, however, make it much less attractive than a system of government regulation of food safety.

The fifth justification for government intervention is that corporate and individual financial exposures to the losses from a major terrorist attack are inherently limited by the nation's bankruptcy laws. For example, assume that a specific firm could suffer two types of terrorist attack: a very severe attack and a somewhat more modest one. Under either type, the losses would exceed the firm's net assets, and the firm would declare bankruptcy. Any losses beyond those that would bankrupt the firm therefore would be irrelevant to the firm's owners. Since the outcome for the owners would not depend on the severity of the attack, they would have little or no incentive to reduce the likelihood of the more severe attack even if the preventive steps were relatively inexpensive. From society's perspective, however, such security measures may be beneficial—and government intervention to address catastrophic possibilities in the presence of the bankruptcy laws therefore can be justified.

The sixth justification for government intervention is that the private sector may expect the government to bail it out should a terrorist attack occur—note the financial assistance given to the airline industry by the government following the September 11 attacks. Such expectations create a "moral hazard" problem: private firms, expecting the government to bail them out should an attack occur, do not undertake as much security as they otherwise would. If the government cannot credibly convince the private sector that no bailouts will occur after an attack, it may have to intervene before an attack to offset the adverse incentives created by the expectation of a bailout.

The seventh, final justification for government intervention involves incomplete markets. The most relevant examples involve imperfections in capital and insurance markets. For example, if insurance firms are unable to obtain reinsurance coverage for terrorism risks (that is, if primary insurers are not able to transfer some of the risk from terrorism costs to other insurance firms in the reinsurance market), some government involvement may be warranted. In addition, certain types of activities may require large-scale coordination, which may be possible but difficult to achieve without government intervention.

These market shortcomings provide a justification for targeted government intervention. But providing a high degree of protection for all possible targets would be prohibitively expensive and practically impossible. Focusing on high-impact attacks helps to narrow the range of private sector settings in which government intervention is warranted.

When government intervention is needed, the best approach is to use government regulation to alter the incentives offered to the private sector for better protecting itself. That can be done either by providing firms with certain advantages when they adopt appropriate measures (the carrot approach) or by imposing costs on those that fail to adopt such measures (the stick approach). In both cases, the goal would be the same: to introduce a difference in the cost of the activities, accomplished either by reducing the cost of the first activity (for example, an investment in security) or by raising the cost of the second activity (for example, business as usual).

Consider the case of trucking. Truck drivers can be subjected to more intensive background checks, and advanced technologies can be used to monitor trucks and ensure the security of their cargo in real time. The government could directly subsidize such steps, for example, by providing tax credits to firms that adopt them. Or it could mandate insurance for trucking firms, thereby relying on insurances firms to impose costs (for example, through higher premiums) on firms that fail to adopt appropriate security measures. The government also could combine either of these approaches with some form of regulation, such as allowing better-protected cargo trucks to travel closer to population centers than less-protected trucks, thereby providing time and money savings to firms that invest in protecting their trucks.

A key distinction between the carrot and the stick approaches is who pays. Government subsidies or tax credits spread the cost of homeland security spending in a particular private market across the entire population rather than only the stakeholders (the owners of businesses, the workers, and consumers of the product) in that sector itself. The stick approach—either through regulation or insurance or some combination thereof—instead concentrates costs on the stakeholders in a particular sector. If particular sectors are inherently more dangerous than others, society may want to encourage activity in other, safer sectors when it has a choice—and such encouragement would be better provided by requiring stakeholders to bear the full cost of protection. The reason is that imposing the cost on the stakeholders rather than the general public would raise the cost of the most dangerous activities. The market would thus discourage such activities (through higher prices), which would help to mitigate the risk of a terrorist attack in the most dangerous sectors.

Before turning to a discussion of specific industries, we first examine these generic approaches to improving security in the private sector.

Subsidies

Perhaps the most obvious way of strengthening incentives for adopting protective measures in the private sector is to provide a government subsidy; for example, some policymakers have proposed issuing tax credits. This approach, however, is generally flawed, and not just because of the substantial budget imbalance facing the nation.

Subsidies or tax credits can encourage unnecessarily expensive investments ("gold plating") in security measures. The problem is particularly severe in the case of investments that provide protection against terrorist attack but also have substantial other benefits to firms. Even if they do not encourage firms to undertake excessively costly investments with minimal homeland security benefits, subsidies or tax credits can provide benefits to firms that would have undertaken the investments even in the absence of the tax subsidy—raising the budget cost without providing any additional security. In other words, subsidies or tax credits "buy out the base" of what firms already are doing to protect themselves against terrorist attack. Subsidies or tax credits also do a poor job of differentiating between high-risk and lower-risk sectors, yet clearly the degree of government intervention should vary depending on the circumstances. In other words, designing and implementing subsidies or tax credits is likely to be just as cumbersome and inefficient as designing direct regulations.

Insurance as a Mechanism for Improving Incentives

An alternative is to provide incentives for adopting better security measures through the insurance system. At first glance, terrorism insurance may seem counterproductive: firms and individuals with insurance against terrorist attack would appear to lack incentives to take appropriate precautions against an attack. However, where such insurance is available, it typically comes with provisions (such as a deductible) to make certain that the insured bears at least some of the cost of an attack and thus has an economic incentive to avoid attacks or minimize their consequences. More important, the insurance companies themselves have an incentive to encourage risk-reducing activities. Indeed, insurance firms are well positioned to provide incentives for mitigation efforts—steps that firms take ahead of time to protect themselves against terrorist attack. The terrorism insurance market therefore could guide protective efforts. Best practices would be encouraged through graduated rate structures that encourage individual owners to adopt prudent and cost-effective technologies and procedures for protecting their firms and the people within them.

Three critical questions arise with regard to using insurance in this way. The first is whether firms will voluntarily purchase the insurance. Terrorism insurance coverage among large firms has expanded noticeably: take-up rates were quite low in 2003 but nearly doubled in 2004, reaching almost half of large firms in mid-2004.[7] Despite the recent increases, however, take-up remains well below 100 percent.[8] In the absence of universal take-up, at least among firms that own critical infrastructure, the incentives provided by the insurance industry are much less likely to produce adequate risk reduction. Furthermore, voluntary insurance markets often suffer from the classic problem of "adverse selection," in which riskier firms are the ones that are more likely to purchase insurance, potentially creating a spiral of rising premiums and decreasing take-up.

The shortcomings of voluntary terrorism insurance raise the issue of whether insurance should be mandatory, at least for large firms or key sectors. Mandatory insurance would not only facilitate risk-mitigation efforts on a broader scale and allow the insurance industry to spread its risks more effectively but also reduce the likely demands on government following any attack in the future.[9] In France, terrorism insurance is mandatory.[10] Former deputy homeland security adviser Richard Falkenrath has suggested that Congress mandate inclusion of terrorism insurance in all commercial insurance policies.[11] In our view, terrorism insurance should indeed be required on all commercial policies, perhaps above some minimum threshold of several million dollars to avoid unnecessary administrative costs in settings unlikely to produce high-impact terrorist damage.

The second question is whether the insurance industry will be able to develop the tools needed to evaluate terrorism risk. Models of terrorism risk at the level of zip codes or specific locations are now available from firms such as Risk Management Systems, EQECAT, and Applied Insurance Research Worldwide.[12] Although these models represent significant advances, they are inherently limited not only by the paucity of historical data on terrorist attacks but also by the difficulty of predicting how terrorist behavior will evolve over time. For example, one model assumes that risk is mostly concentrated in high-visibility targets; another assumes that attacks at low-visibility targets could be employed to sow confusion and broad fear.[13] The key issue is not whether the models are fully reliable; they clearly are not.[14] Instead, the fundamental question is whether the models could become good enough to provide the basis for an insurance-oriented approach to protection. From that perspective, especially compared with the alternative of failing to provide incentives for private efforts or relying exclusively on government regulation, the models seem relatively insightful. And it should be possible for them to be informed by government risk analyses as well. The president has issued a directive requiring the secretary of homeland security to coordinate national protection efforts in infrastructure sectors such as the information technology, telecommunications, transportation, and chemical industries; it also requires the government as a whole to prioritize protection activities.[15]

The third, final question is whether the insurance industry requires a government backstop to play the role envisioned for it here. Some economists argue that the risks can be spread across private financial markets without government intervention.[16] Other economists and market observers, however, argue that capital market imperfections impede the ability of insurers to provide coverage against catastrophic risks such as those involved in terrorist activities. In such cases, a government backstop may be required. Alan Greenspan, for example, has testified that he has "yet to be convinced" that the terrorism insurance market could operate effectively without a government backstop.[17]

In December 2005 President Bush signed into law the Terrorism Risk Insurance Revision Act (TRIRA), a two-year extension and revision of the Terrorism Risk Insurance Act (TRIA). Under the program, insurance firms are required to offer terrorism coverage and the government agrees to pay a specified share of insured losses in the event of a terrorist attack. TRIRA tightens various aspects of the original program, including raising the deductible that applies before government assistance is triggered. Although some of these revisions are in the right direction, significant changes are still warranted. A substantial flaw in the current program is that no fee is imposed by the government for the backstop. (The government would recover a certain amount of its losses after the fact, but it would do so through a surcharge on all commercial insurance policies rather than on only those with terrorism insurance components.) As a result, the government program effectively subsidizes terrorism insurance, with all commercial policyholders liable to pay for part of the subsidy. A better approach would have the government charge a premium based on how much protection the insurance firm itself wants.

A Mixed System of Insurance and Regulation

An insurance-based system could be combined with a larger policy of requiring regulatory standards and third-party inspections. A mixed regulatory standards–insurance system already operates in many other areas, such as home construction and ownership and licensing of motor vehicle operators. Local building codes specify minimum standards that homes must meet. But mortgages also generally require homeowners to carry home insurance, and insurance companies provide incentives for making improvements that exceed code requirements—for example, by reducing the premium if a homeowner installs a security system. Similarly, governments specify minimum standards that drivers must meet in order to operate a motor vehicle, but they also require drivers to carry liability insurance for accidents arising from the operation of their vehicles. Meanwhile, insurance companies provide incentives for safer driving by charging higher premiums to those with poorer driving records.[18]

A mixed system of minimum standards coupled with mandatory insurance not only can encourage actors to perform safely but also can provide incentives for innovation to reduce the costs of achieving any given level of safety. The presence of minimum regulatory standards also helps to attenuate the moral hazard effect from insurance. Minimum standards also could provide guidance to courts in determining negligence under liability laws.[19] A mixed system also has the advantage of being flexible, a key virtue in an arena where new threats will be "discovered" on an ongoing basis. In situations in which insurance firms are particularly unlikely to provide proper incentives to the private sector for efficient risk reduction (for example, because insurers lack experience in those areas), regulation can play a larger role.

Third-party inspections can be coupled with insurance protection to encourage companies to reduce the risk of accidents and disasters. Under such schemes, insurance corporations would hire third-party inspectors to evaluate the safety and security of plants seeking insurance. Passing the inspection would indicate to the community and government that a firm complies with safety and security regulations. The firm also would benefit from reduced insurance premiums, since the insurer would have more confidence in the safety and security of the firm.

This system takes advantage of two potent market mechanisms to make firms safer, while freeing government resources to focus on the largest risks. Insurance firms have a strong incentive to make sure that the inspections are rigorous and that the inspected firms are safe, since they bear the costs of an accident or terrorist attack. Private sector inspections also reduce the number of audits the regulatory agency itself must undertake, allowing the government to focus its resources more effectively on those companies that it believes pose the highest risks. The more firms decide to take advantage of private third-party inspections, the greater the chances that high-risk firms will be audited by the regulatory agency.

Studies have shown how such a program could be implemented in practice. In Delaware and Pennsylvania, the state departments of environmental protection have worked closely with the insurance industry and chemical plants to test this approach in ensuring chemical facility safety.[20]

Required Steps in Specific Industries and Sectors

The steps required to improve security vary across industries. It is important to maximize protection, particularly against catastrophic attack, in a manner that is cost effective and that provides benefits outside the homeland security realm when possible. But applying these principles to specific industries and sectors requires considerable detailed technical analysis on a case-by-case basis.

One common theme throughout much of the discussion below, however, is that although appropriate safeguards generally are expensive to implement immediately, it is often relatively painless to build them into new systems. For example, given that al Qaeda appears to have considerable interest in attacks with biological agents and given the continued difficulty of treating the symptoms of such attacks quickly and effectively (especially on a large scale), it behooves the United States to adopt defensive measures where they are cost effective.[21] Air intakes on buildings can be put well above street level and beyond the reach of anyone without access to restricted areas.[22] Filters might be built into air circulation systems to impede the distribution of any chemical or biological agent introduced into a building—and a slight over-pressure maintained within buildings to reduce the risk that agents will infiltrate from the outside.[23] Addition of filters may be practical only when entire heating, ventilation, and air conditioning systems are being replaced.[24] Still, over time, considerable progress is quite feasible. Many modern heating and air circulation systems have the kinds of sensors, adaptable flows, and other features that could help protect against the effects of terrorist attack as well as optimize a building's functioning and the quality of its air under normal circumstances.[25] This shows how measures taken in part to promote homeland security can have other benefits.

Protecting key buildings against attacks involving explosives is difficult, but it sometimes is warranted when high casualties or other severe damage to society could result from a given attack (and when any attack probably could be prevented by taking reasonably inexpensive measures). To take another example, elevators might be designed to descend to the nearest floor in the event of a power outage—a wise investment against the possibility of electrical system overloading as well. (In the public sector, streetlights could be given low-energy diode emitters powered by batteries as a backup to the main power system.)[26]

Truck bombs, which have been the weapon of choice of al Qaeda in most attacks since 9/11, will remain a threat in the future. Defending against them can involve constructing new, prominent buildings at a certain setback from streets, as has occurred with a number of new U.S. embassies in recent years. Further desirable measures, at least for the highest-profile buildings, can involve using shatterproof glass or coatings having comparable effects on the lower floors and closing underground parking garages or at least inspecting people and vehicles entering them. One also might worry about large bombs being assembled piece by piece by individuals using smaller bags to carry components into a building. This threat may argue for controlling access to symbolically important buildings in particular. At present, outside New York, very few major buildings have any checks or controls on entry.[27]

The Chemical and Nuclear Industries

The U.S. chemical industry remains quite vulnerable to terrorist strikes.[28] As Richard Falkenrath testified in January 2005: "To date, the federal government has made no material reduction in the inherent vulnerability of hazardous chemical targets inside the Untied States. Doing so should be the highest critical infrastructure protection priority for the Department of Homeland Security in the next two years."[29] A DHS study ranked a terrorist act that released chlorine, along with nuclear and anthrax attacks, as among the most deadly plausible scenarios for the United States to worry about in the future, giving further credence to Falkenrath's view.[30] As argued in chapter 1, it is precisely such types of vulnerabilities that demand the most urgent attention.

Voluntary measures have been adopted by some chemical plants, notably those of members of the American Chemistry Council, but they represent a minority of the nation's total chemical facilities. Hardening plants against sophisticated attacks by well-trained terrorists could be uneconomical and in many cases unnecessary. Thousands of chemicals are produced in the United States, but only some 300 are very dangerous and about half that number pose the most extreme threats. There are tens of thousands of chemical plants but only 4,000 to 8,000 where the improper release of an agent could kill 1,000 or more individuals.[31] But a more systematic approach that requires at least a periodic assessment of vulnerabilities and commonsense safeguards is imperative.[32] Former Senator Jon Corzine introduced a bill to do just that, but it has not been passed by Congress.[33]

There also are situations in which less-dangerous chemicals can be used in place of highly toxic ones. Reducing dependence on chlorine for drinking water purification is the most notable example. In these cases, combining the good sense of chemical plant owners with the guiding hand of the insurance market is the ideal mechanism for improving safety.[34]

Another key challenge is securing nuclear materials.[35] Power plants are now protected fairly well. But the cooling ponds used for storage of spent fuel may not be protected against certain types of attacks, such as from air-planes, nor are many areas where low- to medium-grade waste is stored.[36] These latter materials can be used to make "dirty bombs." While such weapons might not kill large numbers, they could cause enormous economic costs (due to cleanup) and disruption (if a city center or other important area could not be used during cleanup). Here the most practical defense is significantly improving security for sites where such materials are found, at home and abroad.[37]

Passenger Trains, Buses, and Boats

On March 11, 2004, a simple terrorist strike against trains in Madrid killed some 200 people and injured another 1,500. The July 7, 2005, London attacks, killing more than fifty people, underscored that Madrid was not a fluke. This worry applies not only to trains, but in similar ways to buses, ferries, and cruise ships. Yet not nearly as much attention has been given to this issue as to, for example, airplane security.[38]

Several experimental efforts have been made to monitor passengers and cargo entering American trains. However, such efforts tend to rely heavily on labor-intensive methods such as using dogs to detect explosives. The challenge is the speed at which people must move through train stations and the number of passengers involved, particularly for heavily traveled local train and subway systems.[39] For example, the New York subway system carries nearly 4 million passengers a day, who get on and off at 468 stations, while all U.S. airports together handle just 1.5 million people a day.[40]

Some additional safeguards are desirable for trains and buses. Emergency communications systems can be improved; stations protected by perimeter fencing, guards, and monitoring; tunnels hardened; and spot checking made more common. Further federal funding is appropriate here; insurance markets are unlikely to be of much help since much train infrastructure is publicly owned.[41] The American Public Transporation Association has called for more than $7 billion in added funding for mass transit systems, including trains, over the next three years—thirty times the expenditures of the last three years combined.[42] Indeed, there is a strong case for substantial funding increases.[43]

But the additional $7 billion strikes us as too much. More logical is a grad-ual, incremental increase that continually evaluates the benefits of new and experimental measures as they are introduced. The fact of the matter is that, almost regardless of expenditure level, security will not be perfect on trains and buses. Controlling access of all passengers at all times seems unrealistic.

Tightened security measures can be used for special events or in the case of intelligence alerts suggesting particular cause for concern. For example, police officers were put on every subway train in New York the day after the July 7, 2005, London bombings.[44] But, unfortunately, this vulnerability is one of those that are so difficult to address that they underscore the need for preventive homeland security activities—border patrols, prevention efforts by police departments and the FBI, and so forth—as well as continued intelligence operations and offensive action abroad.

A Democratic attempt to add $1.7 billion to the 2006 budget for rail security failed in Congress.[45] The Democratic idea was sound but the amount was, for the reasons noted above, probably too much. That said, an increase in the range of hundreds of millions of dollars would have been appropriate and should be pursued for the 2007 budget.

The situation is similar for passenger ships and ferries. Some improvements in security are warranted, but that said, vulnerability is a fact of life.[46] Given that most such attacks, however tragic they might be, would not be catastrophic in the terms we use in chapter 1, a cost-benefit analysis—and the state of available technology and security procedures—suggests that only limited investments of the type already under way are warranted at this time.[47]

Cargo Trains, Trucks, and Barges Carrying Hazardous Materials

Trucks, trains, and barges are the chief means of transporting hazardous materials in the United States today. At present there are few restrictions on who can drive trucks and where trucks can go—except, of course, that as a matter of public safety, tunnels and certain other very specific sections of road are sometimes deemed off limits to certain classes of highly toxic or flammable materials. Background checks have been begun for drivers of especially dangerous classes of chemicals and other substances. But efforts to authenticate a driver's identity by using biometric indicators remain in the pilot testing stage.[48] Moreover, Mexican and Canadian drivers on U.S. roads are not being checked in the same way.[49] Some municipalities have similarly decided to find substitutes for the most lethal sorts of chemicals often carried by trucks (such as chlorine) when possible. Some companies train their employees in security precautions and monitor key facilities such as fuel depots. But these efforts are at present scattershot.[50]

Permitting this state of affairs to continue is highly imprudent. Leaving aside the issue of truck bombs, many trucks carry potentially lethal materials that could kill thousands of people if dissipated in densely congested parts of cities. To reduce the risks, several steps can be taken. First, background checks must be done comprehensively and quickly for drivers transporting substances such as gasoline and chlorine. Names and fingerprints must be compared to entries on terror watch lists. Second, truck storage yards must meet minimal safety standards with regard to limiting access and monitoring perimeters. Third, safety features should be used on the doors of trucks that transport dangerous materials to reduce the odds that materials would be stolen for subsequent use in a terrorist attack. Given the danger involved, not just to the drivers of the trucks and others directly involved but to society as a whole, minimal safety standards are important enough to be imposed by regulation rather than by relying entirely on the insurance markets.

As an additional precaution, trucks carrying certain highly toxic substances should be banned from the centermost part of cities unless escorted by security guards and outfitted with tracking technology as well as automatic braking technology.[51] Economic incentives would thus come into play, with firms measuring the costs of protective technology against the economic benefits of being granted greater access to densely populated regions. The chlorine gas tragedy in South Carolina in January 2005 underscored the need for upgrades to security in this realm as well.

When substituting safer chemicals for dangerous chemicals is not possible, specific trains should be rerouted away from the center of cities when necessary and practical. In early 2005, the District of Columbia prohibited shipments of hazardous materials through parts of the nation's capital. A more systematic national effort is appropriate as well.[52] (The most lethal substances should be banned outright from city centers; others could be permitted, as noted above, when companies adopt best practices, such as automatic tracking and braking technology, for their trucks.)

Finally, safety standards should be enforced. For example, it is unwise that half of the nation's 60,000 train cars that frequently carry poisonous gases are obsolete or otherwise in poor shape.[53]

The Food and Water Industries

Other areas where not enough has been done to prevent attacks are the food industry and the country's water infrastructure. The case for doing more in regard to food can be debated. There are no known cases of al Qaeda or its affiliates attacking the food supply, but that hardly means that the organization, which has already proved itself to be innovative, will not attack it in the future. And certain types of attacks, such as pouring a small amount of botulism toxin into a milk truck leaving a farm, could literally cause tens of thousands of deaths.[54]

As he left the Bush administration, Tommy Thompson, former secretary of health and human services, said that he worried "every single night" about large-scale food poisoning.[55] But infrastructure for monitoring food supplies and quickly detecting any signs of contamination is insufficient. Some additional funding has been added for food safety investigators and laboratories to check for deliberate contamination. But no demands have been placed on the nation's more than 50,000 food processing sites to improve site security. Some voluntary measures have been adopted by the industry—and FDA and USDA have preferred to keep them voluntary, in part to avoid collecting data that could later be made available under the Freedom of Information Act. But these have been spotty.[56]

Requiring sites such as food processing centers to carry terrorism insurance (against any liability for poisoning that occurs on their premises) may provide the simplest and soundest means of addressing this vulnerability in a cost-effective way. At a minimum, it could lead to more uniform adoption of commonsense protective measures, such as more systematic patrolling and monitoring of the perimeters of facilities. As suggested by the Democratic members of the House Select Committee on Homeland Security, each state or region should also have the ability to quickly test foods for a wide range of possible contaminants. This can allow spot checking of food under normal circumstances and prompt efforts to contain the consequences of any attack should one occur.

As for water, it is extremely difficult to contaminate large water systems because of the amount of material needed for lethal doses. That means that protecting drinking water reservoirs, for example, need not extend to the level of providing complete assurance that no person on foot is ever near a reservoir at any time. Protective systems that keep trucks away from such reservoirs and monitor foot traffic well enough to ensure that substantial numbers of people are not able to gain entry to a reservoir would generally suffice. As for water treatment facilities, these can be viewed largely as any other chemical plant—with risk and appropriate security measures determined by the nature of the chemicals in use. A reasonably high level of protection is required to the extent that chlorine is employed, but nothing beyond what would be properly applied to many other facilities in the chemical industry.[57]

A second problem with water concerns the potential for attacks on dams to flood metropolitan areas and create conditions not unlike those produced by Hurricane Katrina—though this time without warning. Risk assessments have been completed for the nation's major dams.[58] The amount of high explosive needed to destroy most of them—together with improved site security near most—limits the likely danger associated with this type of terrorist scenario, but it does not eliminate the risk entirely by any means. At a minimum, this worry is further reason for the nation to digest fully the lessons of Katrina—and figure out how to mount large-scale responses to such catastrophes within hours rather than days. This observation has implications for many agencies, including NORTHCOM. The military should not lead the response to the vast majority of natural disasters or terrorist strikes, in terms of taking command of any effort. But leaving aside such issues, as well as the question of whether posse comitatus should be modified, the U.S. armed forces have physical capacities rivaled by no other national institution, and at a minimum the nation needs to be better prepared to organize and deploy them fast in future crises.

Energy Infrastructure

It will not always be possible to know what infrastructure to protect and what not to protect, until after the fact. Take, for example, the Alyeska pipeline in Alaska—or any other oil pipeline. It is possible to use a rifle to disrupt the flow of oil, and in fact that has happened before, though in an act closer to vandalism or hooliganism than terrorism. Pipelines are of course attacked in Colombia, Iraq, and elsewhere, so the threat is hardly implausible. That said, taking steps to try to prevent such attacks would clearly be very difficult in some places, short of setting up dense security perimeters (or burying the pipelines). Moreover, attacks on oil pipelines would be unlikely to cause any loss of human life. This is the type of threat that should be in a second or even third tier of importance.[59] Some measures—such as protecting chokepoints, ensuring capacity for quick shutdown of damaged pipes, and protecting the pumping stations (and key electronics) of pipeline systems—are warranted, but comprehensive protection is not, at least not in most places.[60]

Boston, the only major city in the United States to have a nearby liquid natural gas terminal, provides another energy example, of greater concern given the potential loss of life involved in any attack. Tankers were not allowed to come into Boston harbor to service the terminal during the 2004 Democratic convention, suggesting that there is a real basis for worry. (Explosions of such tankers could cause structural damage to buildings a third of a mile away and burn the skin of people a mile away.)[61] But has the danger really passed now that the convention is over? This question suggests that it would be prudent to move the terminal—if not immediately, then at least when major renovation is needed on the existing infrastructure.[62]

Skyscrapers, Major Buildings, and Other Structures

In the United States, most large buildings, famous public facilities, sports stadiums, concert halls, and shopping malls are open to the public—and thus to terrorists armed with explosives, chemicals, or biological pathogens. Most such structures lack filters that could trap contamination that gets inside, and few have the type of air circulation system that would reduce the danger of such contamination in the first place. And few have commonsense protections against car and truck bombs, which al Qaeda continues to employ frequently and effectively around the world, even in the post-9/11 era.

The appropriate degree of protection clearly depends on the nature of the target. For the nation's 500 skyscrapers, 250 largest arenas and stadiums, large train stations and airports, and any other location where many thousands of people gather in confined spaces, special efforts are sensible when practical. New buildings might even be built a certain distance back from streets (as is the case with many U.S. embassies today), tougher building codes employed, and parking garages kept physically separate from buildings. But these sorts of sweeping measures clearly are not practical in all cases.[63]

Existing structures can be equipped with shatterproof glass on lower floors. Vehicles entering parking garages can be searched, and in some cases their movements can be restricted. When air circulation systems are renovated, air intakes should be moved above street level and monitored. Reverse pressure air systems and good filters are among the other options. Again, insurance markets can offer owners incentives to adopt such measures.[64]

Conclusion

The number of sites that might be targeted in the United States is daunting, and a rigorous means of protecting the country comprehensively, even if conceivable, is unaffordable. But the United States has a more limited number of sites of particular interest—places where thousands of individuals routinely congregate, for example, or important centers of economic activity—where the symbolic and political significance of any attack could be huge. Most such sites are in the private sector, which owns 85 percent of the nation's infrastructure, though an important number are public. By focusing on key locations and by using insurance markets and related mechanisms to give private owners incentives to adopt best practices at reasonable cost, the country's vulnerability to truly catastrophic terrorism can be substantially mitigated. Since 9/11, we have moved toward that objective. But we have a great distance still to go.

Notes

1. Congressional Budget Office, "Federal Terrorism Reinsurance: An Update," January 2005, p. 13. Some industries (such as transportation, energy, utilities, and financial services) have increased spending modestly. See Benjamin Weiser and Claudia H. Deutsch, "Many Offices Holding the Line on Post-9/11 Security Outlays," *New York Times*, August 16, 2004; and the Conference Board, *Corporate Security Management: Organization and Spending since 9/11* (New York: 2003), p. 5.

2. Peter R. Orszag, "Homeland Security and the Private Sector," testimony before the National Commission on Terrorist Attacks upon the United States [9/11 Commission], 108 Cong., 1 sess., November 19, 2003.

3. Frank Cilluffo, "The Mission of Homeland Security," *NYU Review of Law and Security: Are We Safer?* (Fall 2004): 38.

4. It is also possible, at least in theory, for private firms to invest *too much* in antiterrorism security. In particular, visible security measures (such as more uniformed guards) undertaken by one firm may merely displace terrorist attacks onto other firms, without significantly affecting the overall probability of an attack. In such a scenario, the total security precautions undertaken can escalate beyond the socially desirable level—and government intervention could theoretically improve matters by placing *limits* on how much security firms would undertake. Unobservable security precautions (which are difficult for potential terrorists to detect), on the other hand, do not displace vulnerabilities from one firm to another and at least theoretically can reduce the overall level of terrorism activity. For an interesting application of these ideas to the Lojack automobile security system, see Ian Ayres and Steven Levitt, "Measuring Positive Externalities from Unobservable Victim Precaution: An Empirical Analysis of Lojack," *Quarterly Journal of Economics* 108 (February 1998). For further analysis of evaluating public policy in the presence of externalities, see Peter Orszag and Joseph Stiglitz, "Optimal Fire Departments: Evaluating Public Policy in the Face of Externalities," Working Paper, Brookings, January 2002.

5. The Coase theorem shows that under very restrictive conditions, the negative externality can be corrected by voluntary private action even if the role of government is limited to enforcing property rights. But the Coase theorem requires that all affected parties be able to negotiate at sufficiently low cost with each other. Since virtually the entire nation could be affected indirectly by a terrorist attack, the costs of

negotiation are prohibitive, making the Coase theorem essentially irrelevant in the terrorism context.

6. See Howard Kunreuther and Geoffrey Heal, "Interdependent Security," *Journal of Risk and Uncertainty* 26 (March-May 2003): 231–49; and Howard Kunreuther, Geoffrey Heal, and Peter Orszag, "Interdependent Security: Implications for Homeland Security Policy and Other Areas," Policy Brief 108, Brookings, October 2002.

7. Congressional Budget Office, "Federal Terrorism Reinsurance: An Update," p. 6; and Erwann Michel-Kerjan and Burkhard Pedell, "Terrorism Risk Coverage in the post-9/11 Era: A Comparison of Public-Private Partnerships in France, Germany, and the U.S," Risk Management and Decision Processes Center, Wharton School, University of Pennsylvania, Working Paper 2004-029, October 2004, p. 22.

8. Some economists argue that many firms *should* not insure themselves against terrorist attack, since the owners of the firm can mostly if not entirely diversify that risk. Kent Smetters, "Insuring against Terrorism: The Policy Challenge," Working Paper 11038 (Cambridge, Mass.: National Bureau of Economic Research, January 2005).

9. Howard Kunreuther and Erwann Michel-Kerjan, "Policy Watch: Challenges for Terrorism Risk Insurance in the United States," *Journal of Economic Perspectives* 18 (Fall 2004): 211.

10. Michel-Kerjan and Pedell, "Terrorism Risk Coverage in the post-9/11 Era."

11. Richard A. Falkenrath, statement before the Senate Committee on Homeland Security and Governmental Affairs, 109 Cong., 1 sess., January 26, 2005.

12. Congressional Budget Office, "Federal Terrorism Reinsurance: An Update," p. 4.

13. Ibid.

14. The insurance industry operates in many areas in which models are nowhere close to fully reliable, including tort cases. See Smetters, "Insuring against Terrorism."

15. President George W. Bush, "Homeland Security Presidential Directive/HSPD 7: Critical Infrastructure Identification, Prioritization, and Protection," December 17, 2003 (www.whitehouse.gov/news/releases/2003/12/print/20031217-5.htlm).

16. Smetters, "Insuring against Terrorism." See also appendix B in Congressional Budget Office, "Federal Terrorism Reinsurance."

17. "Senators Trying Again to Extend Terrorism Insurance Plan," *CongressDaily*, February 18, 2005.

18. To be sure, crucial differences exist between the terrorist case and these other examples. For example, stable actuarial data exist for home and auto accidents, but not for terrorist attacks. Nonetheless, it may be possible for insurers to distinguish risks of loss based on differences in damage exposure given a terrorist incident. Some financial firms already are trying to devise a basic framework for evaluating such risks. See, for example, Moody's Investors Service, "Moody's Approach to Terrorism Insurance for U.S. Commercial Real Estate," March 1, 2002.

19. For a discussion of the potential benefits of a mixed system of building code regulations and mandatory catastrophic risk insurance in the context of natural

disasters, see Peter Diamond, "Comment on Catastrophic Risk Management," in *The Financing of Catastrophe Risk,* edited by Kenneth Froot (University of Chicago Press, 1999), pp. 85–88.

20. For further information, see Howard Kunreuther, Patrick McNulty, and Yong Kang, "Improving Environmental Safety through Third-Party Inspection," *Risk Analysis* 22 (March 2002): 309–18.

21. Judith Miller, "U.S. Has New Concerns about Anthrax Readiness," *New York Times,* December 28, 2003, p. A20; and Philip Shenon, "Terrorism Drills Showed Lack of Preparedness, Report Says," *New York Times,* December 19, 2003.

22. Gregory Wright, "Is Your Building's HVAC Safe against Terrorism?" *HVACR News* 24 (May 2004).

23. U.S. Army Corps of Engineers, "Protecting Buildings and Their Occupants from Airborne Hazards," draft, October 2001; Energy Information Administration, "Building Characteristics: Building Use Tables," table 12 (www.eia.doe.gov/emeu/ consumption); letter from Michael C. Janus, Battelle Corporation, December 1, 2001, to Michael O'Hanlon; and Ann Gerhart, "Tom Ridge, on High Alert," *Washington Post,* November 12, 2001, p. C1.

24. Department of Health and Human Services, *Guidance for Protecting Building Environments from Airborne Chemical, Biological, or Radiological Attacks* (May 2002).

25. Jon C. Lund, "Smart Buildings," *IEEE Spectrum* (August 2003): 18–23.

26. Peter Fairley, "The Unruly Power Grid," *IEEE Spectrum* (August 2004): 22–27.

27. Terry Pristin, "Different Cities, Different Security for Buildings," *New York Times,* July 9, 2003, p. C6.

28. For further discussion of homeland security and the chemical industry, see Congressional Budget Office, "Chemicals and Hazardous Materials," in *Homeland Security and the Private Sector,* December 2004.

29. Falkenrath, statement before the Senate Committee on Homeland Security and Governmental Affairs.

30. Eric Lipton, "U.S. Report Lists Possibilities for Terrorist Attacks and Likely Toll," *New York Times,* March 16, 2005, p. 1.

31. Richard D. Farmer, *Homeland Security and the Private Sector* (Congressional Budget Office, December 2004), pp. 21–28.

32. Government Accountability Office, *Homeland Security: Voluntary Initiatives Are Under Way at Chemical Facilities, but the Extent of Security Preparedness Is Unknown,* GAO-03-439 (March 2003), summary page.

33. Office of Senator Jon S. Corzine, "Fact Sheet on Senator Corzine's Chemical Security Legislation," November 17, 2003 (www.corzine.senate.gov/priorities/ chem_sec.html); and Rick Hind and David Halperin, "Lots of Chemicals, Little Reaction," *New York Times,* September 22, 2004, p. A31.

34. A related topic concerns the safeguards applied to the sales of certain lethal chemicals. Not enough has yet been done to ensure proper oversight in that regard. For example, a full decade after the Oklahoma City bombing tragedy, only three states

have notable regulations on the sale of ammonium nitrate fertilizer. Oklahoma joined South Carolina and Nevada in implementing simple measures like requiring identification from anyone wishing to buy such fertilizer and tracking sales of such materials to allow for investigation of any problems that may result. Others should follow their lead. In cases where simple, commonsense, minimal-cost regulations can be devised, they are hardly inconsistent with the general approach advocated here: using market incentives when possible but mixed approaches including some regulation when sensible. See Associated Press, "National Briefing—Oklahoma: Rules to Regulate Selling of Fertilizer," *New York Times*, February 18, 2005, p. A17.

35. See Farmer, "Civilian Nuclear Power," in *Homeland Security and the Private Sector*.

36. Shankar Vedantam, "Storage of Nuclear Spent Fuel Criticized," *Washington Post*, March 28, 2005, p. 1.

37. Peter D. Zimmerman and Cheryl Loeb, "Dirty Bombs: The Threat Revisited," *Defense Horizons* 38 (Washington: National Defense University, January 2004); and Joby Warrick, "Smugglers Targeting Dirty Bombs for Profit," *Washington Post*, November 30, 2003, p. 1.

38. Arnold M. Howitt and Jonathan Makler, "On the Ground: Protecting America's Roads and Transit against Terrorism" (Brookings, 2005).

39. Baronet Media, "Washington Tests High-Security System for Trains," *Vigilo Risk*, June 9, 2004, p. 7.

40. Gregg Easterbrook, "In an Age of Terror, Safety Is Relative," *New York Times*, June 27, 2004, p. 1.

41. Baronet Media, "House Committee Seeks $1 Billion for U.S. Rail Security," *Vigilo Risk*, June 23, 2004, p. 7.

42. David Randall Peterman, "Passenger Rail Security: Overview of Issues" (Washington: Congressional Research Service, July 29, 2005), pp. 2–3.

43. Nicole Gaouette, "Senate Is Split on Spending Bill for Domestic Security," *Los Angeles Times*, July 12, 2005.

44. Sewell Chan, "In Added Security Measure, Officers Are Riding the Rails," *New York Times*, July 8, 2005.

45. David Rogers, "Homeland Budget Accord Is Reached," *Wall Street Journal*, September 30, 2005, p. 2.

46. In addition to the threat of explosives being placed in cars or planted directly on ferries and other ships, there is a risk of scuba divers attacking ships. See Jim Gomez, "Terror Plots May Reach New Depths," *Chicago Tribune*, March 18, 2005. Sometimes certain risky ports or waterways can be avoided overseas, but clearly this is not a completely reliable method of protection. See David Wood, "Terrorism Fears Divert Navy Supply Ships from Suez Canal," *Newhouse.com*, January 13, 2005.

47. Eric Lipton, "Trying to Keep the Nation's Ferries Safe from Terrorists," *New York Times*, March 19, 2005, p. 18.

48. William H. Robinson, Jennifer E. Lake, and Lisa M. Seghetti, "Border and

Transportation Security: Possible New Directions and Policy Options" (Washington: Congressional Research Service, March 29, 2005), pp. 9–10.

49. Transportation Security Administration. Information available at www.tsa. gov/public/display?content=09000519800d3fd3&print=yes (January 6, 2005).

50. See David Johnston and Andrew C. Revkin, "Officials Say Their Focus Is on Car and Truck Bombs," *New York Times*, August 2, 2004, p. A13.

51. Stephen Flynn, *America the Vulnerable: How Our Government Is Failing to Protect Us from Terrorism* (New York: HarperCollins, 2004), pp. 118–22.

52. Eric M. Weiss and Spencer S. Hsu, "90-Day Hazmat Ban Is Passed; Measure Will Bar Shipments in DC," *Washington Post*, February 2, 2005, p. B1.

53. Walt Bogdanich and Christopher Drew, "Deadly Leak Underscores Concerns about Rail Safety," *New York Times*, January 9, 2005, p. 1.

54. Rick Weiss, "Report Warns of Threat to Milk Supply," *Washington Post*, June 29, 2005, p. A8.

55. Mike Allen, "Rumsfeld to Remain at Pentagon; Thompson Quits at HHS, Warns of Vulnerabilities," *Washington Post*, December 4, 2004, p. A1.

56. General Accounting Office, *Food-Processing Security*, GAO-03-342 (February 2003), pp. 1–7.

57. Government Accountability Office, *Homeland Security: Agency Plans, Implementation, and Challenges Regarding the National Strategy for Homeland Security*, GAO-05-33 (January 2005), pp. 84–93.

58. Claudia Copeland and Betsy Cody, "Terrorism and Security Issues Facing the Water Infrastructure Sector," in *Homeland Security and Terrorism*, edited by Russell Howard, James Forest, and Joanne Moore (New York: McGraw-Hill, 2006), p. 200.

59. See, for example, Andrea R. Mihailescu, "Alaska's Vulnerable Oil Pipeline," *Jane's Terrorism and Security Monitor*, September 1, 2004.

60. One area where it behooves the United States to improve vigilance is in the vulnerability of power, communications, transportation, and water infrastructure to electromagnetic pulse from a high-altitude nuclear detonation. Terrorists are unlikely to carry out such an attack, but a nation-state could, and the nature of preparations against such an attack are akin to homeland security activities and so worthy of brief mention here. Protecting all electronics from such an attack is impractical (and modern electronic systems, with their low power requirements and low-voltage tolerances, are inherently more vulnerable to such attacks than were vacuum tubes). But the country's infrastructure should not be allowed to fail catastrophically after such an attack; the period of recovery could last many months, during which time the country would have to function like a pre-modern society. Devising protection for key nodes of major infrastructure is estimated to cost about 1 to 3 percent of total system cost, if done when a system is first being built. But retrofitting protections onto existing equipment might be an order of magnitude more expensive, implying costs reaching well into the tens of billions of dollars. This suggests a two-track approach to protection, redressing glaring vulnerabilities when feasible in the short term (that

is, hardening key electronics used by major infrastructure or purchasing backup systems) while planning to gradually eliminate other vulnerabilities as infrastructure is modernized in the coming years. See Commission to Assess the Threat to the United States from Electromagnetic Pulse (EMP) Attack, *Report of the Commission to Assess the Threat to the United States from Electromagnetic Pulse (EMP) Attack*, vol. 1, Executive Report 2004 (www.iwar.org.uk/iwar/resources/emp/04-07-22emp.pdf [February 17, 2005]); and Frank Gaffney, testimony before the House Committee on the Budget, 109 Cong., 1 sess., February 16, 2005.

61. Justin Blum, "Report Assesses Risks of Attack on Tankers," *Washington Post*, December 22, 2004, p. E1.

62. Associated Press, "Collins Suicide Attack Warning," Lloyd's List, July 5, 2004, p. 12.

63. See Michael E. O'Hanlon and others, *Protecting the American Homeland: One Year On* (Brookings, 2003).

64. See Eric Lipton and James Glanz, "New Rules Proposed to Help High-Rises Withstand Attacks," *New York Times*, March 6, 2002, p. A1; letter from Michael C. Janus, Battelle Corporation, December 1, 2001, to Michael O'Hanlon; Gerhart, "Tom Ridge, on High Alert"; and Arden Bement, director, National Institute of Standards and Technology, statement before the Committee on Science, U.S. House of Representatives, 107 Cong., 2 sess., March 6, 2002.

5

BORDER PROTECTION

MICHAEL O'HANLON

Border protection is a critical pillar of homeland security. It can keep dangerous people and materials out of the country before they even get into a position to attack. In other words, it is preventive in nature, exhibiting one of the most important characteristics of optimal homeland security policy identified in chapter 1.

Border protection should not be principally viewed as a literal defense of the nation's perimeter; it is not tantamount to the creation of a moat around the United States. Rather, it is a set of efforts that exploits the fact that people and goods are relatively easily monitored when they go through checkpoints. In other words, movement across borders allows spotlighting to occur. To be sure, some border protection functions represent something closer to the direct physical protection of borders—most notably, the efforts of the Border Patrol along the long perimeters of the United States as well as some activities of the Coast Guard and the Department of Defense. But the spotlighting role is even more critical. Its failure is what allowed the nineteen hijackers who perpetrated the September 11 attacks to enter the country. Similarly, the nation's lack of accurate knowledge about what goods are coming across its borders has much more to do with holes in the official inspection process—that is, with the spotlighting function—than with the weaknesses of its walls.

Done right, border security activities can offer benefits beyond the homeland security sphere. Digitized and computerized border security measures can allow more secure and rapid movement of people and goods in and out of the United States. They also can provide better knowledge of where ships and goods are in transit. That in turn translates into, among other things, a greater ability to prevent or respond quickly to other dangers, such as piracy and ship accidents, that can afflict trade and travel.

U.S. geography generally helps in the effort to monitor borders and to use them as a means of funneling goods and routing people through places where spotlighting is possible. But the country has two long land borders that remain very difficult to guard, and they are far from the only major challenge facing the domain of homeland security. This chapter considers a number of problems, as well as the general matter of aviation security, which is in part a matter of border protection. Its conclusion, in short, is that there is no magic bullet for keeping illicit goods and undesirable people out of the country and no easy analytical way to deduce what level of increased inspection or monitoring would be sufficient to ensure national security. However, the ongoing efforts since 9/11 have been headed in the right direction, and the gradual increase in capacity for monitoring borders as well as goods should continue. Similarly, integration of terrorist watch lists also is proceeding in generally sensible directions. But the pace of progress is often too slow. In addition, some additional policy steps, such as much more uniform standards for drivers' licenses, are called for.

Monitoring People

There has been progress in regulating the movement of people into the United States and monitoring them thereafter. It is much harder for individuals to gain access to this country while disguising their true identities, particularly anyone on a terrorist watch list. Notably, someone on a watch list who is trying to fly into a U.S. airport from abroad is unlikely to get through under his or her own name and indeed is unlikely to be allowed entry even under a false name if his or her fingerprints already are on file. This is a major step forward since 9/11.

Other useful measures have been adopted. For example, the student and exchange visitor information system (SEVIS) now appears to be functioning quite well in helping to track foreigners in the United States on student visas.[1] Those who overstay their visa can be more quickly identified and located.

Increasingly, biometric indicators also are being used to control foreign travel. The U.S.-VISIT program requires foreign visitors to submit to finger-printing (of their right and left index fingers) and having a digital photo-graph taken on arrival in the United States. A complementary program, the State Department's biometric visa program, requires visa applicants to have their fingerprints taken before they travel to the United States; the finger-prints are then compared with those in a DHS database (known as IDENT) consisting of some 5 million individuals, some of whom are ineligible for a U.S. visa. When visitors arrive in the United States, the fingerprints taken by DHS under the U.S.-VISIT program also are checked against those on their visa (for those required to have a visa) to confirm that the individual in ques-tion is indeed the one to whom the visa was granted.[2]

But a great deal remains to be done. For example, phasing in the U.S.-VISIT program will take at least one more year to complete given current plans, especially at smaller entry and exit points along U.S. land borders.[3]

To reduce the chances that individuals planning terrorist attacks will find a legal way into the country and then overstay their visa, it would be useful to record exits from the United States in real time. Those remaining longer than they should could then be more easily identified and pursued, as the 9/11 Commission recommended.[4]

A remaining problem in air travel security arises from what is known as the visa waiver program (VWP), discussed in chapter 3. Until digitized pass-ports with biometric indicators are widely used by qualifying countries, the visa waiver program will continue to constitute a substantial loophole in U.S. border security, given the prevalence of stolen and forged passports around the world (numbering at least 20 million, according to Moises Naim's book, *Illicit*).[5] While individuals entering under the program are still checked upon entry, officials have less ability to interview them thoroughly when required if questioning must be done at the actual border. This circumstance argues for some other level of screening of individuals from VWP countries before they can board flights for the United States. For example, DHS security per-sonnel could be deployed at foreign airline check-in counters in certain VWP countries (as Israel does with El Al flights).[6]

Terrorist watch lists also need to be improved. The United States has con-solidated some dozen watch lists into a single terrorist screening database (TSDB) using more extensive data in the terrorist identities database (TID). (The effort to construct the TID began with the previous gold standard of ter-rorist watch lists, the State Department's TIPOFF list. That list was subse-quently scrubbed and expanded by consolidating it with other databases.)

Some new specialized watch lists with limited information (which are easier to share with people who do not have a security clearance) are being created as well, to assist in monitoring aircraft passengers and improve the accuracy with which their names are matched against those of suspected terrorists.[7] Thankfully none of the watch list consolidations have turned into a complete fiasco, as the FBI's attempts to computerize its case files unfortunately have.[8] But the consolidation and integration process has been slow.[9] And according to a 2005 report from the Department of Justice's Inspector General, the integrated watch list contains important flaws, including many key omissions. Finally, as the 9/11 Public Discourse Project reported in December 2005, there is not yet a comprehensive version of the TSDB being used to screen airline passengers.

Even digitized passports with biometric indicators cannot track new recruits with no known ties to terrorist organizations; it is therefore important to recall that these sorts of tracking efforts have inherent limitations. This is one clear example of the reason why a multi-tiered strategy for homeland security is imperative.

Screening also works in the opposite direction, keeping good people out while they wait for security reviews to be completed. This is true, for example, for foreign students, who in many cases when screened through the so-called Visas Mantis program have had to wait months for their visas. Improvements have been under way in these programs, including a change allowing students to get a single visa for an entire period of study rather than requiring annual renewal. But there are still long delays.[10] This problem also applies to individuals trying to enter the country to conduct business, seek medical care, or pursue other important matters.

The student problem has not become truly severe. While there was a 2.4 percent decline in foreign student enrollment for the 2003–04 academic year compared with that for the year before, the number of foreign students remained greater than in 2000 or any previous year.[11] Indeed, the overall number of foreign students in the United States was 4.5 percent greater in 2004–2005 than just before the September 11, 2001, attacks, though there was a decline of 14 percent in Middle Eastern students.[12] And the U.S. figures were not notably worse than those witnessed in the United Kingdom. That said, the problem could intensify again—and could affect some of the most talented individuals in the broader foreign student pool, convincing disproportionate numbers of them to go elsewhere. Further measures to address this problem, such as increases in government capacity for processing paperwork, are therefore warranted.

In situations involving certain non-Western countries, U.S. technical and financial help may be needed to ensure good border security and travel controls. The simple fact of the matter is that the interest of the United States in tracking the movement of many terrorists is greater than that of developing countries. Even when that is not the case, many countries will not have the resources to do all that they should do given the urgency of the threat. Seen in that light, President Bush's June 2003 East Africa counterterrorism initiative (EACTI) is a good step in the right direction. It provides $100 million to improve border control, police capability, airline security, and related homeland security operations in a region that has been hit hard by terrorist violence.[13] The latter includes the 1998 U.S. embassy bombings in Kenya and Tanzania and the 2002 attacks on a hotel and airplane in Kenya (the latter, thankfully, was not successful), not to mention ongoing civil strife in places such as Somalia. This is enough money to make a real difference in a region of relatively low incomes, but the funding apparently was taken in large part out of existing programs, meaning that its net beneficial effect is difficult to ascertain.[14] And similar programs probably are needed in other regions, such as Central Asia.

Ensuring adequate capacity to screen individuals and issue visas as well as a proper means for verifying their identities helps the United States beyond the homeland security arena. It can expedite the movement into the country of people who can contribute to the economy and who ideally can become goodwill ambassadors as well as important contact points for the United States once they return home. As argued previously, whenever a homeland security program has benefits beyond the immediate objective of reinforcing national security, it is especially worthy of serious consideration and serious support.

The Special Problem of Land Borders

The preceding discussion pertains generally to the movement of individuals to and from the United States, but monitoring the movement of people at land borders poses special problems. It also offers unique opportunities, underscoring this book's theme about the need for greater international cooperation in the "homeland" security effort. To the extent that the governments of Canada and Mexico make it hard for terrorists to use their country as a staging base or way station, the United States benefits from an added line of defense of its own territory. That does not make its own border enforcement job unimportant, but it does allow a somewhat greater (and more realistic) margin for error at that inherently difficult line of defense. If Canada and Mexico improve their own monitoring of persons traveling into and out of the United States, only modest additional improvements may be needed in U.S. border security along the nations' mutual frontiers, and other lines of protection in the broader homeland security arena may become more effective.

The United States has 216 airports, 143 seaports, and 115 land facilities that are official ports of entry, at a total of 317 locations. Land facilities generally involve car and truck traffic, which is especially difficult to regulate. Moreover, of course, land borders between official points of entry are very hard to control. At many official checkpoints, passengers in cars are not checked as long as they are in vehicles with legitimate license plates. That policy should be changed. Care must be taken to do it in a way that does not seriously slow movement at checkpoints, with resulting negative consequences for commerce as well as convenience of travel. That suggests that the change in policy will have to be gradual, to allow time for more inspectors to be hired and new procedures to be developed, such as adding lanes at checkpoints. Given typical car passenger loads, it may be necessary to increase staffing by as much as 100 percent.[15]

Open land borders also are a serious problem. For example, U.S. land management agencies are responsible for the 30 percent of the borders owned by the federal government. Yet they have only 200 full-time law enforcement officers, a number increased by just 20 percent in the first two years after September 11.[16] Such numbers cannot begin to credibly monitor or prevent off-road border crossings.

Such limited vigilance of U.S. land borders is a mistake. It can deprive the country of the opportunity to spotlight people effectively at official points of entry, thereby blunting one of the very best homeland security tools that the United States and the international community in general possess. There are relatively few dependable ways to search for terrorists among the huge throngs of individuals on the planet; this needle-in-a-haystack effort requires some means of rendering people visible, and official border crossings can do that. So it is especially important to ensure that individuals pass through such locations when traveling.

Take, for instance, the sparsely guarded Canadian border, which can be an important means of entry.[17] The Patriot Act led to a tripling of the number of U.S. agents along that enormously long and porous border, but the total remains just under 1,000. There is little reason to think that that number is adequate.[18] The United States also needs an integrated plan involving increases in random patrols and better equipment for surveillance and mobility along the U.S.-Canada border, as well as better cooperation with Ottawa in the effort.[19] There has been movement in the right direction. DHS is developing a way to increase response capability anywhere to within an hour of notice of a problem and to improve monitoring as well. This might not help with the "lone wolf" terrorist sneaking through the woods, but it could pick up illicit vehicle movements or groups of individuals. Five DHS bases near the Canadian border are being created to help in the effort.[20] Overall, this border is better protected than before, and it soon will be monitored even more effectively. But the absolute amount of U.S. capability is still extremely modest, suggesting an enduring problem.

Although few Canadians would pose major terrorism-related concerns, Canada's efforts to monitor its own borders against terrorist infiltration are wanting in a number of areas. For example, its coast guard does little to monitor Canada's long shorelines and passenger manifests of cruise ships coming ashore are not examined.[21] This underscores the importance of Canada improving its own regulations regarding visitors to the country, but it also means that the United States must assume that foreign terrorists may try to reach this country through its northern neighbor.

A greater worry is the Mexican border, where despite the presence of almost 10,000 border agents an estimated 4,000 illegal aliens cross each day. They are mostly Hispanics but also include individuals from countries such as Afghanistan, Egypt, Iran, and Iraq, who pose a greater risk of possible terrorist infiltration.[22] Intelligence reports express concern that al Qaeda may indeed try to exploit the porosity of this border.[23]

Adding 1,000 employees costs the government about $100 million on average. Therefore a rough estimate of the cost of the above proposals to increase monitors at borders is $1 billion a year, if the doubling of inspectors recommended to monitor passengers in vehicles crossing the border is matched by comparable increases in other aspects of the border protection effort. Accurately estimating the appropriate number of additional inspectors is beyond the scope of this analysis, but the above number gives a reasonable ballpark figure. The number of inspectors has grown by 5,000 over the last decade, with some beneficial effect on the estimated infiltration rate. Indeed, the increase possibly reduced the rate by one-third, though it is admittedly difficult to be sure of the exact numbers as well as the true causes of any decline. It makes sense therefore to continue on the same trajectory while also introducing new operational procedures and new technologies—such as unmanned aerial vehicle patrols, the sea wall near San Diego, and the America's Shield Initiative, which involves multispectral sensors and cameras as well as magnetic and seismic detectors.[24]

The right policy is to keep increasing Border Patrol personnel year by year in significant numbers and then attempt to modify procedures to improve border monitoring. As experience is gained, how many employees will be enough can be determined more accurately. Unfortunately, the Bush administration's request for additional border agents in 2006 totaled just 210 individuals, a far cry from the scale of increase that would be appropriate, given the present porous nature of the country's perimeter.[25] But Congress wisely added $600 million to the president's request, including enough funds for 1,000 additional agents.[26]

IDENT, the database used by DHS's Border Patrol, is not fully integrated on a national scale with other databases. IDENT uses a photo and two fingerprints, whereas the FBI's IAFIS (integrated automated fingerprint identification system) uses all ten fingerprints. Reportedly, all U.S. Border Patrol stations now have interoperable systems capable of accessing IAFIS records and cross-checking the Border Patrol's IDENT entries against those records. But Border Patrol agents cannot access the consolidated name-based terrorist watch list (TSDB) maintained by the Terrorist Screening Center at their stations.[27]

Another problem is that the consular identification cards issued by some foreign governments, including Mexico, to their own citizens can be fraudulently obtained fairly easily.[28] They are often used for identification in the United States. Lax standards for such cards cannot be tolerated. The United States may need to consider contributing seed money to encourage Mexico in particular to develop more rigorous, real-time databases of possible terrorists as well as better ID technology of its own. At present, the United States has a plan to require visitors crossing the Canadian or Mexican borders to present a passport or one of four other hard-to-counterfeit documents. But that plan is not due to be implemented before December 31, 2007.[29]

Summing up, the land border security problem poses three special challenges. One—making sure that smaller border crossing posts receive up-to-date technology to become full participants in new efforts such as U.S.-VISIT—is mostly a matter of taking the problem seriously and providing adequate funds. The second—improving screening of passengers in cars and working toward a standard by which all who pass through a land border are checked—is more demanding conceptually, though surely doable. However, it will require development of new procedures that could slow crossings dramatically, so considerable work is needed to add inspectors and increase the numbers of lanes at key crossings. The third—closing U.S. land borders to illegal infiltration, which is, of course, linked to broader U.S. immigration policy—is a problem for which solutions have not yet been successfully conceptualized, even in theory. To mitigate the problem, more technical and human resources to monitor borders are generally well advised, but they are unlikely to solve it, underscoring again the need for a multi-tiered approach to homeland security—one that begins by pushing America's borders "outward" and improving cooperation with other countries' parallel homeland security efforts.

There also is a clear major benefit to improving border monitoring beyond the homeland security domain. It is an important means of reducing illegal immigration, with all of its associated economic and political repercussions. Focusing on land border controls within a homeland security strategy therefore is consistent with the principle that the United States should be especially keen to pursue programs with multiple benefits. Indeed, the United States and Canada might push this logic one step further and consider another crossing point in the Detroit-Windsor area, where more than $100 billion of trade between the two countries occurs annually. If built outside of the immediate urban areas, it would not only provide backup in case a major bridge were destroyed but reduce traffic congestion under normal conditions.[30]

Domestic and International Air Travel

Overall, air travel is an area in which homeland security measures have been serious and effective. That is entirely appropriate, given al Qaeda's focus on airplanes and the success it achieved using them on September 11, 2001, as well as the large effects on the economy sure to result from any aircraft downing, even if loss of life were modest. Since certain specific vulnerabilities still remain, they merit attention and redress.

For example, as the 9/11 Commission recommended, screening for explosives on passengers themselves should be implemented—starting now with passengers selected for special scrutiny and eventually extending to all passengers. Available technology may not be perfect, but it is sufficiently effective to be worth the investment. The downing of two Russian aircraft on August 24, 2004, that killed ninety people may well have been caused by hexogen explosive on the persons of two passengers, despite security measures at Russia's Domodedovo Airport that are quite similar to those used in the United States.[31] Detectors for such explosives are neither particularly large nor particularly expensive, with one estimate for the national cost of a detector network in the ballpark of several hundred million dollars.[32] However, they do take some time to use, so one would need several per metal detector to maintain the pace of inspections if all passengers were to be screened.

Commercial cargo transported on passenger jets generally remains unscreened, with less than 5 percent of all shipments being inspected. That figure is inadequate. Either screening methods that can be applied more frequently should be developed or hardened cargo holds should be installed on planes.[33] One approach would be to accept that there is no need for 100 percent screening (Congress already has rejected such a standard).[34] Rather, better use of public-private partnerships could focus inspections. There is a known-shipper program for this purpose, but it is too easy to join the program (many members are not believed to follow robust security procedures).[35] Unless these procedures can be improved, Congress may be well advised to reconsider its rejection of the 100 percent screening standard.

Alternatively, and probably a better idea, the nation's civilian airliner fleet might be equipped with hardened luggage holds. According to one (possibly optimistic) estimate, they could be purchased for just over $100 million in investment costs and maintained with about $11 million in additional annual operating costs.[36] They can defend against not only terrorist acts but also accidental explosions, providing an additional benefit beyond the security sphere.

The lack of safeguards on private aircraft also is a worry. Although airspace restrictions have been established around some cities, they typically are no more than twenty to thirty miles wide, meaning that an intruder could reach the center of a city within about three minutes after violating the zone. Warning could be even less if a plane authorized to land at a given airport were diverted at the last minute. Fighter patrols near most major cities are not continuous enough to reliably respond to all such intrusions. So the risk of planes being flown into large buildings remains, albeit to a lesser degree than before.[37] The solution is to require an increasing fraction of aircraft pilots to undergo background checks, starting with those operating larger private planes. Should an incident occur nonetheless, much larger stay-away zones may need to be created.

At present, the level of security of foreign airliners reaching the United States often falls short of standards for American carriers. That should not be tolerated, given the demonstrated severity of the threat and al Qaeda's historic interest in attacks using aircraft. Foreign airlines can fly into the United States without air marshals. The United States has sometimes canceled flights or required air marshals on specific flights when it had reason to worry about a particular individual. But this approach requires exquisite intelligence.[38] Meanwhile, al Qaeda prisoner interrogations have suggested the possibility of future hijacking schemes in the United States, perhaps with terrorists using overseas airports with lesser levels of security as initial ingress points to the global air transportation system.[39] The problem is not just with possible hijackings. Much international air cargo is not screened for security purposes at all.[40] In addition, there are ample indications that screening of passengers for dangerous materials is not yet adequate abroad, just as it is not adequate in the United States.[41]

Cargo Inspections, Port Security, and the Coast Guard

The U.S. cargo inspection system clearly has improved. The number of inspectors grew by about 40 percent from 2001 through 2004. Total numbers of inspections reportedly grew by a larger fraction, about 60 percent, largely because new technologies and procedures allowed greater efficiencies, such as the vehicle and cargo inspection system (VACIS), which uses gamma-rays to image the contents of a container nonintrusively. In addition, inspectors now carry radiation monitors that provide at least some indication of the possible presence of radioactive materials (or at least those that are unshielded).[42] These methods lead to many false positives, so they are not panaceas, but they are much better than letting cargo go unscreened.

The container security initiative (CSI) places American inspectors in many overseas ports so they can work with local inspectors to examine some containers before they are shipped to the United States. Almost all of the world's top twenty ports have joined this program.[43] The Customs-Trade Partnership against Terrorism (C-TPAT), involving at least thirty-four foreign ports and 8,000 companies as of mid-2005, improves security standards for ports and containers and uses the incentive of faster processing and inspection to encourage companies to participate. But since CSI operates only in certain ports and because C-TPAT is voluntary, both are only partial solutions. They help steer inspectors toward the most suspicious cargo but hardly rule out the need for many inspections. The Coast Guard demands crew manifests and shipping information ninety-six hours before any ship reaches U.S. ports so that it can inspect those it finds questionable before they make land.[44]

Despite the progress, only about 12 percent of all containers entering the country in recent times have been inspected, including just 5 percent of all seaborne containers.[45] The latter figure is up from 2 percent before 9/11 (though some officials have suggested that the improvement has been somewhat less impressive).[46]

The 5 percent figure for ship-borne containers is probably a factor of two to five less than it should be. The need for greater vigilance is particularly evident in light of the U.S. view that al Qaeda has ties to the global shipping industry, underscored by Admiral James Loy, then the commandant of the Coast Guard, in 2003.[47] Unless the United States is highly confident that it knows who all such individuals may be and thus that it can carefully inspect all containers that might be used to facilitate terrorist attacks—a dubious proposition—it needs to worry more generally about that possible link. Intelligence on container shipping has improved as a result of the container security initiative and others, but not nearly enough to impart confidence that inspecting one of every twenty containers entering the country through U.S. ports is enough to provide reliable protection. For one thing, CSI and the associated program, C-TPAT, are not yet working well enough. C-TPAT is not yet verifying the security practices of most participating companies, meaning that those companies' inspections of the cargo that they carry cannot yet be relied on to reduce the burden on U.S. government inspectors.[48]

Rather than inspect only those containers deemed suspicious, it seems more appropriate to seek some positive indication of the safety of all types of containers. At least half of all world trade comes from the largest shippers and major ports; a good deal of the remainder can be vouched for through more painstaking work with smaller suppliers and shippers. Most of these containers do not need to be routinely inspected, but some still should be randomly checked. That means that anywhere from 15 to 30 percent of all cargo cannot be deemed safe without physical examination. Much, perhaps most, of that cargo should in fact be inspected.

If it would suffice to inspect 10 percent of all containers, that goal may be within reach, simply by adding inspectors and working out faster procedures at the busiest ports. But if it were deemed important to inspect 20 to 30 percent of all containers, more radical change might be needed, including the redesigning of major ports to prevent backlogs. For now, that latter goal would be excessively disruptive and expensive to pursue, especially given the possibility of a more efficient solution. It may ultimately be needed, however. And as a matter of political reality, it will almost surely be quickly demanded, as a minimum level of effort, if a weapon of mass destruction is smuggled into the United States despite the current level of effort.

Ideally, all containers not loaded and shipped by dependable and regularly monitored shipping companies, using tamper-proof seals as well as global positioning devices, would be scanned through an approach like VACIS. They would then be further inspected if there were reason for alarm and in some cases on a random basis as well.[49] Implementing this concept is not simply a matter of buying the needed equipment and adding inspectors, although those steps obviously are essential; it also can involve expanding infrastructure at various entry and exit points. That can be true for seaports. It is also true at many land border crossings, where the size of current facilities does not always allow for needed machinery and inspection zones.[50] This type of system can improve the general safety of shipping, help track shipments at sea, and otherwise offer benefits outside the immediate homeland security and counterterrorism arena.

Another set of challenges concerns noncontainer ships. Liquid natural gas ships near cities are a great concern. In addition, some have speculated about the possibility of a nuclear weapon being hidden within an oil tanker. A straightforward if minimal precaution might be to require of tankers the same type of preregistration, notification of movements, and safety and inspection standards now required of container ships by the United States. Tankers not meeting the standards might be inspected, at least occasionally.[51]

There is also the matter of the vulnerability of ports themselves—whether to direct attack against ships, to infiltration by illicit ships, or to infiltration by individuals. The Coast Guard has estimated that improving standards to prudent levels would require nearly $10 billion nationwide, of which only a small fraction has been spent.[52] Clearly much more remains to be done. This problem requires attention abroad as well, since foreign ports are where terrorists might have the greatest incentive to try to sneak dangerous materials (or people) into containers bound for American shores.

The Coast Guard, for its part, has made substantial progress in homeland security since 9/11. Notably, it has stopped numerous ships while enforcing new post-9/11 regulations requiring clear ship registration and notification procedures. Even so, capabilities are thin enough that major vulnerabilities remain. For example, officials concede that threats such as an explosive-laden small boat (like the one that attacked the USS *Cole* in Yemen in 2000) would be very hard to stop.[53] Admittedly, even a major expansion of the Coast Guard might not prevent such attacks, but it could allow more effective monitoring of suspicious situations.

Four years ago, the Coast Guard was too small for its pre-9/11 missions. While its budget has grown considerably since the 9/11 attacks, its ship and aircraft fleets and personnel have increased only about 10 percent. Indeed, through 2003 at least, it had substantially reduced the number of hours its ships and airplanes devoted to fisheries enforcement, search and rescue operations, environmental protection, and illegal drug interdiction, by 16, 22, 26, and 44 percent respectively.[54] Despite the cutbacks in some areas, the overall tempo at which Coast Guard assets are employed is up nearly 40 percent compared with pre-9/11 levels.[55]

To restore previous levels of capability for all key missions, the Coast Guard would need another $1 billion in its annual budget to pay for more force structure and personnel.[56] That said, it appears to have found some efficiencies in how it carries out non–homeland security missions. So a more modest increase totaling $300 million to $500 million a year in added funds may suffice (assuming that the Coast Guard's Deepwater modernization project is properly funded, in the range of $1 billion annually—a level that Congress has sometimes wavered in providing).[57] That would both ensure that traditional Coast Guard missions are done well and provide surge capacity for homeland security operations in the event of an acute crisis in the future.[58]

Notes

1. General Accounting Office, *Homeland Security: Performance of Information System to Monitor Foreign Students and Exchange Visitors Has Improved, but Issues Remain*, GAO-05-440T (March 17, 2005), pp. 1–4.

2. General Accounting Office, *Border Security: State Department Rollout of Biometric Visas on Schedule, but Guidance Is Lagging*, GAO-04-1001 (September 2004), pp. 1–9.

3. Lisa M. Seghetti and Stephen R. Vina, *U.S. Visitor and Immigrant Status Indicator Technology (US-VISIT) Program* (Washington: Congressional Research Service, October 14, 2004).

4. National Commission on Terrorist Attacks upon the United States [9/11 Commission], *The 9/11 Commission Report: Final Report of the National Commission on Terrorist Attacks upon the United States* (New York: W. W. Norton, 2004), pp. 388–89.

5. Anthony Davis, "Document Forgery Operations Expand in Thailand," *Jane's Intelligence Review*, February 2005, pp. 36–39.

6. Robert S. Leiken, *Bearers of Global Jihad? Immigration and National Security after 9/11* (Washington: Nixon Center, March 2004), pp. 102–29.

7. Sara Kehaulani Goo, "Airlines Must Hand Over Records; TSA Requests Passenger Data to Test Its Screening System," *Washington Post*, November 13, 2004, p. A7; and Omar Khan, "Screening in Need of Sense," *Washington Post*, April 26, 2005.

8. Harry Goldstein, "Who Killed the Virtual Case File?" *IEEE Spectrum* 42 (September 2005): 24–49.

9. Sara Kehaulani Goo, "Panel Criticizes Screening Plan," *Washington Post*, September 24, 2005.

10. General Accounting Office, *Border Security: Improvements Needed to Reduce Time Taken to Adjudicate Visas for Science Students and Scholars*, GAO-04-371 (February 2004), pp. 1–4.

11. Institute of International Education, "Open Doors 2004 Report on International Educational Exchange," New York, 2004 (www.opendoors.iienetwork.org/?p=49931[November 21, 2005]).

12. Robert Satloff, "The Brain Drain That Wasn't," *Weekly Standard*, July 25, 2005, p. 11.

13. See William Pope, deputy coordinator for counterterrorism, opening remarks, East Africa Counterterrorism Initiative Conference, Kampala, Uganda, April 21, 2004 (www.state.gov/s/ct/rls/rm/2004/31731.htm).

14. Stuart E. Eizenstat, John Edward Porter, Jeremy M. Weinstein, and the Commission on Weak States and U.S. National Security, *On the Brink: Weak States and U.S. National Security* (Washington: Center for Global Development, 2004), p. 57.

15. Ruth Ellen Wasem and others, *Border Security: Inspections Practices, Policies, and Issues* (Washington: Congressional Research Service, May 26, 2004), pp. 2, 11.

16. General Accounting Office, *Border Security: Agencies Need to Better Coordinate Their Strategies and Operations on Federal Lands*, GAO-04-590 (June 2004), pp. 3–4.

17. Leiken, *Bearers of Global Jihad?* p. 118.

18. Blas Nunez-Neto, "Border Security: The Role of the U.S. Border Patrol" (Washington: Congressional Research Service, May 10, 2005), p. 18.

19. David Z. Bodenheimer, "Technology for Border Protection: Homeland Security Funding and Priorities," *Journal of Homeland Security* (August 2003), p. 7.

20. Michael Hill, "New Base to Monitor Border in Northeast," *Washington Post*, October 11, 2004, p. 21.

21. Standing Senate Committee on National Security and Defence, *Canada's Coastlines: The Longest Under-Defended Borders in the World* (Ottawa: Canadian Parliament, October 2003), pp. 151–60.

22. Donald L. Barlett and James B. Steele, "Who Left the Door Open?" *Time*, September 20, 2004, pp. 51–66.

23. Bill Gertz, "Goss Fears WMD Attack in U.S. 'A Matter of Time,'" *Washington Times*, February 17, 2005, p. 3.

24. Nunez-Neto, "Border Security: The Role of the U.S. Border Patrol," pp. 5–7, 11.

25. See Bill Richardson, "Emergencies on Border Are a Plea for Federal Help," *Arizona Republic*, August 26, 2005.

26. David Rogers, "Homeland Budget Accord Is Reached," *Wall Street Journal*, September 30, 2005, p. 2.

27. Nunez-Neto, "Border Security: The Role of the U.S. Border Patrol," pp. 7–8, 29.

28. General Accounting Office, *Border Security: Consular Identification Cards Accepted within United States, but Consistent Federal Guidance Needed* (August 2004).

29. Lara Jakes Jordan, "U.S. Sticks with Passport Plan," washingtonpost.com, September 1, 2005.

30. Standing Senate Committee on National Security and Defence, *Borderline Insecure* (Ottawa: Canadian Parliament, 2005), pp. 47–61.

31. Frances Fiorino and Alexey Komarov, "False Sense of Safety," *Aviation Week and Space Technology*, September 6, 2004, p. 43.

32. Michael Pan and others, "Safety Second," *New York Times*, August 8, 2004, p. 4-11.

33. 9/11 Commission, *The 9/11 Commission Report*, pp. 390–93.

34. Dan Reed, "Air Cargo Stowaway Shows Security Lapse," *USA Today*, September 10, 2003; Graham Allison, *Nuclear Terrorism: The Ultimate Preventable Catastrophe* (New York: Henry Holt and Company, 2004), p. 111; and Baronet Media, "U.S. House Rejects Plan to Inspect Passenger Jet Cargo," *Vigilo Risk*, June 23, 2004, p. 5.

35. Jennifer E. Lake and Blas Nunez-Neto, *Border and Transportation Security: Appropriations for FY2005* (Washington: Congressional Research Service, November 5, 2004), p. 30.

36. Bartholomew Elias, *Air Cargo Security* (Washington: Congressional Research Service, October 15, 2004), pp. 9–22.

37. David Hughes, "Local 'Battle Stations,'" *Aviation Week and Space Technology*, March 24, 2003, p. 35.

38. Eric Lichtblau, "U.S. Orders Foreign Airlines to Use Armed Marshals," *New York Times*, December 30, 2003, p. 1; and Sara Kehaulani Goo, "Terror Concerns Cancel British, Mexican Flights," *Washington Post*, January 2, 2004, p. 1.

39. Sara Kehaulani Goo and Susan Schmidt, "Memo Warns of New Plots to Hijack Jets," *Washington Post*, July 30, 2003, p. 1.

40. Allison, *Nuclear Terrorism*, p. 201.

41. Reuters, "Italy: Five Airports Fail Security," *New York Times*, October 16, 2003, p. A8.

42. See William K. Rashbaum and Judith Miller, "New York Police Take Broad Steps in Facing Terror," *New York Times*, February 15, 2004, p. 1.

43. Frank Hoffman, "Border Security: Closing the Ingenuity Gap," in *Homeland Security and Terrorism*, edited by Russell Howard, James Forest, and Joanne Moore (New York: McGraw-Hill, 2006), p. 145.

44. Ruth Ellen Wasem and others, *Border Security: Inspections Practices, Policies, and Issues*, pp. 19. 34–35, 40.

45. M. R. Dinsmore, "Make Our Ports Safer," *Washington Post*, September 17, 2004, p. A27.

46. The Honorable Cresencio Arcos, director of international affairs, Department of Homeland Security, "The Role of the Department of Homeland Security Overseas," Heritage Lecture no. 840, Heritage Foundation, Washington, D.C., June 7, 2004, p. 4.

47. Steven Kroft, "On the Waterfront," CBS News, August 3, 2003 (www.cbsnews.com).

48. See for example, Eric Lipton, "Loopholes Seen in U.S. Efforts to Secure Overseas Ports," *New York Times*, May 25, 2005, p. A6.

49. Stanford Study Group, "Container Security Report," Center for International Security and Cooperation, Stanford University, January 2003, pp. 19–20; Hans Binnendijk and others, "The Virtual Border: Countering Seaborne Container Terrorism," *Defense Horizons* 16 (Washington: National Defense University, August 2002), p. 7; and Homeland Security Task Force, *Defending the American Homeland* (Washington: Heritage Foundation, 2002), p. 25.

50. Democratic Members of the House Select Committee on Homeland Security, *America at Risk: Closing the Security Gap,* 108 Cong., 2 sess., February 2004, pp. 51–53.

51. Jonathan Medalia, "Port and Maritime Security: Potential for Terrorist Nuclear Attack Using Oil Tankers" (Washington: Congressional Research Service, December 7, 2004).

52. John F. Frittelli, *Port and Maritime Security: Background and Issues for Congress* (Washington: Congressional Research Service, October 14, 2004), p. 17.

53. John M. Doyle, "Enforcement of U.S. Maritime Rules Has Foreign Carriers Scrambling," *Homeland Security and Defense* 3 (July 8, 2004), p. 6; and Lloyd's, "The Back Page," July 5, 2004, p. 12.

54. See General Accounting Office, *Coast Guard: Relationship between Resources Used and Results Achieved Needs to Be Clearer*, GAO-04-432 (March 2004), summary page.

55. Captain Steve Vanderplas, U.S. Coast Guard, "Arm the Coast Guard for the War on Terror," *Proceedings* (August 2004): 36–39.

56. John Birkler and others, *The U.S. Coast Guard's Deepwater Force Modernization Plan: Can It Be Accelerated? Will It Meet Changing Security Needs?* (Santa Monica, Calif.: RAND, 2004), pp. 63–94.

57. Julia Malone, "Coast Guard, Lauded for Storm Aid, Needs Rescue," *Houston Chronicle,* September 18, 2005.

58. Ronald O'Rourke, "Homeland Security: Coast Guard Operations—Background and Issues for Congress" (Washington: Congressional Research Service, August 2, 2004), pp. 3–4.

6

THE ROLES OF DOD AND FIRST RESPONDERS

MICHAEL O'HANLON

The U.S. homeland security effort has several major government players—including not only the Department of Homeland Security, but the Department of Justice (with the FBI) and the intelligence community. But there also are other agencies within the U.S. government that can have important functions within the homeland security mission. Their roles would generally be to support the efforts of the major actors, but in certain instances they could make the predominant contributions.

The most important additional federal player is the Department of Defense (DoD). Within the homeland security arena, its efforts would be directed by the assistant secretary of defense for homeland defense. Operationally, its activities would be spearheaded by the new Northern Command as well as the National Guard. In addition to the DoD, state and local governments—and especially their first responders—could be crucial.

In the homeland security context, both DoD and the first responder community often are viewed as responders to catastrophes. This is one of the reasons that they are supporting agencies, rather than lead players, in most scenarios—they would play their largest and most visible roles after the paramount effort, trying to prevent an attack, had failed. But of course, consequence management is very important; it quite possibly could save thousands of lives and help restore some degree of societal normalcy after a major terrorist strike. And just as important, DoD and first responders can actually help prevent attacks in the first place, especially if provided the necessary tools. In that sense, they can play key roles at the stage of the process in which homeland security is optimally pursued—the preventive stage.

The Department of Defense

There are two central questions for the Department of Defense in the homeland security debate today. First, what is its overall relationship with the rest of the government—and DHS in particular—in protecting the U.S. homeland from possible terrorist attack? Second, should its force structure—in particular that of the Reserves and the National Guard—be significantly modified in light of the new threats facing the country?

DoD's role is primarily in the arena of homeland defense—a subset of homeland security activities focused primarily on directly protecting specific assets or infrastructure from attack and on mitigating the consequences of any successful attacks that do occur.[1] DoD has tended to emphasize several specific areas of its homeland defense efforts. For example, it has continued to patrol airspace as well as collaborate with the Coast Guard to monitor waters near the United States. It also has established several task forces to address possible terrorist attacks within the United States. For most scenarios, its role would be to support DHS, a general principle of most of its homeland security activities, as encoded in U.S. law.[2]

Northcom

After September 11, 2001, the U.S. military added a major command to its operational structure—one focused on the American homeland. In previous decades, DoD had devoted attention to direct protection of the nation's territory only through NORAD (North American Aerospace Defense Command), run jointly with Canada, as well as various ballistic missile defense programs. It had not created a broader organization similar to the regional commands focused on the greater Middle East, the Pacific, Europe and Africa, or South America. But with the creation of Northern Command (Northcom) on October 1, 2002, the U.S. military added an organization designed to carry out the general defense of North America as well as the oceans out to several hundred miles' distance from the U.S. shoreline.[3]

Creation of Northcom reflected recognition of the fact that now the military will sometimes play a significant role in homeland security—specifically, in those aspects described as homeland defense. It will, as noted above, generally play a supporting role, since most counterterrorist efforts involve painstaking work to track or secure modest numbers of individuals and modest quantities of dangerous materials. The FBI, DHS, and the intelligence agencies are better suited to such work, and DoD's recent strategy document on the subject explicitly rules out any Department of Defense jurisdiction over such matters.[4] But there are times when DoD's capacity for providing large numbers of people and assets quickly is extremely important. For example, military reservists were mobilized to monitor traffic near bridges and tunnels and to protect high-value infrastructure such as airports and nuclear power plants after 9/11. DoD also has deployed troops to events such as State of the Union addresses, national political conventions, the 2004 G-8 summit in Georgia, and the funeral of former President Ronald Reagan. (Sometimes troops were deployed under the formal authority of governors, as National Guard forces can be, in part so that they would not be constrained by posse comitatus legislation, which severely restricts the use of federal troops in domestic law enforcement activities.)[5]

Like that of the other commands, Northcom's administration is modest in scale. Located at Peterson Air Force Base in Colorado, Northcom has a dedicated staff of about 1,200, including about 800 military personnel and 400 contractors, and a budget of just under $200 million.[6] But it has the ability to call on forces not normally devoted to its mission if a crisis occurs. (Planning for such activities has improved, but the Katrina experience strongly suggests that much more needs to be done.) It also has jurisdiction over NORAD (a command still jointly maintained with Canada and now focused on missile as well as air threats[7]) as well as a subordinate command in the Washington, D.C., area and a joint task force for civil support at Fort Monroe, Virginia.[8] NORAD might usefully be broadened to include maritime surveillance as well and to coordinate use of combined multinational land forces in response to an emergency. It also might be extended to involve Mexico as well as Canada and the United States.[9]

Of the DoD activities focused most directly on protection of the North American continent, the national ballistic missile program has received the greatest amount of attention. It need not be analyzed in detail here because it receives substantial scrutiny elsewhere—and because it is most doubtful that terrorists could get their hands on large rockets. A SCUD launch from a modified ship is not entirely out of the question for a rogue state, but even this type of ballistic missile threat would likely be beyond the reach of a terrorist.

Less frequently discussed is defense against a type of missile that could also be launched at American targets from beyond U.S. borders but that is much more likely to be available to terrorists—the cruise missile. Many variants weigh only a ton or so, a fifth to a tenth as much as a SCUD, and could easily be placed inside a shipping container. If missiles were armed with a chemical or biological agent in particular and properly outfitted to disperse the agent in an efficient way, such attacks could—particularly with a potent biological agent—kill many tens of thousands.[10] DoD's homeland defense strategy document does discuss this subject but acknowledges that present capabilities are highly limited and localized.[11]

The U.S. military services have numerous programs related to cruise missile defense. Most of them are designed to protect forward-deployed forces within reasonably limited geographical zones. In theory, many of the capabilities that they are working toward could be linked into a national defense of some kind, assuming proper systems integration and networking. But this could be done only at large cost and with very significant operational challenges, such as a high risk of shooting down small aircraft.[12] Additional sensors and a host of interceptor missile bases deployed around the country's perimeter would ultimately be needed if the cruise missile threat were to be addressed seriously. Cost estimates for such capability begin around $20 billion.[13] That presupposes that some outstanding technical challenges, such as reliable discrimination of cruise missiles from other flying objects, could be solved; it may be a decade before such a defense is truly practicable.[14]

DoD could have other specific roles in homeland security as well. It possesses robust communications networks that DHS and other agencies may need to employ in the event of catastrophic attacks that leave normal communications nonfunctional due to massive power outages or other systemic infrastructure failures, as witnessed to a substantial degree in Hurricane Katrina in 2005.[15] Its technology development efforts also are potentially quite useful to the homeland security mission in a broader sense. For example, unmanned aerial vehicles already are used at times in border surveillance; aerostats could be used as well. Unmanned aerial systems also might help with monitoring of key infrastructure.[16]

The National Guard and the Reserves

Since 9/11, a number of analysts and politicians have advocated giving the National Guard or other elements of the U.S. military reserves a much greater role in homeland security. Some say explicitly that they should therefore have a lesser role in military operations abroad; others leave such a conclusion unsaid, though it is implied by their main argument.

The weight of evidence would seem to argue against major changes in the role of the reserve component, however. Having it involved in overseas combat missions is central to the post-Vietnam notion that the country should go to war only when its citizenry is broadly involved in the decision and in the conflict itself. Because the active-duty military is much smaller as a percent of the total national population than in past decades and because it is somewhat concentrated in certain geographic areas, this goal is best accomplished by continuing to use the National Guard and reserve units of the military. Changing this approach could be extremely expensive, since reserve component ground forces cost on average less than half as much as active-duty units of comparable size and capability.[17] Replacing even 100,000 reservists with additional active-duty troops could be expected to add $10 billion to the annual military budget. Moreover, in the absence of a catastrophic terrorist attack, reservists focused just on this country would likely have little to do. Natural disasters have rarely required more than 5 percent of the nation's reservists even at peak demand.[18]

In addition, reservists are not well positioned to become the nation's primary line of defense against threats to the homeland. Most would arrive too slowly to any location where a tragedy occurred to be nearly as useful as firefighters, police, and health workers. Whether an attack involved chemical or biological agents, radiological weapons, a collapsed building, or even a nuclear detonation, victims of serious injuries would generally have to be treated before most reservists could be activated. Most immediate security for the site in question would have to be provided by police, who could be on the scene quickly, rather than by reserve infantry units, which might typically require twelve to twenty-four hours to mobilize. Dispensing antibiotics or other medications on a massive scale could in theory be done by reservists. In fact, since to date state and local governments have failed to develop workable plans for distribution, it may be prudent to have that option as a backup.[19] But that would not require dedicated forces, only a certain number of units given rudimentary training in dispensing medications. It might also be done by local citizens—first responders or a homeland security reserve corps (made up in part of retired first responders and health care providers) or even local Rotary and Kiwanis club members.[20] But the problem will need to be taken more seriously for that to happen.

It is important to have a certain number of reserve infantry units and related forces dispersed around the country and available should a catastrophe occur (or should multiple mass-casualty catastrophes occur, a possibility that DoD planning assumptions explicitly acknowledge[21]). But their tasks would likely consist of maintaining public order, protecting certain types of workers and facilities, and perhaps ultimately cleaning up chemical or biological agents—not preventing terrorism or carrying out immediate consequence management. Therefore they would not require training, equipment, or assignments that were particularly different from what they currently have.

This is not to say that reservists are unimportant for homeland security. For example, there are a number of nuclear-biological-chemical response teams in the reserve component. They include the Army National Guard's thirty-two WMD civil support teams, which consist of roughly twenty-two individuals each. The guard is expanding the number of such teams to have one in each state, while also creating about a dozen larger regional response units with 120 personnel each.[22] (The active-duty Marine Corps also fields its 400-person Chemical Biological Incident Response Force, based in Indian Head, Maryland.)[23]

There may be a case for additional, modest initiatives. For example, it may be sensible to create a new type of small, dedicated unit to undertake possible homeland security missions. While such a unit would not be the first to reach victims, it could be on the scene within several hours to twenty-four hours, to begin, for example, the process of cleaning up after a chemical or biological attack. It could also provide the nucleus and technical expertise, as well as the command capability, for a larger force, which might be needed after a true catastrophe. Unit members could train using appropriate scenarios and work out rapid response procedures relevant to domestic emergencies. If such measures involved, say, 5,000 to 10,000 individuals, start-up costs could be up to about $1 billion and annual operating costs thereafter would likely be several hundred million dollars.[24]

It is important to ensure that the reserves do not include too many firemen, police officers, or other first responders from any given community who could be deployed overseas. Otherwise there is the risk that, should another terrorist attack (or even a natural disaster) occur in the United States, a community's first responder community may be too stretched to be effective. What is the proper ceiling on how many first responders might be reservists in any given locality? Presumably by the time any element of the first responder community starts to have double-digit percentages of its total strength in the military reserves, it could be handicapped by a large-scale military operation abroad. But there are other ways to mitigate the risks inherent in such situations, short of deciding who can and cannot join the Reserves. For example, the National Guard has been working to ensure that no state ever has more than half of its reservists deployed away at a time—and generally much less than that. In addition, specific exemptions can be granted to individuals if a given locality would be hurt too severely by activation of a unit (this is especially likely to be relevant in small communities). An additional part of the solution would involve honing procedures for sharing the assets of the Reserves and the National Guard among states, perhaps coordinated through new Guard regional commands. This type of rethinking should make it feasible to use the reserve force structure for overseas missions without compromising its ability to respond to plausible demands at home.[25]

The Role of State and Local Governments

Since September 11, 2001, homeland security has been a job largely for the federal government, especially in terms of guarding borders, protecting the country's most valuable infrastructure during heightened alerts, and developing antidotes to biological agents. The role of state and local governments as well as of the nation's first responders has been viewed primarily as providing a quick reaction to and consequence mitigation for any attacks that occur despite the best efforts of the federal system, although they also have helped with border protection efforts and surveillance of key facilities and assets.

Whether this image was an understandable initial strategy after the al Qaeda attacks, it is flawed. In addition to other problems discussed elsewhere in this book, it skews the proper role played by other layers of government within the United States. In particular, it risks overemphasizing the consequence management mission of state and local governments while underemphasizing their role in prevention.[26] It also can foster a mind-set in which homeland security funds are used in an unfocused and largely parochial way, flowing to states and localities with little ranking of priorities and little sense of strategic purpose.

This is not intended to be a sweeping indictment of everything that has been done at the state and local level. The programs to prepare first responders to deal with chemical, biological, or large-explosive attack date back to 1996 and the Nunn-Lugar-Domenici legislation following the Oklahoma City tragedy. While these programs have not always been efficient or focused, they have improved, and they are funded at a level of resources roughly appropriate to the task at hand. Also, some cities have practiced evacuation plans and other rapid-response options (others should as well).

But preventive efforts have been quite lacking, especially outside of New York City. No police forces in the country except New York's have created more than skeletal counterterrorism units to integrate their normal police work with counterterrorism efforts. The FBI has some capacity for such efforts, but it is limited. The nation's larger cities also need their own dedicated counterterror teams, and the federal government should help fund the creation and operation of such units.

The First Responder Community and Consequence Management

In recent years, some have called for allocating $10 billion to $20 billion in additional annual resources to the first responder community—police, fire, and rescue units—in order to provide equipment and training to help mitigate the damage caused by any successful terrorist attack. Resources would include gear to protect them against the effects of weapons of mass destruction, large-scale specialized training, more teams to handle possible building collapse, and radio systems that are interoperable between different types of responders within a given jurisdiction.[27]

Such ideas go too far. For example, it is not necessary to equip all of the several million first responders in the United States with state-of-the-art chemical protective gear or interoperable communications systems. Equipping specialized teams within each major jurisdiction with such capabilities and creating several mobile communications headquarters with interoperable technology are less expensive and more quickly doable propositions.[28] It is not necessary to have every firefighter's radio talk to every police officer's radio; a certain number of mobile interoperable communications vans, which can be quickly deployed to a problem site, are a more cost-effective solution. They allow for quick coordination and cross-communication through the squad or team leaders of each type of organization—capabilities that would have been enough to save many firefighters on September 11, 2001, in New York City. A large city could purchase several dozen, at $1 million each, for a reasonable cost of several tens of millions of dollars.[29]

Preexisting shortfalls in local police, fire, rescue, and hospital capabilities for traditional missions must not be confused with homeland security needs, nor should they be funded with homeland security dollars.[30] Current national spending in the range of $5 billion a year is roughly adequate for first responders, especially now that actual disbursements to state and local governments also are starting to flow at more appropriate rates than in the immediate post-9/11 period.[31]

Still, important jobs are waiting to be done. For example, it appears that very little work has been done on developing clear and realistic evacuation plans for parts of major urban areas should a nuclear explosion produce a cloud of radioactive debris, which could put tens of thousands of lives at risk, in addition to those lost in the initial blast. The Katrina hurricane experience underscored the importance of such planning not only for terrorist attacks but also for certain types of natural catastrophes. But proper emergency preparedness is less a matter of increasing resources to be spread among hundreds of thousands of first responders than of carrying out proper planning and coordination—as well as ensuring that funds are spent to address true national vulnerabilities rather than compensate for local deficits in traditional first-responder capacities.[32]

Poor Resource Allocation and Other Financial Problems

There are numerous unfortunate effects of using homeland security dollars in large measure to redress preexisting shortfalls in traditional first responder capabilities. Notably, in the first years after 9/11, the funding formulas devised for helping states with homeland security created a situation wherein a lightly populated state such as Wyoming received $10 per capita from DHS for emergency preparedness while New York, a much more likely target, received just $1.40.[33] Indeed, this incongruous situation persisted into 2004, with that year's funding providing $19 million to Wyoming but only $177 million to California and $104 million to New York—a per capita difference of more than five to one, in the wrong direction.[34]

That situation had been partially rectified by the time the 2005 budget was passed. Of the $3.5 billion fund for local preparation, about $830 million was allocated directly to cities and particularly to high-profile cities: New York was allocated 25 percent of the $830 million total; Washington, 9.3 percent; Los Angeles, 7.4 percent; Chicago, 5.4 percent; and Boston, 3.1 percent. Together, these five cities received half of the funds in that fund.[35] In the administration's 2006 budget request, about $3 billion was to be allocated according to threat-based guidelines.[36]

States and localities also need ways to obtain equipment and training more efficiently once they gain access to funds. Relevant measures include forming municipal or statewide cooperative arrangements to buy equipment in bulk—something that the federal government now encourages by allowing municipalities (not just states) to apply for funding.[37] They also include developing legal instruments such as standing purchase orders to allow for rapid acquisition of needed materials and establishing national standards for proper equipment and training practices to guide states and localities.[38]

In addition, as the level of government most capable of emergency spending, the federal government should provide funds more quickly and comprehensively for overtime costs related to heightened alerts and expedite reimbursement practices.[39] It should also clearly allow the use of federal funds to hire personnel at the state and local level specifically for homeland security.[40]

Emphasizing Prevention

At present, the FBI generally runs joint terrorism task forces in major American cities, and it is starting to do a better job of working with state and local police forces in such efforts. For example, a joint center operated by the FBI and New York state police opened in Albany in 2004 to provide police with quick checks of suspicious individuals to see whether they are on any terrorism watch list.[41]

But the FBI suffers from a number of limitations. First, it is rather small. With fewer than 15,000 agents nationwide, it can devote no more than a modest number to any city. Some 1,100, naturally the largest figure, are in New York. (By comparison, New York is a city with 40,000 police officers, of whom some 10,000, realistically speaking, can be mobilized for specific acute needs, such as protecting the Republican National Convention that was held there in 2004.)[42] Other large cities generally have at most a few hundred FBI officers. As Louis F. Quijas, the head of the FBI's law enforcement coordination office, put it: "We've got 11,000 FBI agents and 800,000 local cops. They are the force multiplier in the war on terrorism."[43]

Without enough raw numbers, it is impossible for the FBI to walk the streets. For example, the FBI cannot realistically monitor events such as conventions of propane gas suppliers and users, self-storage business entrepreneurs, apartment building owners, or pest control company owners. Terrorists might try to infiltrate such events to learn tactics or gain access to needed equipment, and a homeland security strategy emphasizing prevention should try to identify them in such situations.[44]

Second, by most accounts the FBI remains slow to change its organizational ethos, which is to carefully develop solid legal cases against specific suspects. It often hoards information gained through its investigations. In one concrete example, according to former agent Mike German, the FBI was slow to make a serious attempt to infiltrate suspected terrorist groups—even after 9/11.[45]

The above problems are, at least in principle, fixable. But there also is a more inherent limitation to the FBI, alluded to above. The FBI is not out on the streets in the way that local police have to be. The latter routinely conduct community policing activities, pursue sham money handling operations, uncover businesses that provide false IDs or facilitate smuggling or illegal immigration, and develop trusted sources—often getting tips on suspicious characters thereby. Many times, police simply are better placed to operate as general collectors of terrorism-related intelligence.

The country therefore needs to beef up its local police intelligence and counterterrorism operations. New York devotes some 500 officers to such tasks, but it is an exception. Los Angeles has about thirty-five personnel, Chicago fewer than ten. Yet these cities are far from immune to attack; indeed, Los Angeles already was targeted, in the Millennium Plot.[46] Part of the problem is that too many localities, even major ones, assume that they will not be targets in the future simply because they have not been in the past, or even if they have been. And at a time of generally tight budgets, additional local monies have been hard to find.[47]

Dedicated counterterrorism personnel can help uncover terrorist cells. They can develop lists of possible targets requiring special protection during alert periods and, to the extent possible, better permanent protective measures (such as safeguards for parking garages, more use of shatterproof glass or protective window film in places, and protective cordons near air intakes).[48] They can work with public officials, developers, and construction firms to ensure that new structures with likely appeal as terrorist targets implement commonsense safeguards.[49] Many such things are now happening in New York City and to an extent in Washington; few are happening in most of the rest of the country.

To spur more law enforcement institutions in large cities to get into the terrorism prevention business, matching federal financing could be offered to them to hire more personnel. Since localities would have to provide some of the money in any matching-fund approach, they would be less likely to abuse it, and cities that saw no particular terrorism threat (rightly or wrongly) would not be obliged to take advantage of the program. It might be provided through a COPS II–type program, modeled after the Clinton administration's idea of using federal funds to help pay for more local police around the nation.[50] The scale of the effort would be much smaller, however—about 10,000 officers nationwide—and hence much more affordable (under $1 billion a year).

Most resources from such a program should flow to the nation's several dozen largest cities. The police forces of the others are not large enough to operate dedicated counterterrorism units efficiently. Moreover, they are somewhat less likely to be targeted by terrorists—the Oklahoma City experience notwithstanding—than are the international symbols of the United States, such as its largest cities. Since risk assessment is as much art as science, it will be impossible to determine a scientifically correct apportionment for larger cities and smaller ones. The latter should not be cut out of a program entirely, but it makes sense to give them substantially less than their per capita share.

It might be wisest for smaller cities to set up coordination centers with the FBI or to provide short segments of counterterrorism training for some mid-career police officers. These types of approaches may be more practical than creating dedicated counterterrorism units in places where a critical mass of personnel is not easily attainable.

There are subjects besides police department counterterrorism capacity that require attention at the state and local level. Notably, the issue of gun regulation should be seen in part as a homeland security issue. At present individuals on terror watch lists often succeed in getting guns, and in fact it is not illegal for them to do so. Nor can the government check to determine whether a suspected terrorist has in fact purchased a gun recently.[51] In addition, the so-called gun show loophole remains, meaning that no background check of any kind is required for individuals buying weapons from private distributors at gun shows.[52] In the age of terrorism, such oversights in the law need to be corrected.

Notes

1. Department of Defense, *Strategy for Homeland Defense and Civil Support* (Washington: 2005), p. 5 (www.defenselink.mil/news/June2005/d20050630homeland.pdf).

2. Doug Sample, "DoD Official Outlines Homeland Defense Progress," *American Forces Information Service News Articles*, June 14, 2005 (www.dod.mil/news/Mar2005/20050316_202.html).

3. U.S. Northern Command, "U.S. Northern Command's Strategic Vision," Internal Working Paper, October 1, 2003, p. 2.

4. The Honorable Paul McHale, assistant secretary of defense for homeland defense, statement before the Senate Committee on Armed Services, 108 Cong., 2 sess., March 25, 2004, p. 7 ; and Department of Defense, *Strategy for Homeland Defense and Civil Support*, p. 5.

5. David Kelly, "Command Shifts amid Fears of Terrorist Attacks on Ports," *Los Angeles Times*, November 6, 2004.

6. Telephone conversation with Lieutenant Colonel Sean Kelly, Northcom public affairs office, February 1, 2005.

7. Government of Canada, *Defence: A Role of Pride and Influence in the World* (Ottawa, 2005), p. 22.

8. Josh White, "New Headquarters Will Guard Capital Area," *Washington Post*, September 21, 2004, p. 6; John Conger, "Unique CBRNE Training Issues Face Joint Task Force-Civil Support," *Homeland Security* (April 2004) (www.homelandsecurity. org/journal/articles/Burmood_Lucas_conger.html); and James Jay Carafano, "Shaping the Future of Northern Command," *CSBA Backgrounder* (Washington: Center for Strategic and Budgetary Assessments, April 25, 2003).

9. Council on Foreign Relations, Canadian Council of Chief Executives, and the Consejo Mexicano de Asuntos Internacionales, *Building a North American Community* (New York: 2005), p. 11.

10. Office of Technology Assessment, *Proliferation of Weapons of Mass Destruction: Assessing the Risks* (Washington: 1993), p. 54.

11. Department of Defense, *Strategy for Homeland Defense and Civil Support*, pp. 25–26.

12. Loren Thompson, *Cruise Missile Defense: Connecting Theater Capabilities to Homeland Needs* (Washington: Lexington Institute, 2004).

13. Michael E. O'Hanlon and others, *Protecting the American Homeland: One Year On* (Brookings, 2003), p. 15.

14. Randy Barrett, "Cruise Missile Defense System at Least 5–8 Years Away," *Space News*, July 5, 2004, p. 6.

15. Adrian A. Erckenbrack and Aaron Scholer, "The DoD Role in Homeland Security," *Joint Forces Quarterly* 35 (October 2004), p. 35.

16. See Amy Butler, "Upcoming UAV Roadmap to Include Homeland Security Missions," *Defense Daily*, December 16, 2004, p. 1.

17. Lane Pierrot, *Structuring U.S. Forces after the Cold War: Costs and Effects of Increased Reliance on the Reserves* (Congressional Budget Office, September 1992).

18. Frances Lussier, *Structuring the Active and Reserve Army for the 21st Century* (Congressional Budget Office, 1997), pp. 13–14.

19. Richard Falkenrath, "Homeland Security and Consequence Management," in *The Challenge of Proliferation: A Report of the Aspen Strategy Group*, edited by Kurt M. Campbell (Washington: Aspen Institute, 2005), p. 136.

20. Randall J. Larsen, *Our Own Worst Enemy: Why Our Misguided Reactions to 9-11 Might Be America's Greatest Threat* (Washington: National Legal Center for the Public Interest, 2005), p. 19.

21. Department of Defense, *Strategy for Homeland Defense and Civil Support*, p. 9

22. Bradley Graham, "War Plans Drafted to Counter Terror Attacks in U.S.," *Washington Post*, August 8, 2005, p. 1.

23. William K. Rashbaum, "Sniffing New York's Air Ducts for Signs of Terror," *New York Times*, April 22, 2003, p. 1; Department of Defense, "Chemical Biological Incident Response Force, 2004," March 4, 2005 (www.dcmilitary.com/baseguides/navy/indianhead/ih_biological.html); and Thomas X. Hammes, "Responding to Chemical and Biological Incidents at Home," *Joint Forces Quarterly* 36 (2005).

24. Lynn E. Davis and others, *Army Forces for Homeland Security* (Santa Monica, Calif.: RAND, 2004), pp. xi–xv.

25. Associated Press, "National Guard in Short Supply, Some States Fear," *Honolulu Advertiser*, May 17, 2004; and Sarah Kershaw, "Governors Tell of War's Impact on Local Needs," *New York Times*, July 20, 2004, p. 1.

26. For a similar argument, see James Jay Carafano, Paul Rosenzweig, and Alane Kochems, "An Agenda for Increasing State and Local Government Efforts to Combat Terrorism," *Heritage Foundation Backgrounder*, February 24, 2005.

27. See Warren B. Rudman, Richard A. Clarke, Jamie F. Metzl, and an Independent Task Force, *Emergency Responders: Drastically Underfunded, Dangerously Unprepared* (New York: Council on Foreign Relations, 2003).

28. Homeland Security Advisory Council, U.S. Department of Homeland Security, *A Report from the Task Force on State and Local Homeland Security Funding* (Washington: June 2004), p. 13.

29. See Michael O'Hanlon and Jack Weiss, "Prepare Our Cities for War with Iraq," *Washington Times*, December 31, 2002. Another estimate is that national costs could total $350 million for the necessary investment. See Michael Pan and others, "Safety Second," *New York Times*, August 8, 2004, p. WK11.

30. James Fossett, "The Current State of Homeland Security," in *The Role of 'Home' in Homeland Security: The Federalism Challenge* (New York: Rockefeller Institute of Government, 2003), p. 31; and Gilmore Commission, *IV. Implementing the National Strategy*, Fourth Annual Report of the Advisory Panel to Assess Domestic Response Capabilities for Terrorism Involving Weapons of Mass Destruction (Arlington, Va.: RAND), p. 35.

31. Statement of William O. Jenkins Jr., director, Homeland Security and Justice Issues, General Accounting Office, "Emergency Preparedness: Federal Funds for First Responders," GAO-04-788T, May 13, 2004.

32. John Mintz, "U.S. Called Unprepared for Nuclear Terrorism," *Washington Post*, May 3, 2005, p. A1.

33. See Rudman, Clarke, Metzl, and an Independent Task Force, *Emergency Responders: Drastically Underfunded, Dangerously Unprepared*, p. 18.

34. See National Commission on Terrorist Attacks upon the United States [9/11 Commission], *The 9/11 Commission Report: Final Report of the National Commission on Terrorist Attacks upon the United States* (New York: W. W. Norton, 2004) , p. 20; and Department of Homeland Security, Office for Domestic Preparedness, *Fiscal Year 2004 Homeland Security Grant Program* (July 23, 2004) (www.ojp.usdoj.gov/odp/docs/fy04hsgp_appkit.pdf).

35. Eric Lipton, "Big Cities Will Get More in Antiterrorism Grants," *New York Times*, December 22, 2004, p. A20.

36. President George W. Bush, *Budget of the United States Government, Fiscal Year 2006* (Washington: February 2005), p. 156; and David Rogers, "Homeland Budget Accord Is Reached," *Wall Street Journal*, September 30, 2005, p. 2.

37. House Resolution 3266, ultimately passed into law in 2005, allows for such funding mechanisms; see Select Committee on Homeland Security, "H.R. 3266—The Faster and Smarter Funding for First Responders Act," July 30, 2004 (www.homeland.house.gov).

38. There also are some types of preparatory steps outside the realm of major budgetary expenditures that should still be considered. These could include designating schools as emergency medical treatment centers in advance of any attack and making sure that citizens know the very simple basics about how to respond to various kinds of possible terrorist attack. The tendency among Americans to avoid making basic preparations to deal with any attacks—like designating a meeting place away from home should there be a strike near their house—also needs to be addressed. Further development of citizen volunteer corps, for simple tasks such as helping guide people to disaster shelters, providing first aid, or transmitting messages when communications systems are disrupted, is also an area worthy of activity (though not one we explore here in detail). See Stanley I. Greenspan, "We're Not Ready for a New 9/11," *Washington Post*, July 12, 2004, p. A17; Lynn E. Davis and others, *Individual Preparedness and Response to Chemical, Radiological, Nuclear, and Biological Terrorist Attacks* (Santa Monica, Calif.: RAND, 2003), pp. xiii–xxiv; John Mintz, "Public Less Fearful of Terrorist Attack," *Washington Post*, July 21, 2004, p. A12; Amanda Dory, *Civil Security: Americans and the Challenge of Homeland Security* (Washington: Center for Strategic and International Studies, September 2003), pp. v–ix, 70–75; and David M. Simpson and William Strang, "Volunteerism, Disasters, and Homeland Security: The AmeriCorps National Civilian Community Corps and Community Preparedness," *Journal of Homeland Security and Emergency Management* 1, no. 4 (2004).

39. Homeland Security Advisory Council, U.S. Department of Homeland Security, *A Report from the Task Force on State and Local Homeland Security Funding*, pp. 1–3; General Accounting Office, *Homeland Security: Communication Protocols and Risk Communication Principles Can Assist in Refining the Advisory System*, GAO-04-682 (June 2004), pp. 34–36.

40. Kiki Caruson, "Mission Impossible? The Challenge of Implementing an Integrated Homeland Security Strategy," *Journal of Homeland Security and Emergency Management* 1, no. 4 (2004), p. 17.

41. David Johnston, "Terror Data to Be Shared at New Center Near Albany," *New York Times*, May 24, 2004.

42. David Johnston, "Fears of Attack at Conventions Drive New Plans," *New York Times*, July 5, 2004, p. 1.

43. Dan Eggen, "Bridging the Divide between FBI and Police," *Washington Post*, February 16, 2004, p. A25.

44. William K. Rashbaum, "Police Tactic against Terror: Let's Network," *New York Times*, August 14, 2004, p. B1.

45. Eric Lichtblau, "Another F.B.I. Employee Blows Whistle on Agency," *New York Times*, August 2, 2004, p. A15.

46. The 9/11 Commission, *The 9/11 Commission Report*, executive summary, p. 4 (www.9-11commission.gov).

47. On the challenges faced by municipalities during alerts, see Jack Weiss, "Orange Crunch," *New York Times*, January 14, 2004, p. A19. Los Angeles spends $1 million a week on overtime pay and related costs every time it goes on orange alert; see also Lisa Friedman, "Cities Still Aren't Prepared," *Los Angeles Daily News*, June 24, 2003. In another example, Amtrak spends $500,000 a month for police overtime when on heightened alert. See General Accounting Office, *Transportation Security: Federal Action Needed to Help Address Security Challenges*, GAO-03-843 (June 2003), p. 21. And in a different type of example, just to illustrate the potential costs involved, security costs in Boston and New York at the Democratic and Republican conventions in 2004 were in the range of $50 million and $75 million respectively. See David Johnston, "Fears of Attack at Conventions Drive New Plans," *New York Times*, July 5, 2004, p. A1.

48. On protective window film, see Lauren Bayne Anderson, "Demand for Window Film Spikes after Terror Alerts," *Washington Post*, August 3, 2004, p. E1.

49. William K. Rashbaum and Judith Miller, "New York Police Take Broad Steps in Facing Terror," *New York Times*, February 15, 2004, p. A1; and Patrick D. Healy and William K. Rashbaum, "Security Issues Force a Review at Ground Zero," *New York Times*, May 1, 2005, p. 1

50. Michael O'Hanlon and Jack Weiss, "How Police Can Intervene," *Washington Times*, August 18, 2004.

51. Government Accountability Office, *Gun Control and Terrorism: FBI Could Better Manage Firearm-Related Background Checks Involving Terrorist Watch List Records*, GAO-05-127 (January 2005), pp. 3–5; and William J. Krouse, "Terrorist Screening and Brady Background Checks for Firearms" (Washington: Congressional Research Service, July 25, 2005).

52. Helen Dewar, "Gun Bill Dies after Sponsors Drop Support," *Washington Post*, March 3, 2004; and editorial, "Misfires on the Hill," *Washington Post*, December 31, 2003.

7

TECHNOLOGY DEVELOPMENT
AND TRANSPORTATION SECURITY

MICHAEL D'ARCY

Technology makes a unique contribution to safeguarding the United States against terrorist threats. As Michael Chertoff, the secretary of homeland security, has noted, "Technology can provide tremendous added value in the quality of security across virtually every sector of the homeland."[1] Some threats are themselves reliant on modern technology, such as weapons of mass destruction or shoulder-launched surface-to-air missiles. Others, such as bombs and firearms, are more basic yet still capable of large-scale damage. Technology can mitigate a range of such threats, either by detecting them before they can cause harm or by minimizing their effects. This potentially powerful contribution to homeland security means that resources should be marshaled intelligently, backed by the consistent support of research and development programs, to ensure that technology is used effectively and develops as rapidly as possible. At the same time, policymakers should be aware that technology's limitations and costs—as well as public acceptance, economic impact, and civil liberties—set boundaries on what may be done. Scientific progress can be slow and fitful, and policymakers should therefore remain realistic when assessing the technological capabilities likely to emerge over the coming years.

This chapter describes some ways in which the U.S. government is attempting to ensure the timely development of suitable technology and thereby capitalize on its recognized potential. It then

129

considers how technology can enhance aspects of homeland security broadly related to the transportation of people and goods. This focus, and that of chapter 8, which analyzes countermeasures against weapons, is in keeping with this book's general philosophy (and that enunciated by the Department of Homeland Security following publication of its Second Stage Review in July 2005)—which is that preventing and preparing for catastrophic events should take precedence over defending against smaller-scale attacks that, though lethal, do not threaten mass casualties or serious, long-term damage to the nation's economic and social well-being.

Transportation is vulnerable to attack. Mass disruption and great human and financial loss can follow such an attack. Furthermore, the use of transport is often integral to preparing and perpetrating attacks and therefore offers a potential "chokepoint" at which terrorists can be apprehended. The technologies analyzed here include those related to the secure identification of travelers; the prevention of explosions in modes of transport, especially air travel; and the inspection and tracking of cargo. In each case an assessment is made of how technology can help to combat a threat or address a need, what the current possibilities and limitations are, how the technology may develop in the foreseeable future, and what steps should be taken to use it in the best way possible. Where unit costs for the technology are quoted, they should be taken as giving a general indication of the order of magnitude of the expenditure that would be required to develop, procure, or deploy the technology.[2]

Technology Development: The Role of the U.S. Government

The government supports technology development and deployment for homeland security though several departments, including the Department of Defense, the Department of Energy, and the DHS, and in numerous ways, including the direct sponsorship or hosting of research and the creation of legal and institutional frameworks to facilitate the transition from development to implementation. The government has the ability to support research that, even though it may not yield immediate success or lead to profitable products, could produce technology that greatly enhances U.S. security. Two government entities in particular have a responsibility for fostering leading-edge technology through the efforts of the government and private sectors. These are the Defense Advanced Research Projects Agency (DARPA), an agency in the Department of Defense that is devoted to promoting technological innovation to enhance national security, and the Homeland Security

Advanced Research Projects Agency (HSARPA), which is operated by the Science and Technology Directorate of the DHS. DARPA has existed in various forms since 1958, whereas HSARPA was established in 2002. They differ somewhat in their philosophy and modus operandi.

DARPA traditionally has emphasized high-risk, high-payoff research, thus aiming to ensure that the United States will never be "technologically surprised" and to accelerate the transition of technology from the long-term research and development (R&D) stage to practical implementation. Although the problems to be tackled are defined at a high level within DARPA, the ideas for tackling them are developed from below, so proposals are sent by research groups to program managers, who allocate funding. In addition to solicited proposals, DARPA also accepts unsolicited ones, and so, wisely, it is open to unforeseen opportunities. Its structure aims to ensure flexibility in determining what research to support: grants are made for relatively short periods of time (three years) and program managers have great discretionary authority in making funding decisions. They themselves remain in their position for only four to six years, as it is believed that short tenures minimize institutional obstacles to innovation.[3] When DARPA awards grants to commercial entities, the private company may make a profit from any marketable goods (especially dual-use technologies) that result. This incentive is an important part of a strategy to harness the resources of the private sector. In FY2005, DARPA had a total budget of more than $3 billion, as in FY2006. With such a large budget, DARPA traditionally has supported "blue skies" research, for which no practical application is imminent. This is an important means by which the United States can remain at the forefront of innovation, and, in the long run, it increases the likelihood of developing technology that can tackle currently intractable problems. DARPA's list of achievements encompasses a wide range of military technologies as well as water purification devices, hybrid engines, and, above all, the infrastructure for the Internet.[4] It is not without problems, however. The short-term nature of the funding can be difficult to reconcile with the inherently long-term nature of many types of research. The possibility that funding can be cut mid-term and on the decision of a single person fails to recognize the way that research laboratories function, including the time taken to build up infrastructure and human resources. It also may deter high-quality applicants for funding. Notwithstanding these difficulties, DARPA has been responsible for much innovation, and such work must not be jeopardized by recent efforts to concentrate more narrowly on applied projects that are of more obvious relevance to homeland security.

HSARPA is a smaller operation than DARPA, with a FY2005 budget of around $300 million.[5] It is only one route by which the DHS Science and Technology Directorate supports technology development, but, given its particular responsibility for ensuring innovation and rapid technology transfer, it is a particularly important one in the long term. It issues contracts "to engage businesses, federally funded research and development centers, universities, and other government partners in performing its mission to gather, generate, and develop ideas, concepts, and advanced technologies to protect the homeland."[6] To carry out its function, HSARPA issues solicitations for ambitious technological projects, to which R&D entities respond. As in DARPA, the funding and administration of projects is carried out by program managers with technical expertise who have "ownership" of the programs. The differences between DARPA and HSARPA extend beyond the scale of the enterprise, however. The main one is that HSARPA is much more needs-driven than DARPA, and its solicitations identify the required technology and the specifications (such as technical capabilities, cost, size, and so forth) that must be met. Eighty-five to 90 percent of HSARPA funds are for identified DHS requirements, with the remainder going to "revolutionary research."[7] Submission of unsolicited proposals is permitted, and, as with DARPA, marketable commercial products may result from funded research. Since HSARPA has been in existence for only three years, it is difficult to judge the success of its approach because research initiated by the first tranche of solicitations is still in progress. From the perspective of enhancing America's technological capabilities for homeland security over the longer term, the relatively limited support of high-risk research is an obvious shortcoming. DARPA's track record provides a clear positive example of the benefits of such research. However, there is no reason to believe that HSARPA will not be successful in hastening the development of specific, field-ready items that plug existing gaps in security. The vast difference in the funding of DARPA and HSARPA means that the latter cannot afford to gamble as much on exotic programs, and until its funding is increased it is sensible for HSARPA to focus on projects that are more likely to reach a successful, and obviously useful, conclusion.

The short length (three years) of the contracts awarded to the scientists employed by HSARPA can be a problem. The lack of job security may well deter many people at the most productive stage of their careers, leading to a large untapped pool of expertise. Whether designed to achieve a high-caliber operation or to minimize labor costs, it is not a prudent policy. A better approach would be to make it possible for practicing scientists to take up a position with HSARPA that offered them a long-term career track while allowing them to retain their expertise and familiarity with cutting-edge science and technology, not forcing them entirely to the bureaucratic or managerial side. An option whereby scientists and engineers could retain their affiliation with their university or company while still being employed by HSARPA could be explored.

Another role that the government can play in encouraging private sector innovation to enhance homeland security is to neutralize the deterrent effect of company liability for possible technological failures. To that end, the Support Anti-Terrorism by Fostering Effective Technologies Act of 2002 (Safety Act) provides liability protection in the event of a terrorist attack for suitably qualified technologies and services that, for reasons of liability risk, would otherwise not be developed or made available. By the end of October 2005, the DHS had received 245 pre-applications and 122 full applications for protection since the enactment of the Safety Act. However, only twenty-nine of the applications had received designation (recognition of antiterrorism utility) and certification (granting of liability protection), while sixteen had received designation only.[8] In view of the technologies' potential benefit, the rate at which applications are processed must be dramatically increased and the process must be incorporated directly into the R&D procurement process to streamline deployment.[9]

The Safety Act does not offer coverage for technology deployed *in anticipation* of an attack in the case where no attack subsequently occurs. That would seem to be a serious shortcoming in the case of medical countermeasures, particularly vaccines, for which the relevant considerations are somewhat distinct from those related to other technologies. Vaccines are usually administered prophylactically, anticipating a threat whose probability is not well known and that may never materialize. Sufficient testing of a vaccine to guarantee against adverse reactions in persons receiving it may not be possible; sometimes there may not be any people infected by a particular pathogen, while the deliberate infecting of healthy people is, for certain pathogens, unacceptable. Anthrax is a classic example of this type.[10] Furthermore, the natural variation in the human population means that one cannot be sure, on the basis of an inevitably limited trial, that no adverse reactions will result from the vaccine. For these reasons there should be at least some liability protection for prophylactically administered medications even if there is no subsequent terrorist attack. The successor to the Bioshield Bill (see chapter 8) ought to address this issue.

Might there be other preventative technologies that also would benefit from liability protection in advance of a possible attack? Nonmedical countermeasures are not subject to the same intrinsic limitations on testing as medical ones are, and therefore there is less reason to excuse a malfunction or failure resulting from incomplete testing or inadequate development. Hence liability should not be waived for nonmedical technologies, and in this regard the Safety Act is correct.

The Homeland Security Act of 2002 called for establishment of a technology clearinghouse "to encourage technological innovation in facilitating the mission of the Department."[11] This clearinghouse is not yet operational. It would be a valuable resource, increasing the access of both the private sector and the federal, state, and local governments to reliable information about available technologies, including an assessment of the technologies' utility. It also would give an indication of current technology gaps, thus guiding government research support and private sector innovation, and it could give the DHS under secretary for science and technology a greater role in coordinating science and technology development. The FY2006 Department of Homeland Security Appropriations Act makes no mention of this clearinghouse.[12] This omission should be rectified by mandating the establishment of the clearinghouse at the earliest possible opportunity.[13]

Secure Identification of People

In conventional passports a photograph is used to identify the bearer. This is too vulnerable to forgery, especially if the image is printed on a piece of photographic paper, as it traditionally has been. Entry into the United States is easy for a traveler who uses a forged American passport or a passport from a country that participates in the visa waiver program (VWP). Nationals of such countries can enter the United States for up to ninety days without a visa. Even with a genuine passport, "look-alike" travelers have been known to gain entry to a country under a false identity. It is clear that a more secure form of identification is needed, particularly for the United States and VWP countries, one that is more difficult to forge and more reliably identifies the bearer. To that end "e-passports"—passports that contain biometric data stored on a chip—are currently being developed, and Congress has mandated that the VWP countries begin to use them, as will the United States itself. E-passports are not cheap; the cost to European countries of collecting facial and fingerprint biometric data, plus the associated software and databases, has been estimated at €1.5 billion to €3 billion ($1.8 billion to $3.6 billion), while the cost of including the biometric data chip may run between €10 and

€15 ($12 to $18) per passport.[14] The potential enhancement to border security is substantial, however.

The various technological challenges associated with e-passports meant that many VWP countries could not meet the October 2005 deadline set by Congress to begin issuing them.[15] (The United States would not have begun issuing the passports by that time, either.) For this reason the deadline for biometric passports was extended to October 2006, but, as an intermediate step, the VWP countries were required to include digitally laser-printed images in their passports from October 2005.[16] That will yield some improvement in security, since it is more difficult to fraudulently insert such pictures into a passport. The extra year for e-passport development will allow the VWP countries to settle the technological problems; it also should be used to address the question of which biometric information, in addition to the usual personal data contained in a passport, should be contained in the chip.

The International Civil Aviation Organization (ICAO) has been working since May 2003 on establishing specifications for e-passport hardware based on internationally recognized standards defined by the International Organization for Standardization (ISO).[17] An electronic reader communicates with the chip, at a distance of four inches or less, by radio frequency waves. The chips are much less susceptible to forgery or alteration than are conventional passports because they are digitally signed. However, there remain several technological issues to be resolved, including the e-passports' durability (they should last ten years),[18] the interoperability of the chips and readers, the placement of the chips in the passports, the verification of the digital signatures, and the prevention of unauthorized reading of passport data.[19] The latter is a particular concern; despite the small optimum working range between reader and chip, it has been shown that chip data can be accessed from a range of up to thirty feet.[20] This would make unauthorized reading ("skimming") of the personal data on the chip possible, jeopardizing travelers' privacy and potentially their safety. Furthermore, the communication between chip and reader was, as originally envisaged, not encrypted, meaning that eavesdropping would be possible.

The Department of State currently is working on a modification to the design of the e-passport to prevent access to chip data while the passport is closed.[21] Beyond that, the technique of "basic access control," which will be used by various European countries to access chip information in their e-passports, is under consideration for use with U.S. e-passports. This encrypts the information transferred between chip and reader, and the transfer cannot take place unless some of the machine-readable printed data on the passport are first input into the system. It therefore represents a much more secure method of accessing stored biometric data and should be adopted by the United States for use with its e-passports.

The choice of biometric is subject to several considerations. The biometric must uniquely identify the bearer, it must be acceptable to the public, and it should permit automated matching. Automation speeds up and, properly implemented, makes more trustworthy the process of matching the biometric data submitted by a traveler at the point of entry with that contained in the chip. This procedure is called "one-to-one matching"(verification). If sufficiently reliable, automated matching also can permit database searching, which is termed "one-to-many matching" (identification). ICAO has decided that the e-passport chip will store a facial image of the traveler, the biometric that is most universally accepted; other biometrics can be included at a country's discretion. While a facial image is a simple and well-accepted means of checking identity, it is not completely secure because appearances can change. Furthermore, the current unreliability of automated facial image matching means that a U.S. Customs and Border Protection (CBP) official would have to perform the match visually, which is no improvement over the existing procedure. Searching image databases for wanted travelers would not be possible, either. Since searching terrorist or criminal watch lists carries great potential for improving security, it should be a goal of the technology implementation.

Relying solely on the facial biometric is therefore unwise. The National Institute of Standards and Technology (NIST) has found that it is necessary to control the subject's pose and the lighting carefully in order to get a probability greater than 90 percent of successful matching to a stored image; this is difficult to achieve, especially in an airport.[22] Since failure to match would result in time-consuming secondary questioning, a matching accuracy rate even in the middle of the 90 to 100 percent range is inadequate. It would render searching of a large database unfeasible, because it would yield too many false matches. Sufficient improvements in facial recognition technology may take place in the future to allow reliable matching, but superior alternatives already exist. The most obvious is fingerprinting. All foreign entrants to the United States, whether they are VWP participants or visa holders, submit two index fingerprints upon entry, which are stored in a central database. NIST has found that using two fingerprints has a 99.6 percent success rate for one-to-one matching for the current quality of fingerprints obtained by the US-VISIT program. That is an acceptable level of performance for identity verification and also allows the possibility of database searching. This approach's main disadvantage is that 2 to 5 percent of the population cannot provide fingerprints, which means that use of more than one biometric would be prudent.[23]

The US-VISIT program already allows the matching of the fingerprints submitted to those of known or suspected criminals. Fingerprint matching of visa applicants to criminal watch lists also takes place at overseas Department of State posts,[24] and, in a partnership between the DHS and Department of Justice, electronic fingerprint matching technology that compares prints from all ten fingers against the FBI's nationwide IAFIS criminal database is being used to apprehend convicted criminals as they attempt to enter the United States.[25] Over the period September 2004 to December 2005 this initiative succeeded in identifying 606 homicide suspects and 154,530 suspected criminals.[26] Improved interoperability of the fingerprint systems is needed, however.[27]

Using ten fingers for identification increases reliability and reduces false matches. For that reason the DHS has decided that in the future, first-time visitors under the US-VISIT program will have to provide all ten fingerprints; only two prints will be required for verification of the entrant's identity thereafter, as at present.[28] Likewise, all ten fingerprints will be taken from visa applicants. There are logistical difficulties associated with collecting all ten fingerprints. It has been estimated that it would currently double the enrollment time at an airport,[29] leading to vastly increased waiting times for incoming passengers, so additional points of inspection at borders will be necessary, in addition to the new finger scanners.[30] However, the advent of ball scanners, which can read all ten fingerprints when a person grasps the ball, will reduce the ten-fingerprint scan time to the same as that required for two prints, and the development and deployment of such scanners should be pushed hard. In remarks made prior to standing down as secretary of homeland security, Tom Ridge recommended, as does NIST, that U.S. passports include all ten fingerprints in the biometric data.[31] EU countries intend to include fingerprint as well as facial data in their e-passport chips. The United States should do likewise (as in the case of the new government worker ID cards).[32] That would permit more reliable identification of all travelers, not just those using visas or traveling from VWP countries.

Data obtained by scanning the iris of a person's eye constitute another possible biometric. Iris scanning is quick (unlike retina scanning), and, in principle, offers an extremely low probability of false matching because of the uniqueness of the iris and the quality of the fitting algorithm. This technology has been deployed in the Netherlands, the United Arab Emirates,[33] and Afghanistan[34] and was installed in a number of U.K. airports in 2005. In 2001 the U.K. National Physical Laboratory conducted tests in which iris recognition registered no false matches in more than 2.7 million comparisons, making 1.5 million comparisons per minute. That was at least twenty times faster than any of the other biometrics studied (face, fingerprint, hand geometry, vein, and voice recognition).[35] However, the failure-to-enroll (FTE) rate—that is, the proportion of scans that do not succeed in properly reading or registering the biometric data—of iris scans is not well understood, and it appears to vary widely.[36] For that reason there currently is no objective evidence that the iris is a superior biometric in practice to even a single fingerprint. In Canada, where iris recognition is used in the CanPass program (which expedites customs clearance for "trusted travelers") it was found that 15 percent of the users had to be helped to enroll using the iris biometric, 12 percent were not successful in doing so, and 5 to 10 percent appeared unable to provide a sample (due to factors such as drooping eyelids).[37] Furthermore, unlike for fingerprints, there is no existing database of iris images against which one-to-many matching for suspicious persons may be performed. If the FTE rate can be reduced, iris recognition would appear to be a promising technology for the future, but it should not be relied on at present.[38] As mentioned above, redundancy in the biometrics used is a good idea; use of ten fingerprints and an iris scan to verify or identify a traveler will, when feasible, cover the vast majority of travelers. The possible misuse of such information, which may be used for identification and access in numerous facets of life and, unlike a Social Security number, cannot be changed, reemphasizes the need to ensure that skimming and eavesdropping to obtain e-passport information are impossible.

Biometric identification can be applied to individuals engaging in activities that offer opportunities to prepare or perpetrate terrorist acts, such as working in an airport or other transportation-related facility, HAZMAT truck driving, and seafaring. Biometric ID cards would be the best way of ensuring that only people who have passed the necessary background checks are allowed to access dangerous materials and vulnerable areas of transport nodes. Background checks should be standardized across states. The original FY2006 budget proposal would have consolidated and coordinated the operations of nine screening programs through a single Office of Screening Coordination and Operations (SCO).[39] The FY2006 budget established the SCO but did not incorporate within it the functions of the separate programs, although some consolidation of oversight within the Transportation Security Administration (TSA) did take place by the establishment of the Office of Transportation Vetting and Credentialing. Depending on the success of the

SCO, these decisions may need to be revisited in the future since more reliable checks, and better integration of the systems used by these programs, are certainly necessary.

Existing security measures for transportation workers, such as photographic or magnetic ID cards or passcodes, are too vulnerable to being breached. This problem is being addressed by the transportation worker identification credential (TWIC) initiative, which establishes a "uniform, nationwide standard for secure identification of transportation workers."[40] The credential is a card that incorporates the holder's fingerprint information and various security features (holograms, background weaving, and so forth) to make tampering difficult; iris and hand geometry data also could be included.[41] As in the case of passports, there should be redundancy of biometrics. To ensure compatibility with all legacy systems—those systems in use that predate the establishment of the DHS—the biometric data are stored in various ways: a chip, a magnetic strip, a 2-D barcode, a linear barcode, and a digital photograph.[42] A seven-month test of the TWIC in numerous settings began in November 2004,[43] and implementation has been rightly deemed a priority by the deputy secretary for homeland security, Michael Jackson.[44]

The Seafarers' Identity Documents Convention, written under the auspices of the International Labour Organization, came into force on February 9, 2005, thus creating a global biometric identification system for the world's 1.2 million seafarers.[45] A 2-D barcode containing fingerprint data is included on the seafarers' identity document; the interoperability of the cards and readers used by different countries has already been tested.[46] As these examples indicate, use of fingerprints is a standard that should be encouraged in all biometric systems because the acquisition and matching technology is well developed, enrollment is straightforward, and the frequency of false matches and non-matches is acceptably low. Of course, the concept should be explained and justified to the public, and understood and accepted by it.

Defending against Explosives and Firearms

Explosives threaten many spheres of activity, particularly travel, but it is not possible to guard all locations in which a terrorist might detonate a bomb. Minimizing the risks depends on intelligence, public awareness, appropriate design of structures, and surveillance, in addition to detecting explosives. If technology develops as hoped, in the future surveillance will not be restricted to monitoring by human guards but will apply "automated scene understanding," for which HSARPA funding awards were made in 2005.[47] This will integrate the use of all available data—from video, radar, seismic, acoustic, and other sources—which would be too much for a single person to process, and will automate the process of identifying suspicious signs or activity.[48] Video-based "intelligent surveillance" is already being used to monitor the U.S.-Mexican and U.S.-Canadian borders, as well as Andrews Air Force Base.[49] Explosive detection systems can be readily implemented only in certain locations, such as airports and government buildings; others, such as public transportation systems and sports venues, present greater difficulties due to the large volume of people who pass any entry point in a short space of time. Still, even here more can be done to safeguard against explosives than is being done at present.

In U.S. airports, passengers pass through metal detectors (magnetometers) on their way to the gate and their hand luggage is X-rayed. The magnetometer is designed primarily to detect firearms and knives, while the X-rays can discriminate to a certain extent between different materials: organic, inorganic, and metallic objects are shown in different colors.[50] When the magnetometer raises an alarm about a passenger, he or she is subjected to a pat-down search; questionable luggage is searched by hand. Screening of all checked baggage for explosives was mandated by the 2001 Aviation and Transportation Security Act; this approach is different from the tiered system of luggage screening used in Europe, which results in the highest level of scrutiny being applied to only a small fraction of luggage (roughly 3 percent in the London airports, for example).[51] This would be a more cost-effective means of improving security than the extensive screening of all luggage, which is currently mandated in the United States.

Two types of system are used to perform explosives screening: the explosive detection system (EDS) and the explosive trace detection (ETD) system. EDS machines use X-rays to produce a three-dimensional image; an object of high density indicates that an explosive may be present and triggers further examination of the baggage using, for example, an ETD machine.[52] The EDS machines are expensive (more than $1 million each), and they have a high false-positive rate, more than 20 percent.[53] ETD systems require an operator to take a swab from a piece of luggage to pick up traces of any explosive, which then is analyzed by ion mobility spectroscopy (IMS). Each unit costs around $50,000, and the false alarm rate is less than 1 percent. False negatives are more of a concern, and a time-consuming process of screening inside the baggage must be carried out to ensure that it is completely free from explosives. For reasons of cost, many more ETD than EDS machines have been deployed, even though the former are slow, labor-intensive devices that limit the rate at which baggage can be processed.[54] Furthermore, much of the screening takes place in airport lobbies. As recommended by the 9/11 Commission, airports should move toward "in-line" screening, which is faster and can be more cost-effective.[55]

Screening capabilities for explosives and firearms need improvement. Magnetometers give no information as to whether a passenger is carrying explosives or nonmetallic (plastic or ceramic) weapons, but several new devices can plug that gap. The primary new system for detecting explosives is a portal costing around $160,000. A burst of air hits the passenger standing in the portal, and IMS analyzers in the roof of the portal screen the resulting particles for explosives; the result is delivered in about fourteen seconds. This is significantly longer than the time taken to walk through a metal detector, so many such portals would have to be deployed in an airport to permit screening of all passengers. The random plus risk-based selection of passengers that currently is employed would not require such a large deployment. These portals underwent trials at airports in fourteen U.S. cities in the first half of 2005, and since then the TSA has deployed around 100 additional portals in the nation's larger airports. In FY2006, it hopes to buy another 195 portals for forty-one more airports.[56] In due course there could be integration of explosive detection and magnetometer technology.

New imaging technologies promise to identify explosives or weapons of any type on the person of passengers. Known as "X-ray backscatter" and "millimeter wave" technologies, they are based on detecting the reflection of various types of electromagnetic waves by the passengers. In each case, different materials reflect the waves differently, so that concealed weapons and explosives can be imaged. For example, in the X-ray technique currently being tested by the TSA, organic materials, including plastic explosives and narcotics, appear as bright white objects.[57] The radiation dosage is very small (0.02 percent of that of a chest X-ray) and therefore poses negligible danger to the passenger.[58] The U.S. government plans to use mobile and parcel scanners based on this technology to scan for plastic explosives.[59]

Millimeter wave systems use an array of sensors to detect the UHF radio waves scattered by a passenger; they allow faster scanning than the X-ray systems because an image covering 360 degrees can be acquired in a single shot.[60] Determination of whether the passenger is carrying anything at all can be made in about ten seconds. Each machine is expected to cost around $100,000.[61] A purely passive type of millimeter wave system also is available, relying on the millimeter waves that all people radiate to form an image.[62] Neither X-ray backscatter nor millimeter wave systems are ready for full deployment in U.S. airports, but both are imminent. Concerns about privacy, owing to the machines' ability to see through clothes, have been remedied in various ways; installation of such machines should be expedited since the current vulnerability to plastic explosives and nonmetallic weapons is high.

Hand-held detectors sensitive to traces of a range of explosives are available and being purchased by the U.S. military, and machines that can check for traces of explosives on the documents submitted by a passenger at check-in are now becoming available; in each case the IMS technique is used.[63] Passengers' hand luggage can be scanned using the X-ray backscatter technique, which discriminates better between different materials than does the usual transmission X-ray imaging. As a result of technology development, EDS systems that are smaller, cheaper, [64] faster,[65] or that can more reliably identify explosives[66] are becoming available. These could allow faster screening of all hand and checked luggage, fewer false positives, and amelioration of airport lobby clutter. (Given that many terminals within major U.S. airports have peak checked baggage screening demand of 3,500 per hour or more, higher throughput capability is vital.)[67] The cost of such systems ranges from $300,000 to around $2 million. Looking slightly further ahead, a number of promising technologies can be seen that could identify explosive materials with greater reliability, speed, or facility than existing techniques.[68] These include quadrupole resonance imaging (a relative of nuclear magnetic resonance imaging),[69] mass spectroscopy,[70] surface-enhanced Raman spectroscopy,[71] terahertz imaging,[72] and "stoichiometrics,"[73] in which a material is subjected to thermal or fast neutrons and the gamma-rays it emits are measured.[74]

The TSA has both near-term (two to five years) and long-term (more than five years) programs for developing and deploying more advanced baggage-screening equipment. Near-term projects aim for incremental improvements, such as combining X-ray diffraction or quadrupole resonance with currently employed EDS scanning technology, or developing screening systems that have a throughput that is a factor of 3 higher than at present, with 75 percent fewer false alarms and better detection capability due to higher spatial resolution.[75] Longer-term projects aim for "revolutionary" developments; previous attempts to achieve such dramatic progress on a shorter schedule were unrealistic and unsuccessful.[76] As specified in the Intelligence Reform and Terrorism Prevention Act of 2004, the focus of this development includes walk-through explosive detection portals, document scanners, shoe scanners, and backscatter X-ray scanners.[77]

Given the existing and forthcoming screening technologies, the fact that not all airline cargo is screened should be questioned. In November 2003 the DHS announced a strategic plan for securing air cargo that involves inspection of high-risk cargo as well as random inspections,[78] and there is now a known-shipper program,[79] though the security of existing programs of this type is questionable.[80] Many of the factors relevant to the question of whether 100 percent of air cargo should be screened mirror those related to sea cargo screening (for example, intelligence-based targeting, supply-chain security, costs, logistical difficulties, and so forth).[81] The crucial difference, however, is that it is much easier to cause catastrophic damage using a small amount of explosive in an aircraft than on a sea freight vessel or in a port. For that reason, 100 percent screening of air cargo for explosives should be seriously considered. The 9/11 Commission recommended that "[t]he TSA should require that every passenger aircraft carrying cargo must deploy at least one hardened container to carry any suspect cargo."[82] However, the idea that any suspect cargo would be carried at all is worrisome. Such hardened containers can lose their ballistic integrity in the course of normal (rough) handling after only a few days, and relying on such containers to protect against an explosion is unwise.[83] Cargo should be loaded onto an aircraft only when it is certain that it is free of explosives. If the concomitant economic disruption makes that impossible, then, at the very least, lighter and more durable hardened containers must be developed and used. They also must be cheaper, so that a greater proportion of cargo (ideally all) can be transported in this way.

Away from airports, it is rarely as feasible to screen carefully for explosives. Public transportation is an obvious target for a bomb attack, as the Madrid and London bombings have demonstrated, but requiring every subway or Amtrak passenger to pass through an explosive detection portal that takes ten seconds to generate a reading is impractical because of the volume of people to be processed. Random checks would be feasible, but gaining public acceptance might be difficult. In the case of a train, a checked baggage regime might make large-scale baggage screening possible, though that would require passengers to change the way that they use train transportation. As a more general solution to the detection of explosives in train and bus stations and other transport locations, sniffer dogs, which cost around $20,000 each, could be used. They have great sensory capabilities; however, they must rest every twenty minutes.[84] Explosive portals and EDS machines could be used for screening the person and belongings of those who wish to enter government buildings and a sufficient number of portals would make screening at a major sport or other public event possible. HSARPA is currently (January 2006) soliciting proposals for the development of devices to detect improvised explosives.[85] Despite this and ongoing research into the other technologies described above, the fact that it is not possible to rapidly screen large numbers of people or to detect explosive traces from long range means that it will not be possible in the foreseeable future to scan large areas for explosives with devices that have a high degree of sensitivity.[86] Locations in which easy public access is essential will remain vulnerable.

Cargo Security

About 25,000 containers arrive and are off-loaded at U.S. seaports every day, to say nothing of the cargo arriving by air and over land. The sheer volume of cargo offers a terrorist possibly the most attractive means of introducing weapons, whether conventional or not, into the country. It is therefore highly desirable to be able to screen incoming cargo for nuclear and radiological materials, explosives, chemical and biological weapons, surface-to-air missiles, firearms, and even unauthorized immigrants, as well as to ensure the integrity of containers in transit.

The United States currently inspects around 6 percent of the incoming sea cargo; the decision to inspect cargo or not is based on intelligence.[87] The containers to be inspected, either upon arrival in the United States or abroad under the Container Security Initiative, are passed through a gamma-ray or X-ray screening portal and swept with a radionuclide identification device (RID). CBP staff have personal radiation detectors to continuously monitor for radiation; dogs, which can detect narcotics, chemicals, and explosives, operate around the cargo containers. Individual items may be X-rayed, and material suspected of being a biological threat is taken for analysis by Department of Agriculture staff.

These measures reduce the likelihood of dangerous cargo, especially material for nuclear and radiological weapons, entering the United States, but they are insufficient. Capabilities for detecting chemical and biological agents lag those for detecting radioactivity. With current infrastructure it is not possible to increase significantly the fraction of cargo inspected, but doing so is necessary in order to take advantage of the deterrent effect of random screening. To increase inspection capacity, wider installation and effective use of existing screening technology—and improvements in its accuracy and speed—are required. New portable technologies for detecting chemical and biological agents will be essential. Furthermore, at present there is no standard way to ensure that a cargo container inspected abroad remains free from tampering in transit. Container doors have seals that are broken when a door is opened, but the entire door handle assembly can be removed without breaking them.[88] A more reliable indicator of container integrity is needed. For greater confidence that shipments have been delivered intact, it would be wise to implement a system whereby containers are tracked in transit.

Screening technology must allow swift and accurate inspections. Delays are very expensive: in 2002 the strike at Long Beach port reportedly cost $1 billion a day. An inspection time of one minute per container would be acceptable for large-scale screening.[89] The rate of false alarms also must be exceedingly low. Given that a cargo ship might have 3,000 containers on board, an acceptable rate might be less than 0.1 percent.[90]

To examine a container's contents, X-ray or gamma-ray imaging machines are used; a container on truck or train can be scanned in less than one minute, so screening a large fraction (say, 20 percent or more) of containers in this way would be feasible. CBP officers are trained so that normally they can make a rapid determination of whether an image indicates that further inspection is necessary.[91] Whether X-ray or gamma-ray systems are used depends largely on circumstances and budget. X-ray scanning is the more mature technology, and it can yield more detailed images, but the machines are bigger, less mobile, more power-hungry, and more expensive. An X-ray machine such as the Eagle costs around $2.5 million,[92] whereas a mobile gamma-ray VACIS scanner costs around $900,000.[93] The gamma-ray scan is adequate for inspecting most containers, but an X-ray scan is vital when high energy is needed to image a container's cargo or penetrate its thick walls (as is true for approximately 10 percent of the containers). Therefore a potential configuration for cargo scanning at a port is to inspect incoming containers by gamma-rays systems, of which several operate in parallel, and to direct only containers that require greater penetration to the port's single X-ray detector.[94] Since the main obstacle to implementing 100 percent scanning of cargo containers is the lack of space at ports in which to install the requisite number of detectors and to route the cargo containers, it is appropriate to focus investment in the smaller, cheaper, and more mobile gamma-ray scanners.

The primary method of detecting chemical weapons and explosives at ports is through the use of dogs.[95] Dogs have the advantages over machines of mobility, sensitivity to vapors, and the ability to scan large volumes rapidly: a canine team can process 400 to 500 packages in about thirty minutes.[96] In accordance with the strategy advocated in this book, which focuses on catastrophic threats, detecting explosives in ports and on land borders should not be a top priority for investment. Explosives are, of themselves, less of a threat than the unconventional weapons or surface-to-air missiles that one might discover in cargo. Furthermore, explosives for bombs can be made using materials readily available within the United States. It does make sense, though, to have ETD machines, at a cost of under $50,000 each, available to check suspicious imports, and vapor-sensing devices could assist in the detection of missiles. A low-tech response to the threat posed by the use of explosives while at sea entails reinforcing shipping containers to make them more blast resistant, at a cost of about $15,000 per container.[97] Screening for explosives before a container departs a port is a more cost-effective and safer—and therefore better—option.

Hand-held devices to identify materials that pose a chemical or biological threat are becoming available at prices that range from around $9,000 to $25,000,[98] but they are of limited utility unless the suspicious substance already has been detected. Small but potent quantities of such materials could be readily concealed in cargo, and the ease with which they could be imported remains one of America's most serious vulnerabilities.

The challenge of tracking and ensuring the integrity of a container over the duration of transit can be met through container security devices (CSDs). New types of seals that would be broken even if the entire door handle were removed intact have been developed, and sensors that can determine whether a container door has been opened en route have been commercially developed.[99] These can be integrated into two different technologies that allow tracking of the containers: radio frequency identification (RFID) and global positioning systems (GPS).

The RFID devices, currently being tested by the DHS, are small, battery-powered units that store information from the sensors to which they are connected.[100] This information, such as the time of an unauthorized opening of a door, is accessed by standard Bluetooth technology (used for communication by laptop computers and mobile phones). The $10 cost of each device, which has a lifetime of ten years, means that rapid and large-scale implementation of this technology will be possible once the CBP-specified target false alarm rate, less than 1 percent, has been achieved. The current false alarm rate for a door-opening is believed to be 5 percent.[101] A longer-term DHS goal is to install a range of sensors on containers to create so-called smart boxes, at a cost of no more than $50 per voyage (based on a DHS assessment of what is economically viable).[102] The sensors could monitor the integrity of the entire container, its previous movements, and the temperature and radiation levels inside. Viable smart boxes are believed to be two years away;[103] development, supported by HSARPA, is ongoing.[104]

The current lack of international standards constitutes a major barrier to adoption of radio frequency identification and tracking technology by the shipping industry.[105] The main disadvantage of RFID-based sensors is that they can convey information only when interrogated. Rail cars have been tracked in the United States for the past thirty years using RFID tags,[106] but waiting until a sea container has been brought to a U.S. port to find out that its integrity has been breached may be waiting too long. Reading information in transit would require bringing, by sea or air, an RF reader into close proximity with the container, a potentially costly and certainly infrequent procedure. Other concerns include the susceptibility of the information on the RFID tags to being read without the permission or knowledge of the owner, the tags' vulnerability to tampering, and cost.[107] Potential difficulties include the fact that the many metal objects in a port act as reflectors for radio frequency signals, possibly making it difficult to read the RF tags, and the fact that if many containers are densely stacked on a vessel, it will not be possible to read all the tags individually.

If it is sufficient to track containers at exit and entry ports and periodically while at sea, RFID is adequate. If not, GPS is a better solution.[108] GPS technology, which is well established, allows tracking of a container in real time: its position, updated every thirty minutes, can be established to within ten meters.[109] As with RFID, sensors can detect whether the container's door has been opened, and an alert can be sent by satellite as soon as a breach is detected; that is a distinct advantage over RFID. False alarms have not been found to be a significant problem in the systems implemented to date. A GPS unit costs around $500;[110] it may be battery- or solar-powered, and it has a lifetime of around ten years.[111] In the future, additional sensors could be installed that would trigger an alarm if, for example, the container were breached in another way or the radiation level inside were to rise above a certain level. The fact that GPS is an established system means that there are no concerns about standards, and widespread installation of such tracking systems could take place as soon as the shipping industry is mandated or induced to do so. A technical obstacle is that, as with RFID tags, it is difficult to communicate with individual containers if they are stacked and tightly packed on a container vessel. Solar-powered systems would also be less useful in such a configuration. Its only disadvantage relative to the RFID-based system is the greater cost.

Customs and Border Protection will require participants in the C-TPAT scheme to use smart box technology once the false alarm rate falls to a commercially viable level. The DHS has not yet committed itself to buying any particular container tracking product, nor has it mandated that containers be fitted with tracking devices, and so the shipping industry has not yet settled on a standard.[112] Present government thinking appears to be leaning toward the RFID system; its low price means that the private sector could bear the entire cost. Establishing a standard and thus energizing the industry should be a matter of priority for the DHS, and any standard will have to be internationally accepted. The International Standardization Organization, with which the World Shipping Council is liaising on the matter, and the World Customs Organization are bodies with which the standards must be cooperatively established.[113] In view of GPS's constant provision of information and ease of use, GPS tracking should be adopted if possible.

In summary, the government should bolster HSARPA by employing high-caliber scientists under more stable conditions. U.S. e-passports should contain secure fingerprint data to optimize reliability and utility. Explosive trace detectors (to be replaced by penetrating imaging, when available) should be installed in all airports to scan high-risk and randomly selected passengers; a greater proportion of air cargo, eventually 20 percent or more, must also be scanned for explosives. The government should deploy more gamma- and X-ray scanners at ports to inspect 10 to 15 percent of cargo containers. As soon as technically feasible, the government should mandate the electronic monitoring of container integrity and GPS-based tracking of in-transit containers.

Notes

1. Michael Chertoff, remarks to the Commonwealth Club of California, July 28, 2005 (www.dhs.gov/dhspublic/display?content=4700 [October 29, 2005]).

2. Actual system costs contain many variables, including personnel, the terms of purchase, and the details of deployment, analysis of which is beyond the scope of this chapter.

3. Defense Advanced Research Projects Agency, "DARPA—Bridging the Gap—Powered by Ideas," February 2005.

4. See "DARPA Legacy" (www.darpa.mil/body/legacy/index.html [March 10, 2005]).

5. HSARPA is under the DHS Science and Technology Directorate, whose spending is almost entirely devoted to R&D; in FY2005 the Science and Technology Directorate accounted for 84 percent of the $1.2 billion DHS R&D budget. See "DHS R&D in FY 2005 Final Appropriations," American Association for the Advancement of Science (AAAS), Washington, November 29, 2005. HSARPA was responsible for disbursing around 30 percent of this sum to industry contractors, research institutions, and universities, and thus had a budget in the region of $300 million. The Department of Homeland Security Appropriations Act of 2006 has allocated to the DHS a $1.3 billion R&D budget in FY2006, of which 99 percent will go to the Science and Technology Directorate. See the AAAS Funding Update on R&D in FY2006 (www.aaas.org/spp/rd/dhs06c.htm [December 12, 2005]).

6. Dr. Charles E. McQueary, under secretary for science and technology, Department of Homeland Security, before the House Committee on Science, 109 Cong., 1 sess., February 16, 2005.

7. David F. Bolka, director, HSARPA, in a presentation to the DHS Industry Forum, Washington, March 8–9, 2004 (www.ctc.org/DHSIF/Bolka.pdf [March 30, 2005]).

8. E-mail to Michael d'Arcy from Tom Burke, DHS, October 31, 2005. The certified technologies include detection devices for explosives and anthrax spores, gamma-

and X-ray screening systems, marine traffic management systems, computerized systems for first responder interoperability, risk assessment by data mining, and various services concerned with risk management and security at government and commercial installations. See the Safety Act website (www.safetyact.gov) for more details.

9. To that end the Department of Homeland Security Appropriations Act of 2006 allocates $7 million for Safety Act technology development.

10. Interview remarks to Michael d'Arcy by Adam Driks, associate professor, Department of Microbiology, Loyola University, Chicago, June 30, 2005.

11. Homeland Security Act of 2002, sec. 313.

12. Department of Homeland Security Appropriations Act 2006 (Public Law 109-90), October 18, 2005.

13. An earlier appropriations bill, H.R. 1817, passed only by the House, did include a measure to establish this clearinghouse.

14. Frank Paul, head of the large-scale IT systems unit, European Commission, quoted by Dan Balaban in "Vendors Taken to Task over E-Passport Flaws," *Card Technology* 10 (February 2005): 26.

15. "France, Britain, Japan Unable to Meet New U.S. Passport Rules," Agence France-Presse, February 1, 2005.

16. The DHS reported that all twenty-seven VWP countries, apart from Italy and France, met the October 26, 2005, digital photo deadline (www.dhs.gov/dhspublic/display?content=4907 [October 29, 2005]).

17. See the ICAO webpage on machine readable travel documents (www.icao.int/mrtd/ [June 27, 2005]).

18. Balaban, "Vendors Taken to Task over E-Passport Flaws."

19. Eric Lipton, "U.S. to Alter Passport Design because of Privacy Fears," *New York Times*, April 28, 2005.

20. Kim Zetter, "Feds Rethinking RFID Passport," *Wired News*, April 26, 2005 (www.wired.com/news/privacy/0,1848,67333,00.html [June 27, 2005]).

21. Interview remarks to Michael d'Arcy by Richard P. McClevey, facilities manager, Office of the Deputy Assistant Secretary for Passport Services, Department of State, June 27, 2005.

22. Interview remarks to Michael d'Arcy by Charles L. Wilson, group manager, Information Access Division, NIST, December 6, 2004.

23. U.S. General Accounting Office, "Technology Assessment: Using Biometrics for Border Security," GAO-03-174 (November 2002).

24. Asa Hutchinson, under secretary for border and transportation security, DHS, testimony before the U.S. Senate Committee on Commerce, Science and Transportation, 108 Cong., 2 sess., June 22, 2004.

25. Department of Homeland Security, press release, September 21, 2004 (www.dhs.gov/dhspublic/display?content=4030 [December 9, 2004]).

26. Department of Homeland Security, press release, "Fact Sheet: Secure Border Initiative," December 8, 2005 (www.dhs.gov/dhspublic/interapp/press_release/press_release_0805.xml [December 12, 2005]).

27. Aliya Sternstein, "Fingerprint Standard Still Elusive," FCW.COM, February 18, 2005 (www.fcw.com/fcw/articles/2005/0214/web-fingers-02-18-05.asp [June 30, 2005]); Blas Nuñez-Neto, "Border Security: The Role of the U.S. Border Patrol" (Washington: Congressional Research Service, May 10, 2005), p. 28.

28. Michael Chertoff, remarks on the Department of Homeland Security Second Stage Review, July 13, 2005 (www.dhs.gov/dhspublic/display?content=4597 [October 29, 2005]).

29. Charles L. Wilson, NIST, December 6, 2004.

30. An increase in the average inspection time at the border from thirteen to nineteen seconds would result in an increase in the peak waiting time from nearly five hours to nearly twenty hours. See "Technical and Policy Issues of Counterterrorism," *Physics Today*, April 2003, p. 39.

31. Alan Cooperman, "Fingerprints Urged for Passports," *Washington Post*, January 13, 2005, p. A6.

32. U.S. General Services Administration, "Smart Card" (www.gsa.gov/Portal/gsa/ep/channelView.do?pageTypeId=8199&channelId=-13480 [February 18, 2005]).

33. John Daugman, reader in computer vision and pattern recognition, Computer Laboratory, University of Cambridge, "Largest Current Deployment of Iris Recognition" (www.cl.cam.ac.uk/users/jgd1000/deployments.html [December 10, 2004]).

34. "Prepare to Be Scanned," *Economist*, December 4, 2004.

35. Tony Mansfield and others, "Biometric Product Testing Final Report," U.K. National Physical Laboratory, Teddington, March 2001.

36. FTE rate ranges from less than 1 percent to more than 12 percent. E-mail to Michael d'Arcy from Charles L. Wilson, NIST, March 29, 2005.

37. Charles L. Wilson, NIST, December 6, 2004.

38. The United Kingdom is including the iris biometric as well as ten fingerprints and a facial image on national ID cards that it plans to introduce in 2008.

39. Angela Kim, "DHS Proposes Reorganization of Screening Programs," *Aviation Daily*, February 9, 2005.

40. U.S. General Accounting Office, "Transportation Security: Federal Action Needed to Help Address Security Challenges," GAO-03-843 (June 2003), p. 46.

41. Interview remarks to Michael d'Arcy by Darrin Kayser, spokesman, Transportation Security Administration, March 29, 2005.

42. Department of Homeland Security, press release, November 17, 2004 (www.dhs.gov/dhspublic/display?content=4119 [March 28, 2005]).

43. Transportation Security Administration, press release, November 17, 2004 (www.tsa.gov/public/display?content=09000519800e0f0f [February 18, 2005]).

44. Angela Grealing Keane, "DHS Identifies TWIC Priority," *Traffic World*, March 11, 2005.

45. International Labour Organization, press release, February 10, 2005 (www.ilo.org/public/english/bureau/inf/pr/2005/7.htm [February 18, 2005]).

46. Tracy Logan, "Seamen Sail into Biometric Future," BBC News World Edition (news.bbc.co.uk/2/hi/technology/3976093.stm [February 18, 2005]).

47. HSARPA BAA Awards, Solicitation BAA-04-05 (www.hsarpabaa.com/main/HSARPAAwards.asp?BAAID=3 [December 12, 2005]).

48. The potential of this technology has been highlighted in the National Critical Infrastructure Protection Research and Development Plan, April 2005, p. 28 (www.dhs.gov/interweb/assetlibrary/ST_2004_NCIP_RD_PlanFINALApr05.pdf [October 30, 2005]).

49. Elaine Shannon, "Eye on the Border," *Time,* May 2004 (www.objectvideo.com/objects/pdf/articles/Time.pdf [February 26, 2005]).

50. Michael Fickes, "Technology Exposing Trouble," *Government Security,* February 1, 2003.

51. Viggo Butler and Robert W. Poole Jr., "Rethinking Checked-Baggage Screening," Reason Public Policy Institute, Los Angeles, July 2002.

52. "In-Line Screening Sets a New Benchmark at Harrisburg, Pa.," *Airport Security Report,* December 15, 2004.

53. Kelly Leone, Transportation Security Administration, and Rongfang Liu, New Jersey Institute of Technology, "Validating Throughput Analysis of Checked Baggage Performance," paper submitted to Transportation Research Board, July 2004.

54. From September 2001 to February 2004, more than 1,100 EDS machines and 6,000 ETD machines were deployed at more than 440 U.S. airports. Cathleen A. Berrick, director, Homeland Security and Justice Section, U.S. General Accounting Office, February 12, 2004, in her statement, "Aviation Security: Challenges Exist in Stabilizing and Enhancing Passenger and Baggage Screening Operations," GAO-04-440T.

55. In-line screening equipment installed at Lexington Blue Grass Airport, Kentucky, broke after sixteen months; see Michael A. Gobb, executive director of Blue Grass Airport, testimony before the House Subcommittee on Aviation, 108 Cong., 2 sess., July 14, 2004.

56. David M. Stone, assistant secretary, Transportation Security Administration, testimony before the Senate Committee on Commerce, Science, and Transportation, 109 Cong., 1 sess., February 15, 2005.

57. Peter Gwynne, "New Screening Technologies Emerge from R&D Labs," IEEE Spectrum Online, June 2002 (www.spectrum.ieee.org/WEBONLY/resource/jul02/screen.html [February 26, 2005]).

58. The American Science and Engineering, Inc., BodySearch system is an example of such a device; see www.as-e.com/products_solutions/body_search.asp (February 26, 2005).

59. "American Science and Engineering, Inc., Receives $6.6 Million Order from the U.S. Government for Multiple Z Backscatter Vans and Parcel X-ray Systems," *Business Wire,* January 5, 2005.

60. Remarks by Rick Rowe, president and CEO, SafeView Inc., at the National Academies Science and Technology Policy Fellows Seminar, Washington, March 2, 2005.

61. Lakshmi Sandhana, "There's No Place to Hide," *Wired News,* August 26, 2002 (www.wired.com/news/privacy/0,1848,54598,00.html [February 25, 2005]).

62. "QinetiQ Passive Millimeter-Wave Imagers" (www.qinetiq.com/home_us/case_studies/case_studies_homeland_security/millimeter_wave_imager.html [February 27, 2005]).

63. See, for example, the detectors developed by Sandia National Laboratory (www.ca.sandia.gov/pubs/factsheets/explosives/microhound.hound0905.pdf [October 29, 2005]).

64. "TSA Certifies Airport Explosives Detection System for Baggage," *Business Wire*, January 25, 2005.

65. Gwynne, "New Screening Technologies Emerge from R&D Labs."

66. Richard Lee, "GE Infrastructure Wins Baggage-Screening Contract," *Stamford Advocate*, January 26, 2005.

67. Mark E. Lunsford and Roger L. Dickey, "In-Line Lite," *Airport International*, December 1, 2004.

68. For a detailed survey of future techniques for detecting explosives, see the Board on Chemical Sciences and Technology, "Existing and Potential Stand-off Explosives Detection Techniques" (Washington: National Research Council, 2004).

69. Joel B. Miller and Geoffrey A. Barrall, "Explosives Detection with Nuclear Quadrupole Resonance," *American Scientist 93* (January-February 2005), p. 50.

70. Syagen Technology, "Explosives Detecting MS" (www.syagen.com/explosives_ms.asp [February 26, 2005]); National Materials Advisory Board, "Opportunities to Improve Airport Passenger Screening with Mass Spectrometry" (Washington: National Research Council, May 2004).

71. Nancy T. Kawai and Kevin M. Spencer, "Raman Spectroscopy for Homeland Security Applications," *Raman Technology for Today's Spectroscopists*, June 2004, p. 54.

72. "U.S. Airports Look to Terahertz Screening," *Physics World*, January 2005, p. 6.

73. Ryan Singel, "Sniffing Out Things That Go Boom," *Wired News*, January 12, 2005 (www.wired.com/news/privacy/0,1848,66241,00.html [February 27, 2005]).

74. G. Vourvopoulos and P. C. Womble, "Pulsed Fast / Thermal Neutron Analysis: A Technique for Explosives Detection," TALANTA 54 (May 2001): 459.

75. Berrick, statement in "Aviation Security."

76. Remarks of Penrose C. (Parney) Albright, assistant secretary for science and technology, DHS, to the Washington Science Policy Alliance, American Association for the Advancement of Science, Washington, March 1, 2005.

77. Intelligence Reform and Terrorism Prevention Act of 2004, Sec. 4013.

78. Transportation Security Administration, press release, November 17, 2003 (www.tsa.gov/public/display?theme=44&content=0900051980069bfe [December 10, 2004]).

79. Transportation Security Administration, press release, April 9, 2004 (www.tsa.gov/public/display?content=09000519800994a4 [February 26, 2005]).

80. U.S. Government Accountability Office, "Cargo Security: Partnership Program Grants Importers Reduced Scrutiny with Limited Assurance of Improved Security," GAO-05-404 (March 2005).

81. Stephen E. Flynn, "Transforming Air Cargo Security in the Post 9-11 World,"

Cargo Network Services (Summer 2002); Bartholomew Elias, "Air Cargo Security" (Washington: Congressional Research Service, September 2003).

82. National Commission on Terrorist Attacks upon the United States [9/11 Commission], *The 9/11 Commission Report: Final Report of the National Commission on Terrorist Attacks upon the United States* (New York: W. W. Norton, 2004), p. 393.

83. "New Aviation Security Requirements Contained in Intelligence Reform Act," *Air Safety Week*, January 3, 2005.

84. Butler and Poole, "Rethinking Checked-Baggage Screening."

85. Homeland Security Advanced Research Projects Agency, "Prototypes and Technology for Improvised Explosives Device Detection" (www.hsarpabaa.com/main/BAA0503_solicitation_notice.htm [February 27, 2005]).

86. See the Board on Chemical Sciences and Technology, "Existing and Potential Stand-off Explosives Detection Techniques."

87. Interview remarks to Michael d'Arcy by Todd Horton, chief, Evaluations and Assessments, and Lisa Clark, program manager, Operations Branch, Container Security Initiative, Customs and Border Protection, February 14, 2005.

88. Ephraim Schwartz, "GE Completes Trial of Smart Shipping Containers," *InfoWorld Daily News*, January 11, 2005 (www.sealock.com/the_problem.html [February 20, 2005]).

89. Interview remarks to Michael d'Arcy by Kim Kennedy, president, K&K International Storage Containers, February 2, 2005.

90. See comments of Kirk Evans, HSARPA director of mission support, quoted by R. G. Edmonson in "Creating the Smart Container: Department of Homeland Security Says It's Making Headway with Advanced Container Security Device," *Journal of Commerce*, December 13, 2004.

91. In the United Kingdom, one in every 150 images thus obtained is insufficiently clear, thus necessitating the unpacking and manual inspection of the container. Maarten van de Voort and others, "Seacurity: Improving the Security of the Global Sea-Container Shipping System" (Santa Monica, Calif.: RAND, 2003), p. 11.

92. Rapiscan Eagle(r) X-ray Inspection System (www.rapiscansystems.com/eagle.html [December 9, 2005]).

93. SAIC, Portal VACIS(r) Inspection System (www.saic.com/products/security/portal-vacis/index.html [February 20, 2005]).

94. Interview remarks to Michael d'Arcy by Rex D. Richardson, program manager, VACIS Imaging IR&D, SAIC, February 9, 2005.

95. For use of sniffer dogs in detecting chemical weapons, see U.S. Customs and Border Protection, press release, "CBP Deploys Chemical Detector Dogs," June 6, 2005 (www.cbp.gov/xp/cgov/newsroom/press_releases/archives/cbp_press_releases/062003/06062003.xml [October 29, 2005]).

96. U.S. Customs and Border Protection, "Frequently Asked Questions" (www.cbp.gov/xp/cgov/border_security/canines/faq.xml [February 22, 2005]).

97. "Transportation Security: Federal Action Needed to Help Address Security Challenges," June 2003, p. 19.

98. Interview remarks to Michael d'Arcy by Eric Montgomery, sales representative, Smiths Detection, February 22, 2005.

99. Ephraim Schwartz, "GE Completes Trial of Smart Shipping Containers," *InfoWorld Daily News*, January 11, 2005; also see China International Marine Containers Group Ltd., "GE and CIMC Complete First Commercial Test of Tamper Evident Secure Container"(www.cimc.com/News/2005-1/200511712126C22287.htm [February 22, 2005]).

100. General Electric, Intermodal Container Security (www.geindustrial.com/ge-interlogix/solutions/intermodal_container_security/commerceGuard.html [February 10, 2005]).

101. As reported by Eric Johnson, "Industry Group Eyes Smart Box Technology in Containers to Combat Terrorism," *Press-Telegram*, February 8, 2005.

102. R. G. Edmonson, "Creating the Smart Container: Department of Homeland Security Says It's Making Headway with Advanced Container Security Device," *Journal of Commerce*, December 13, 2004.

103. Randy Koch, Unisys, as reported by John M. Doyle in "Most Cargo Container Sensors Not Yet Effective, Consultant Says," *Homeland Security and Defense*, November 24, 2004.

104. HSARPA, "Advanced Container Security Device," solicitation notice (www.hsarpabaa.com/main/BAA0406_solicitation_notice.htm [February 22, 2005]). For an example of ongoing development, see "RAE Systems Releases Container Security White Paper Detailing Successful Sea Trial Results," *Business Wire*, January 12, 2005.

105. ABI Research, "Container Security Tracking," Oyster Bay, N.Y., 2004.

106. Interview remarks to Michael d'Arcy by David Baker, CEO and director of engineering, Lat-Lon LLC, February 21, 2005.

107. Jacqueline Emigh, "Needs for Standards, Privacy Top RFID Concerns," *eWeek*, September 16, 2004 (www.eweek.com/article2/0,1759,1646921,00.asp [February 21, 2005]).

108. GPS recently was deemed the most promising technology for electronic container tracking, based on the current security concerns that it could address and the commercial benefits that would accrue in terms of supply chain logistics and enterprise resource planning. See "Steady Growth Projected for Electronic Container Tracking," *GPS World*, February 1, 2005.

109. U.K. Ordnance Survey, "National GPS Network Information" (www.gps.gov.uk/additionalInfo/whatIsGPS_08.asp [February 22, 2005]).

110. For comparison, a forty-foot cargo container costs approximately $2,000.

111. David Baker, Lat-Lon LLC, February 21, 2005.

112. Mary Catherine O'Connor, "Container Tracking Needs Standards," *RFID Journal*, December 9, 2004 (www.rfidjournal.com/article/articleview/1279/1/1/ [February 10, 2005]).

113. Christopher Koch, president and CEO of the World Shipping Council, testimony before the U.S. Senate Committee on Commerce, Science and Transportation, 108 Cong., 2 sess., March 24, 2004.

8

Countermeasures Against Specific Weapons

Michael d'Arcy

The term "weapons of mass destruction" is commonly used to include nuclear, biological, chemical, and radiological weapons. However, grouping all of these weapons together is an oversimplification that masks important differences in the nature of the threat that they present. Nuclear bombs and some contagious biological agents are the only weapons truly capable of mass destruction, since both have the potential to cause millions of casualties. The threat from chemical and radiological weapons is not of the same magnitude, although they certainly are weapons of potential mass *effect*, owing to the human and economic disruption that would ensue from an attack.[1] One characteristic common to all the weapons mentioned is that they are unconventional, and therein lies part of their attraction for terrorists. The public does not have the same understanding of the nature and scale of the threat as it does in the case of conventional explosives, for example, and so the consequent panic and psychological trauma would magnify the effect of a successful attack.[2]

Another weapon whose effect would certainly be widespread is the shoulder-launched surface-to-air missile (also known as a man-portable air defense system—MANPADS), which is used to target aircraft. The likely economic effect of a successful attack on a passenger jet would be catastrophic and global, even aside from the toll in human lives.[3]

155

This chapter discusses how technology can diminish the threat from these weapons of catastrophic effect, what its limitations are, how it may develop in the future, and how the U.S. government should make use of it.

Unconventional Weapons

Technology can be used in three ways to counteract the threat and impact of unconventional weapons of mass effect (WME): detection, effect minimization, and post-attack cleanup. The broad issues regarding cleanup, though not the technical details, are fairly similar for each type of weapon. Cleanup requires planning before a WME attack, and it differs according to the weapon used. For example, some weapon agents dissipate with minimal treatment, while others are persistent. One of the most important questions—besides that of the decontamination method used—concerns the level of cleanliness required to restore a contaminated location to a usable state. Often it will be neither necessary nor feasible to return to the pre-attack level of cleanliness. Although some research has been carried out on this matter for attacks that involve radiological material[4] and anthrax, the federal government has not yet promulgated definitive guidance regarding either the level of decontamination that must be attained after different types of WME attack or even how that level could be determined by local authorities.[5] It is important to fill this gap both to allow first responders and the branches of government specified in the National Response Plan to prepare[6] and to ensure that the public understands and accepts the cleanup operation deemed appropriate and feasible in the aftermath of a given WME attack.

Civil authorities should give more attention to post-attack planning. In addition to scientific determination of the appropriate level of decontamination, public education and consultation on the matter must take place well in advance of an attack. The U.S. government should issue guidance to state and local governments on how to go about the cleanup process and what the goal of cleanup should be. The Environmental Protection Agency (EPA) is the appropriate agency to take responsibility for this. Mostly preventative countermeasures more specific to each type of WME threat are discussed below.

Nuclear and Radiological Threats

The nuclear and radiological threats are very different in nature. Explosion of a stolen or improvised nuclear bomb would cause massive destruction over a wide area and long-term radioactive contamination. Although such an attack is relatively unlikely due to the difficulties inherent in obtaining or building such a weapon, the consequences would be so catastrophic that countering the threat should be accorded the highest priority. A radiological dispersion device (RDD) (sometimes called a "dirty bomb," though it need not involve an explosion) would spread radioactive material around a smaller area, causing few casualties but great disruption and significant economic and psychological damage. In view of the availability of unsecured radioactive waste material around the world, such an attack is much more likely.

Fissile materials ("special nuclear materials"), which can be used to manufacture nuclear weapons, include uranium-233, uranium-235, and plutonium-239;[7] they are identified by the neutrons or gamma-rays produced in their radioactive decay.[8] Radionuclides of particular concern as radiological threats are cobalt-60, strontium-90, cesium-137, iridium-192, plutonium-238 and -239, and americium-241.[9] Some have medical (for example, cobalt-60, iridium-192) or industrial (cesium-137, americium-241) applications in civilian life and so may be kept in less-than-secure locations. Each of these isotopes can be detected by the radiation it emits. For maximum utility, detection should also identify the isotope (by spectroscopy), thus allowing accurate evaluation of a genuine threat and avoidance of false alarms from nonthreatening materials such as ceramic tiles, which are disruptive, reduce public confidence, and necessitate time-consuming and costly inspections. Isotope identification also allows for a lower alarm threshold and hence greater sensitivity.

The borders of the United States are the best point for detecting radioactive material that could be used to make a nuclear bomb or RDD, since, for the most part, the legal importation of goods is controlled there. It also is necessary to have detection capabilities in those areas that are more likely to be the target of an attack. The radiation sensitivity of the currently available passive detectors, which are based mainly on scintillators, is good, since they can detect even small amounts of radioactive material in trucks or cargo containers. Passive detectors are noninvasive, they do not expose people or materials to radiation, and they can be small in size; in addition, they do not require an irradiating source. Their disadvantages are that they may not detect a radioactive source that has been shielded, and they may have difficulty distinguishing a specific source from background radiation. Coupled with the absence of isotope identification, this leads to false alarms.

The importance that the U.S. government attaches to addressing the nuclear and radiological threat was underlined by its establishment in April 2005 of the Domestic Nuclear Detection Office (DNDO) in the Department of Homeland Security, which will integrate and coordinate related efforts

across the federal government. The deployment of radiation detection technology at U.S. borders has been commendably widespread. Customs and
Border Protection (CBP) had been working toward the aim of scanning all
cargo entering the country across its land borders or through its ports by the
end of 2005. Although this goal was not achieved, substantial progress has
been made. By November 2005, more than 600 (passive) radiation portal
monitors had been deployed at the nation's ports of entry.[10] Oakland and Los
Angeles-Long Beach seaports (the latter of which receives approximately
44 percent of all sea cargo destined for the United States) screen all incoming
cargo containers for radiation,[11] while roughly 90 percent of the traffic across
the northern and southern U.S. borders is screened.[12] The radiation portal
monitors cost around $200,000 each, are sensitive to gamma-rays, and can
scan a car, truck, or container for radioactivity in about thirty seconds. Incapable of isotope identification, they are used for the initial detection of a
radioactive source. If the alarm is raised, examination using a hand-held
radioisotope identification device (RID) can be carried out.[13] This examination is performed routinely on sea cargo containers after they pass through an
imaging machine; it takes a couple of minutes. Through the Department of
Energy's Megaports initiative, detector portals also have been installed (at
U.S. expense) in two overseas ports, Rotterdam (Netherlands) and Piraeus
(Greece). As of March 2005, portals were in the process of being installed in
Colombo (Sri Lanka), Algeciras (Spain), and Freeport (Bahamas),[14] and as of
October 2005 agreements for participation in the program also existed for
Antwerp (Belgium), Dubai (United Arab Emirates), and Manila (Philip-
pines). More recent cooperative agreements have been signed with Oman,
China, and Israel. The aim is to install such equipment at the twenty most
important overseas seaports, which are the origin of 70 percent of the container traffic destined for the United States, by 2010.[15] This program is useful,
though its long-term planning has been criticized and the United States has
found negotiations on some high-priority ports difficult.[16] It will not be a
panacea, however; as with the container security initiative (CSI), terrorists
are resourceful and could well target minor or poorly screened ports.

Pager-sized personal radiation detectors (PRDs) are used for preliminary
detection of radioactivity since they are sensitive and provide a fast readout;
they cost between $600 and $2,000 each.[17] According to former CBP commissioner Robert Bonner, the DHS has deployed more than 10,500 PRDs so
that every frontline CBP officer at a U.S. port of entry wears one and has done
so since March 1, 2003.[18] Police and firemen in various jurisdictions (for

example, New York City), as well as HAZMAT teams and Coast Guard staff, are equipped with basic Geiger detectors, costing in the region of $350 each.[19]

The extent of detector deployment within the U.S. interior, especially in cities, is difficult to ascertain since the information is classified, but many fixed sensors have been installed around the country, for both gamma-rays and neutrons.[20] The sensors are sensitive to radiation but prone to giving false alarms.[21] They communicate actively to a central location, thus creating a type of network that can be used to "map" radiation. This is just the type of capability that would be needed in a clandestine radiological attack.

As is evident, the isotope identification capability of the technology deployed thus far remains inadequate, and that is, rightly, the focus of current extensive research efforts. The American National Standards Institute (ANSI) developed new standards to cover personal radiation detectors, hand-held survey meters, portable radionuclide identifiers, and portal monitors in 2003, and in February 2004 the DHS defined the standards to which radiation detectors must conform.[22] The next generation of radiation detectors will be based on germanium, allowing more sensitive detection and precise spectroscopy than at present. Developments in cryogenic cooling have already led to hand-held detectors that can, for example, identify plutonium in a mixture of isotopes, in varying concentrations, in less than one minute and identify it as being weapons-grade (that is, suitable for use in a nuclear bomb) in less than four minutes.[23] Such detectors cost around $68,000 each. A new radiation portal based on this technology is being developed (supported by a contract from HSARPA) that will be as much as twenty times superior to current portals in its ability to distinguish isotopes, allowing more rapid identification with fewer false alarms.[24] A scan of a cargo container will take five seconds or less.[25] Other developments will essentially improve the existing technology, reducing the time taken to detect radiation and increasing the precision of energy and dosage measurement, or integrate it with other functions. For example, next generation PRDs, with a target price of $1,000, will be built into mobile phones and combine the functionality of radiation sensor, cellular phone, personal digital assistant with Internet access, and global positioning system locator.[26] Online connectivity means that they can form a radiation monitoring network, thus producing a radiation map.

The main priority of current deployment efforts must be to scan all traffic across U.S. land, sea, and air borders for radioactivity and to continue to build up the national detector network. As isotope-identifying detectors become available, they must take the place of the less sophisticated models

that monitor radioactivity. As always, technology will seek to reduce the cost and increase the speed, portability, and sensitivity of detectors, whose deficiencies in those areas currently limit the quality of radioactive screening. The DNDO is pushing the development of new technology. Development of off-shore detection capacity would be desirable, because even docking at a U.S. port would represent an opportunity for terrorists to inflict massive damage and casualties if a ship were carrying a nuclear weapon. Screening of the sea around a port over a radius of perhaps ten miles for the radioactivity characteristic of fissile materials would therefore be prudent, if feasible.[27] Buoys fitted with commercially available radiation detectors have recently been developed and deployed by the Defense Threat Reduction Agency at the entrance to the U.S. Navy submarine base at King's Bay, Georgia.[28] The main shortcoming is that shielded radioactive samples cannot yet be detected in this way, so the sensitivity of the detectors and their ability to discriminate against background signals needs to be improved. "Sensor fusion," in which different types of scans are performed simultaneously, can help to overcome the effects of shielding because it gathers complementary information and because the presence of heavy shielding is itself suspicious.[29]

Further ahead, active detectors that irradiate a sample with gamma-rays or neutrons in order to generate a signal will become available; there should be prototypes in the next couple of years. These can help to overcome the effects of shielding and give information on the spatial distribution of radioactive material, thus aiding in threat identification. The cost of each such machine is likely to be several million dollars. Detecting neutrons will always be more difficult than detecting gamma-rays because neutrons are more easily stopped by surrounding material.

Decisionmakers' awareness of what must be done is encouraging, and the government is continuing to make this effort a priority. The FY2006 Department of Homeland Security Appropriations Act allocated $318 million to the DNDO, of which $125 million is for the purchase and deployment of radiation portal monitors at ports of entry and at least $81 million is for research and development (R&D) into nuclear and radiological countermeasures.[30] The development of new technologies is being led by HSARPA, and the DNDO will "put a fence around dollars intended to transform that [nuclear detection] capability towards a next generation R&D effort."[31] In May 2005 work was begun on the construction by the Department of Energy (DoE) and the DHS of a radiological and nuclear countermeasures test and evaluation complex at the DoE's Nevada test site. This complex, which is scheduled to be operational in late 2006, will test detectors in mock-ups of real-life settings such as roads, border crossings, and airport checkpoints.[32] Though some have rightly counseled against excessive reliance on detection technology as opposed to securing stocks of highly enriched uranium, improvement in current detection capabilities is both possible and necessary. The emphasis on research and development therefore is justified.

Chemical Threats

The threat from chemical weapons is well understood, even if it can be difficult to defend against. The main vulnerability arises from lethal industrial chemicals, whether stored or in transit. Many, such as chlorine and ammonia, are kept in large quantities in chemical plants,[33] and approximately 300,000 tons of cyanide are stored by U.S. industry for use in areas such as printing and agriculture.[34] An attack on an industrial chemical plant close to a populous area could cause huge casualties, as proven by the 1984 disaster in Bhopal, India, which is conservatively estimated to have killed 4,000 people.[35] This underlines the importance of securing chemical plants and transport of chemicals in the vicinity or upwind of populous areas.

Aside from industrial stocks, readily available chemicals could be used to mount an attack. Organophosphate pesticides are chemically similar to nerve agents. Moreover, formulas and processes to produce military-grade nerve agents were declassified in the 1960s and 1970s and now are readily accessible through the literature and the Internet. Al Qaeda is known to publicize through the Internet methods of manufacturing chemical weapons that make use of household chemicals. However, although chemical weapons are the easiest of the unconventional weapons to make and obtain, distribution of the toxic agent involved is a major obstacle to a successful attack. Casualties are extremely unlikely to reach the level of those that could result from a nuclear or biological attack. Confined areas, such as an underground transportation system, are the most suitable scenes for a chemical attack; the Tokyo subway attack in 1995, using sarin gas, killed twelve people and injured more than 1,000, but it could have been far more deadly if it had been carried out differently.

Small quantities of some chemicals can be lethal; certain nerve agents can cause death if only a drop comes into contact with the skin, although some gases may require significant inhalation. Hence it may be almost impossible to detect some highly dangerous chemicals before they are released. Prompt detection and identification of chemicals in the event of an attack are essential in allowing rapid evacuation and isolation of the affected region, appropriate treatment of those injured, and initiation of procedures to minimize the spread of the toxic agent. Chemical sensors, costing around $20,000 each, have been operating in the Washington, D.C., subway system since 2003 as part of PROTECT (Program for Response Options and Technology Enhancements for Chemical/Biological Terrorism), which has since been extended to Boston.[36] These sensors perform rapid, automated identification of chemical agents, allowing an agent-dependent response to be swiftly implemented. No other U.S. subway system has been equipped in this way, however, and that gaping vulnerability should be remedied.

False alarms in automated chemical analysis are a concern, and further development is needed in several respects: reducing the size of the detectors; increasing the range of chemical agents that they can detect; increasing the speed, sensitivity, and reliability of identification; and increasing the extent of automation.[37] HSARPA currently is in the process of awarding funding for the development of the next generation of chemical sensors, which will detect vapors of very low concentration.[38] Developmental efforts also are in progress in the United Kingdom to produce cheap (around $10), small (button-sized) sensors to detect about twenty different types of chemicals, making installation on every subway carriage or cargo container, to name but two examples, a feasible proposition.[39] Other types of sensors currently under development are focused on long-range detection of chemicals by using the radiation that they absorb and scatter. That would allow scanning of large areas from a safe distance, which would be valuable when one is protecting mass gatherings of people, for example.[40]

The fact that the chemicals necessary to produce potent weapons are so commonplace means that controlling their sale is not a feasible method of preventing the production of weapons. Since the information needed to produce such weapons is widely available in libraries and on the Internet, preventing its dissemination is impossible. Access to pesticides is more amenable to regulation. However, though it already is necessary to obtain a license for restricted-use pesticides, the licensing process requires only that the application pass the necessary examinations. It would be wise to introduce a background check into the procedure.

More work is needed to develop an immediate response strategy to a chemical attack, in addition to clarifying the cleanup procedure. Questions regarding confinement and ventilation, the safest course of action that people in an affected location can take, identification of the nature of an attack, equipping of first responders, evacuation of the people affected, and treatment of the injured all must be addressed. The appropriate responses should be publicized and practiced so that authorities and responders, in particular, understand what the emergency procedures are and are ready to implement them. Practical steps to mitigate the effect of an attack are possible, but they must be thought through. In an underground mass transit system, inflatable barriers or curtains could be used to stop the spread of an agent. Other procedures depend on the agent: for example, venting the confined space with fresh air might save lives in the event of a mustard gas attack since the gas would be too dispersed, once outside, to cause serious injury. On the other hand, nerve gases could still be lethal even after emerging into the open air, and confinement would then be appropriate. In buildings, evacuation channels must be kept open by, for example, keeping positive air pressure in corridors and stairwells.

The likely spread of any chemical agent released can be modeled by computer, and doing so should be seen as an essential part of any city's preparation for a chemical, biological, or radiological attack.[41] Whether it should be carried out in an institution with an existing modeling capacity or whether a city should develop its own facility for that purpose could be decided on a case-by-case basis. First responders must have adequate means to identify the chemicals released to determine the threat that they present. Handheld detectors (costing in the region of $9,000) that can identify chemical traces in seconds are available as well as larger detectors (costing around $50,000) that can identify unknown solids and liquids in a few minutes; however, large-scale procurement of these products by the DHS has not yet taken place.[42]

Just as important, first responders must know how to recognize the symptoms associated with a chemical attack and how to obtain the appropriate antidote (if one exists) as quickly as possible. It is feasible to minimize the effect of a nerve agent by administering an ATNAA (antidote treatment nerve agent autoinjector) sufficiently quickly. Time is of the essence, however; in the case of the agent soman only two minutes are available in which to administer the antidote if it is to have the desired effect, whereas for VX sixty hours are available.[43] More development of antitoxins is needed; for example, the approach currently used to treat a cyanide attack is forty years old. A faster and simpler technique would be desirable.

Biological Threats

Information on techniques and procedures for cultivating and weaponizing biological pathogens is available on the Internet, so prohibiting the dissemination of that information is impossible. There are strict controls on the possession of medical-grade cultures, but the apparatus for cultivating biological agents (such as incubators) can be purchased easily, and monitoring such purchases might permit nefarious activity to be identified. It must be acknowledged, however, that biological agents can be prepared more readily than can a nuclear weapon, for example. And the threat of natural diseases must not be ignored; though unrelated to terrorism, an outbreak of some diseases could certainly undermine national security. The ongoing concern over the possible jump of the H5N1 avian flu virus to humans should act to spur development and acquisition of countermeasures (vaccines and antiviral drugs).[44] These tools also are integral to the effort to deal with bioterrorism. The Bush administration's announcement of a National Strategy for Pandemic Influenza shows a commendable sense of urgency, but it is too early to judge the efficacy of this effort.[45]

Technology contributes in two ways to countering the biological terrorism threat: first, in helping to detect an attack, and second, in developing medications that can prevent or treat infection. Rapid detection of an attack and identification of the biological agent involved are critical because, in addition to facilitating isolation of the point of attack and evacuation of surrounding areas, they can permit effective treatment of those infected but showing no symptoms. It may take some days, or even longer, for these to appear, by which stage mass infection could have taken place and some sufferers could be beyond cure.

As with certain chemical weapons, it can be very difficult to detect a dangerous quantity of a biological pathogen prior to an attack. An attack can be detected in several ways. The most obvious is to detect the presence of pathogens that have been released into the environment. Current detector technology for pathogens, however, is not as well developed as that for chemical or radioactive materials, and automated detection systems are only now becoming available. Under the BioWatch program, sensors were installed in more than thirty U.S. cities to detect biowarfare pathogens, piggybacking on a pollution-sensor system built by the EPA. Samples are collected from these sensors every day, but only after analysis at the nearest laboratory in the Centers for Disease Control and Prevention (CDC) network can a pathogen be identified. This is a slow, costly, and labor-intensive detection system. There also has been criticism over the lack of preparation in the BioWatch program regarding what to do in the event of an alarm resulting from the positive detection of pathogens.[46] Intensive research is in progress to develop the next generation of pathogen detectors. HSARPA has called for a number of new biosensor types:[47] bioagent autonomous networked detectors (BAND), costing $25,000 or less and capable of performing preliminary analysis before sounding an alert; rapid automated biological identification system (RABIS) devices, costing $50,000 each and capable of identifying a dangerous pathogen level in less than one minute;[48] and instantaneous bio-aerosol detector systems (IBADS), costing (depending on the precise details) up to $50,000 each and capable of carrying out rapid, automated, and reliable identification of bio-aerosols. The BAND and RABIS devices must each be able to scan for at least twenty different pathogens. Several other technologies are ready for implementation, including the autonomous pathogen detector system, which can scan for eleven different pathogens and identify various viruses, bacteria, and toxins in less than one hour, and a handheld pathogen detector for use by first responders.[49]

Although in the future detectors should be the most rapid method of detecting a biowarfare attack, monitoring of reported medical cases, admissions to hospitals, and prescriptions filled can also allow the identification of a disease outbreak. Physicians, who may have been trained some years ago, must be given information on how to recognize symptoms that could result from a biological attack, which might mimic those of a common disease.[50] According to a 2005 report by the Trust for America's Health,[51] almost half of U.S. states do not track disease outbreak information in a way that matches national standards (in 2004 this figure was two-thirds), and nearly 20 percent of the states report that they do not have enough laboratory scientists to manage tests for a suspected anthrax or plague outbreak (though this is a marked improvement over the 2004 figure of 60 percent).[52] This indicates an inadequate capacity to identify an attack.

The idea of using symptoms, as opposed to diagnoses, to identify a biowarfare attack ("syndromic surveillance") has been proposed, and it already is being implemented on a small scale in various jurisdictions. This approach is less hindered by physicians' difficulty in diagnosing unfamiliar ailments quickly and accurately, and it could even include airport surveillance for people carrying disease, which would afford a general public health benefit.[53] Syndromic surveillance also gathers information on statistics such as over-the-counter drug use and work absenteeism. New York City's surveillance program costs $1.5 million a year.[54] A major obstacle to effective national syndromic surveillance, however, is the lack of integration and standardization among different state programs. Individual jurisdictions have their own software systems and analysis algorithms. The CDC does have its BioSense program for disease detection by data analysis,[55] which could become the national standard, but states continue to use their individual systems. Furthermore, sensitivity to the privacy requirements of the Health

Insurance Portability and Accountability Act of 1996 (HIPAA) also is hampering the data sharing necessary for syndromic surveillance. Steps should be taken to integrate and standardize syndromic surveillance efforts, and data sharing that does not identify individual patients must be facilitated.

An adequate stockpile of effective medication and a plan for its distribution are essential to countering bioterrorism. The Strategic National Stockpile (SNS)—now, correctly, returned to the management of the CDC since the signing of the 2004 Project Bioshield legislation—is a distributed stockpile of antibiotics, chemical antidotes, antitoxins, life-support medications, intravenous drugs, airway maintenance supplies, and medical and surgical items.[56] In the event of an emergency, any state in the United States can be reached with supplies within twelve hours. It makes sense for the focus of preparation to be on known pathogens, since those are the ones most likely to be used by terrorists. However, the range of vaccines, antibiotics, and antiviral drugs that the SNS contains does not adequately address the threat. Vaccines do not exist for all the known viral pathogens, and only two new classes of antibiotic have been discovered in the past thirty years, raising the specter of an attack with antibiotic-resistant bacteria.[57] Such bacteria—for example, methicillin-resistant *Staphylococcus aureus* (MRSA)—also constitute a major public health concern.

The National Response Plan, which is an all-hazards approach to dealing with terrorist attacks and laying out the proper roles of various institutional actors and layers of government, goes some way toward preparing for a bioterrorism attack, but the nation's capacity for implementing the response—distributing medications and administering vaccines as appropriate—is inadequate.[58] Over most of the country the state of readiness for distribution of medication is wanting; only seven states and two cities have achieved "green" status for the SNS, indicating adequate preparation for the administration and distribution of medical countermeasures.[59] An idea currently under consideration is to have postal workers perform the task of distributing countermeasures to people's homes, but it requires further planning. These workers must be protected from biological agents at large and guarded against potential assault from people attempting to forcibly take possession of the life-saving goods. That will require the involvement of the police or National Guard, which must be realistically planned and supported; they may be subject to many demands during a period of emergency. One recently suggested method of planning the response to a biological attack is based on risk and decision trees; it is claimed that that would allow the government to "better characterize the costs, risks, and benefits of different policy options and ensure the integration of policy development."[60] In view of the current lack of adequate planning, this recommendation merits consideration.[61] As far as prophylactic administration of vaccines is concerned, recent evidence from the 2003 effort to vaccinate emergency and medical workers against smallpox shows that people are unwilling to subject themselves to vaccines, which normally carry a degree of risk, in anticipation of an attack whose probability is unknown.[62] If the level of threat is sufficiently high to justify the expense and risk, then that must be explained openly. If not, the vaccination program should not be carried out.

The distribution of funds for preparation is a constant bone of contention. Nearly one-third of states cut their public health budgets over FY2003–04, and federal bioterrorism funding decreased by more than $1 million per state in 2004[63] and was not completely restored in 2005.[64] The CDC Cities Readiness Initiative, through which funding is given to twenty-one U.S. cities in order to increase their capacity to deliver medical countermeasures in an emergency, is an appropriate program, but it has been funded at the expense of—not in addition to—state and local efforts.[65] Furthermore, some contend that the focus on bioterrorism is jeopardizing public health, through failure to focus on known and ever-present risks and ailments, the reordering of research priorities (which could undermine U.S. ability to tackle biological pathogens in the long term),[66] and the construction of level 4 research laboratories, which may themselves pose a risk to health by virtue of the virulent pathogens that they house. However, in view of the potentially catastrophic effect of a biological attack, the focus on bioterrorism is largely justified and much of the funding, particularly for the National Institutes of Health (NIH), has been in addition to, rather than instead of, previous support.[67] With suitable precautions it is possible to ensure that virulent pathogens cannot escape from a level 4 research laboratory.

As is often the case in science, unforeseen and collateral benefits almost certainly will result from biosecurity research. The ability to boost the function of the human immune system could be of wide applicability and great value. Priority should be given, whenever possible, to efforts that will be of benefit to both preparations for a biological attack and ordinary public health needs (including preparation for future pandemics, whether of flu or of other illnesses), and a long-term strategy should be adopted so that U.S. research capabilities in the future are not compromised. Technology should not be supported at the cost of investment in the nation's public health infrastructure; if the basic infrastructure is lacking, America will represent an exceedingly vulnerable target both to attacks and outbreaks of more common diseases such as flu. In addition, the United States must not fail to train a cadre of experts who can contribute in the long term to strengthening the nation's defenses against biological threats. Some universities already are offering graduate programs in biodefense, and it has been estimated that the nation needs "at least 7,000 to 12,000 trained biodefenders working for the military, intelligence agencies, law enforcement and first-responder services, and in the medical and engineering fields."[68]

To meet the need for new vaccines and antibiotics it has been deemed necessary to enlist the help of the private sector, with its resources of capital, facilities, and expertise. However, drug companies are unwilling to invest in vaccines against possible bioterrorism agents as there is no guarantee that they will ever be used, and other types of drugs (for, say, heart disease) are much more lucrative. Project Bioshield was developed to entice the private sector to join in the effort to develop new vaccines and other medications, and $5.6 billion was pledged over ten years to fund private sector development of these countermeasures.[69] However, the Bioshield bill has not done enough to engage the private sector.[70] Large companies are still reluctant to get involved because the U.S. government will be the only customer, the profit margins are low, and there are concerns about intellectual property rights (especially during a crisis) and liability in the event of an adverse reaction to a medication. The latter is important because the Bioshield bill allows the Food and Drug Administration to permit the administration of a drug or vaccine during an emergency before it has been fully licensed. The Safety Act provides liability protection to certified technologies in the event of a terrorist attack, but it affords no protection for technology if there is no attack, placing vaccine and drug manufacturers in a potentially vulnerable position.[71] As explained in chapter 7, medical countermeasures are different from other technologies because it may be impossible to test them on infected people until there is an actual outbreak; hence preventative deployment carries a greater risk.

To address these concerns, various bills have been brought before Congress to further increase the attractiveness of vaccine development.[72] Proposals include absolving drug companies from liability and allowing them to extend their patents on particularly lucrative drugs. The latter measure may be a step too far, as it could prevent the proliferation of cheaper, generic drugs with wider societal benefit.[73] To avoid a giveaway to the private sector, the government may have to establish its own laboratories, "Manhattan Project" style, dedicated to developing vaccines, antibiotics, and antiviral drugs.[74] Use of government laboratory facilities was recommended by the Gilmore

Commission several years ago.[75] Concerns would include the necessary capital investment and the business model for producing the medications. One of the bills referred to above, S. 1873, includes a proposal to establish an advanced biomedical research and development agency within the Department of Health and Human Services (DHHS) to coordinate bioterrorism countermeasure development. "Warm base" programs that can commence production on short notice in the event of an attack could be maintained by such government laboratories; otherwise, the government will have to provide support to the private sector.

In the development of countermeasures, there is the question of priorities. Should the three prongs to counter bioterrorism—vaccines, antibiotics, and antiviral drugs—be given equal emphasis? They should. The threat that antibiotics address is different from that addressed by the other two, and, as noted, antibiotic-resistant bacteria are an increasing problem. The uses of vaccines and antiviral drugs are somewhat complementary. An antiviral tends to be applicable to a wider range of pathogens than does an individual vaccine, and it is not possible to determine in advance whether a vaccine or antiviral drug will be agent-specific or of broader applicability. Furthermore, vaccines can be too strong for some people. As an example, the existing smallpox vaccine produces a serious adverse reaction in thirty people per million,[76] of whom one, on average, will die (for a more typical vaccine, only one person per million will suffer a severe reaction).[77] An antiviral drug would be of benefit to somebody who is not strong enough to accept the vaccine. In addition, development of a vaccine usually takes around eight years, and, at a cost of $800 million, it does not always represent the optimum use of money.[78] As with antibiotics, antiviral drugs and vaccines have varying degrees of public health benefit, and development of all three prongs should be supported.

There is an urgent need to address the shortcomings in the management of the SNS, in the plans for response to an attack, and in the preparations for a post-attack cleanup. Recent reports have criticized both the lack of a coordinated plan at the federal level to prepare for a biological terrorist attack[79] and the lack of adequate preparation in most states.[80] Per Homeland Security Presidential Directive 7, promulgated in December 2003, the DHS has the lead role in coordinating the overall national effort to protect critical U.S. infrastructure and key resources, while the DHHS has particular responsibility for public health and healthcare. Hence it falls to the DHHS to rectify the inadequate coordination and provision in the nation's preparations for a biological terror attack and to integrate the efforts at the different levels of government.

Surface-to-Air Missiles

The potential threat presented by man-portable air defense systems (MANPADS) is illustrated by the attacks on a passenger airliner in Kenya in 2002 and on a cargo jet in Iraq in 2003. As of May 2004, between 500,000 and 750,000 MANPADS were believed to be in the world, an unknown number of which are poorly secured and susceptible to theft by terrorists.[81] In November 2004, the U.S. government estimated that 6,000 MANPADS may be outside the control of any government,[82] but there is considerable uncertainty as to the number of missiles in the hands of terrorist organizations; some estimates are as high as 150,000.[83] The U.S. Department of State estimates that at least nine terrorist groups, including al Qaeda, have obtained some type of MANPADS;[84] other estimates range as high as thirty groups.[85] For a buyer with the right connections, the black market price can be as low as $5,000, easily afforded by any moderately funded group.[86] The effective lifetime of a MANPADS is uncertain;[87] some experts maintain that, with proper care, a missile can remain useful for at least twenty-two years.[88] If so, those disseminated during the cold war by the United States and the Soviet Union for proxy conflicts remain a threat.

It is estimated that a commercial aircraft has as much as a 70 percent chance of being lost if hit by a single missile; with two hits, the probability of loss is close to 100 percent.[89] In addition to the intrinsic destruction, the economic impact of a successful attack could be severe. A 2005 RAND report estimated that the direct cost of losing a jet and its passengers would be $1 billion, based on the value of the aircraft and the insurance liability for the dead, and that the total economic impact could be more than $15 billion, assuming a systemwide shutdown of air travel for a week following an attack and a longer-term fall in demand for air travel of 15 to 25 percent.[90] (However, were it possible to keep the majority of planes flying after an attack and to reassure travelers that flying was still the safest form of transportation, much of the negative impact could be avoided. Governments should liaise with the aircraft industry to explore how that could be accomplished.) Various approaches to diminishing the MANPADS threat are possible:

—reducing the number of MANPADS in circulation

—making an attack more difficult by improving airport security or reducing the predictability of aircraft trajectories

—deflecting a missile off course

—destroying a missile in flight

—making airplanes more robust against a hit

To reduce the number of MANPADS at large, the CIA attempted to buy back Stinger missiles in Afghanistan during the late 1980s and the 1990s. Despite pushing the black market price as high as $100,000, it was able to reclaim only seventy of the 900 missiles sold to the mujahedeen in the 1980s.[91] A similar program in Iraq has yielded only a few hundred of the thousands of MANPADS believed to be part of the pre-war Iraqi arsenal.[92] In September 2005 the Department of State reported that, through bilateral and multilateral efforts involving the United States, more than 13,000 MANPADS in thirteen countries in Africa, Central America, eastern Europe, and South East Asia had been destroyed since 2003.[93] The total number of MANPADS destroyed up to that point was 17,000, and the United States had received commitments for the destruction of more than 7,000 more.[94] The moral seems to be that buy-back and decommissioning programs can be useful in reducing the number of MANPADS at large but that they must begin before the weapons fall into the hands of those who are highly motivated to attack the United States and for whom monetary inducements hold little attraction. Nonproliferation treaties and controls on arms sales are crucial in preventing new technology from falling into the hands of those intending to attack the United States.[95]

To assess the other approaches to countering MANPADS, it is necessary to say a little about the characteristics of the weapon.[96] For the most part, MANPADS are guided by infrared heat-seeking devices, whose capabilities vary according to the missile's production era. First-generation missiles, from the 1960s, target the heat of an aircraft's engine but can do so only when chasing the aircraft; the maximum altitude of the target is about one mile.[97] Their simple targeting system is susceptible to confusion by background heat sources, including the sun, and therefore is amenable to being deflected by decoys. These are the most widely proliferated type of MANPADS, believed to be in the hands of al Qaeda, Chechen rebels, the Taliban, the Tamil Tigers, Hezbollah, and the Revolutionary Armed Forces of Colombia (FARC), among others.

The second generation dates from the 1970s and discriminates better against background radiation and decoys; head-on assaults and assaults from the side also are possible. The range of attack is about 2.5 miles, and the maximum altitude of the target is a little less than two miles. These missiles have not been as widely proliferated as the first generation, but al Qaeda and other groups do possess them. The third generation was developed during the 1970s and early 1980s. These weapons have a range of up to four miles, a maximum target altitude of more than two miles (though it is lower if the target is fast moving), and the ability to recognize and reject decoy flares.

They are even less widely proliferated, but they are known to be in the possession of Chechen rebels, and it is likely that al Qaeda and the Taliban also have them.[98] Fourth-generation missiles, only now entering operation, will have greater range. Less common MANPADS include those that are radio controlled by the operator while in flight and those that follow a laser beam spot on the target. Since they are controlled by people, they could be less susceptible to countermeasures. The former are difficult to operate, though. The latter, however, cannot be jammed because there is no communication between ground and missile, and in the future may require only initial target identification by the operator.

To improve airport security, surveillance of the airport perimeter and its environs should be improved; that would help in combating terrorism generally. However, given that the typical climb gradient for an aircraft is between 400 and 500 feet per mile, a plane will have to travel at least twenty miles before it is out of the range of a MANPADS missile. It is unrealistic to expect surveillance to cover an area of 1,200 square miles or more around every airport (or even the 300 square miles associated with a single flight path) to detect anyone intending to perpetrate a missile attack.[99] Furthermore, the MANPADS threat is greater outside the United States than within it (an assessment based purely on the relative numbers of weapons available and number of people inclined to use them), and the United States cannot rely on the capability and willingness of countries all over the world, especially in troubled areas, to perform surveillance to the necessary standard. Varying the approach and departure patterns of the aircraft would be complicated to implement, difficult to reconcile with passenger information needs, and ineffective against patient attackers. Hence it could not be used as a general modus operandi, but it could be used in response to specific intelligence. Increasing the gradient of an aircraft's trajectory would not yield a great reduction in the range of the aircraft's vulnerability (probably no more than a factor of 2),[100] and passengers would not welcome the change.

Measures to reduce an airplane's heat signature in the event of a missile launch are possible, though they are technically challenging because there would only be a matter of seconds to respond following the detection of an incoming missile. Such measures could include shielding or ducting the engine exhaust; mixing exhaust gases with cold ambient air; minimizing the use of auxiliary power units; using lower engine power settings; and reducing engine power to the minimum required to sustain flight at a safe altitude.[101] These measures would reduce the probability of a successful strike.

Ground surveillance to detect missile launches could be implemented in the United States, and proposals to develop a "networked, electro-optic sensor grid," data-linked to the airborne plane, were contained in the FY2004 Department of Defense budget justification. Onboard surveillance would be preferable, since it permits an aircraft to be alert no matter where it is. However, the current high false alarm rate of onboard missile warning systems means that this approach is not ready for implementation. Surveillance makes sense only if useful action can be taken after detection to avoid a hit. Evasive action is a rather unfeasible form of defense since the incoming missile is in flight for less than ten seconds, leaving little time for response, and large commercial airliners are not easily maneuverable.[102] Transport planes might even break up or go out of control if subjected to such extreme stresses. A recently announced alternative uses a directed high-power microwave weapon to damage the electronics of the missile's guidance system; it is believed to be effective against all currently available MANPADS.[103] The cost is estimated to be $25 million per airport if a minimum of twenty-five systems is built, so that it would cost less than $1 billion to protect airports that handle 70 percent of U.S. takeoffs and landings. On the other hand, given that the threat from MANPADS is greater outside the United States, on-board capacity for defense would be preferable.

Different on-board techniques to send a missile off course are available. The first, already widely used by the military, is to shoot out hot flares from the plane to act as decoy targets. Israeli systems based on this approach, using flares that are invisible to the human eye, are being installed on passenger jets, at a cost of around $1 million per system (buying a new Airbus or Boeing jet costs roughly $200 million).[104] With funding from the DHS, a team led by United Airlines is developing a conceptually similar system: after detection of an incoming missile, "pyrophoric" countermeasures (which ignite on contact with air) would be released to guide the missile off course; it is claimed that the two-second burn time means that they do not present a danger at ground level.[105] The difficulty and expense of maintaining such systems are a matter of concern, and laser-based jamming systems may be superior both in this regard and in terms of deflecting modern missiles. Pyrophoric countermeasures, therefore, are unlikely to be a long-term solution to the MANPADS threat.

An infrared (IR) jamming system currently in use employs pulsed heat lamps on the body of a jet to create a diffuse IR signature that makes the missile's IR-based heat sensor less effective. An example of such a product is the

ALQ-204 Matador,[106] which is estimated to cost $3.5 million, including installation and crew training.[107] A more advanced technique, known as a directed infrared countermeasure (DIRCM), involves the use of a turntable-mounted IR laser on the body of the plane to blind the guidance system of a MANPADS missile whose attack is detected. This type of approach has been identified by a White House task force as being the most promising technology, and its development received $120 million in funding for 2004 and 2005.[108] The 2006 budget proposal includes $110 million to "continue to research the viability of technical countermeasures for commercial aircraft against the threat of shoulder-fired missiles," and testing on air cargo planes will be carried out.[109] A current shortcoming is the short mean time between system failures, only 300 hours. That equates to only forty transatlantic flights, roughly a factor of 10 below the acceptable level.[110] According to the DHS, the DIRCM approach is effective against current threats,[111] but there are doubts about its effectiveness against next-generation MANPADS. The DHS has specified various performance, cost, and technical standards that systems to send missiles off course must meet.[112] The cost of the 1,000th unit must be no more than $1 million and the false alarm rate must be no more than 1 per 100 takeoffs or landings. The cost requirements can be met by DIRCM systems,[113] and their maintenance could be easier and cheaper than that of decoy-based systems.[114] Since there are about 7,000 aircraft in the U.S. commercial fleet, mass installation of DIRCM systems will cost many billions of dollars. The RAND report estimated that the purchase cost would be $11.2 billion and the annual operating and support costs would be $2.1 billion ($300,000 per aircraft).[115] Such costs must, however, be compared with the potential cost and upheaval following a successful attack. Provided that proliferation of next-generation MANPADS can be restricted, the DIRCM should, with development, offer a technically feasible defense against MANPADS.

To shoot down shoulder-launched missiles in flight, Northrop-Grumman has designed its hazardous ordnance engagement toolkit (HORNET), which would use a ground-based chemical laser to destroy the missiles.[116] In principle this is attractive; high-power lasers have successfully shot down artillery and slower-moving missiles in the past, albeit under test conditions.[117] However, HORNET is still at the conceptual stage and has been deemed "ineffective" by the DHS.[118] The DHS strategy seems to be to make each plane defensively self-sufficient, which is wise, whereas each HORNET installation covers only a particular space. Furthermore, due to the limited range of the laser's shoot-down capability (around five kilometers), each airport would need a number of such systems to protect the area over which aircraft are vulnerable. Given that Northrop-Grumman estimates that each system would cost "in the low tens of millions of dollars," the cost to protect the thirty-one airports that account for 70 percent of U.S. takeoffs and landings would be several billion dollars.[119] Moreover, as pointed out by RAND (and as in the case of the high-power microwave jamming system), it would be difficult to ensure protection of U.S. aircraft in foreign countries by such a ground-based, and expensive, system. Hence, even when (or if) the technology is proven, the HORNET is unlikely to provide adequate protection.

Aircraft can be strengthened and modified to better resist a missile attack. This is a longer-term project, since even retrofit modifications to existing aircraft are still at the developmental stage and most of the improvements will entail changes in the design of future planes.[120] Particular areas of focus would include hardening and shielding the engines, whose heat signature makes them the target of incoming missiles; adaptive controls that would improve the handling of damaged aircraft; separation of hydraulic and fuel systems from areas likely to be hit; self-sealing fuel-feed lines; fluid shut-off mechanisms in the rear portions of the engines; gas generator systems (to fill empty space in the fuel tanks with inert gas instead of oxygen); and even relocation of the engines away from the wing fuel tanks.[121] Some of these measures could also be beneficial in protecting general aircraft against mechanical failures. In the short to medium term, however, the preventative and attack-thwarting mechanisms described above will take precedence. Preventing a hit will always be preferable, ceteris paribus, to having to withstand it.

The 2005 report from the RAND Corporation advocates a layered strategy, emphasizing that steps to protect airport perimeters, counter the proliferation of MANPADS, and strengthen aircraft against attack should be implemented in addition to the development of countermeasures.[122] This is highly compatible with the discussion above. Export controls must be aimed at preventing proliferation of the next generation of MANPADS, which will be available to advanced countries beginning some time between 2006 and 2010 and against which the technologies discussed above, except the ground-based HORNET and high-power microwave systems, will be of limited utility. The goal is to prevent these new weapons from falling into the hands of non-state actors. Since the existing threat cannot easily be diminished, current DHS support for countermeasure development is appropriate. RAND counseled against mass installation of on-board countermeasures at this time, on the grounds of their current unreliability and exorbitant expense; that is a sensible recommendation. In light of the likely public reaction and wider economic implications in the event of a successful attack on a commercial passenger plane, even if the government and industry leaders can reduce the severity of the consequences, perfecting a countermeasure is an urgent priority.

In summary, the government must put in place the infrastructure necessary to scan all traffic coming across U.S. land, sea, and air borders for radioactivity, with isotope identification capability. To improve biological attack detection, tracking of disease must be standardized across the states and more laboratory scientists trained and hired. States, in cooperation with the DHHS, must develop realistic, robust plans for distributing and administering medications in the event of an attack, while Congress should pass a bill granting liability protection to medical countermeasures administered prophylactically in an emergency. In addition, a greater national effort must get under way to develop medical countermeasures, either by harnessing the power of the private sector or establishing government laboratories. To tackle the MANPADS threat the government should improve the surveillance of airport perimeters, fund the development of infrared countermeasures, pursue further international counterproliferation agreements, and make preparations to keep planes flying and passengers traveling in the wake of an attack.

Notes

1. Some, therefore, have recently proposed restricting the term "weapons of mass destruction" to nuclear and biological weapons only.

2. A program of public education and awareness improvement would be beneficial in demystifying these weapons and enabling people to respond in an appropriate way in the event of an attack.

3. Though, as discussed below, governments can play a role in minimizing the disruption caused by such an attack by helping to avoid a mass grounding of planes.

4. Elizabeth Eraker, "Cleanup after a Radiological Attack: U.S. Prepared Guidance," *Nonproliferation Review* (Fall-Winter 2004).

5. National Research Council, "Reopening Public Facilities after a Biological Attack: A Decisionmaking Framework" (Washington: National Academies Press, 2004).

6. Department of Homeland Security, National Response Plan (December 2004).

7. "First Responders, Remediators Want 'Smart' Radiation Detectors," *Nuclear Waste News*, November 18, 2004.

8. Dennis Slaughter, "Detecting Well-Shielded Highly Enriched Uranium," Lawrence Livermore National Laboratory (rdc.llnl.gov/rdp/uranium.html [February 2, 2005]).

9. *Proceedings of the International Conference on Security of Radioactive Sources,* Vienna, Austria, March 10–13, 2003 (www-pub.iaea.org/MTCD/publications/PDF/pub1165_web.pdf [February 2, 2005]).

10. Robert C. Bonner, commissioner, U.S. Customs and Border Protection, remarks at CBP Trade Symposium, Washington, D.C., November 3, 2005.

11. Department of Homeland Security, press release, June 3, 2005 (www.dhs.gov/dhspublic/display?theme=43&content=4530 [December 12, 2005]).

12. Robert C. Bonner, commissioner, U.S. Customs and Border Protection, remarks to Kansas City Chamber of Commerce, Kansas City, Mo., May 16, 2005.

13. Joseph C. McDonald, Bert M. Coursey, and Michael Carter, "Detecting Illicit Radioactive Sources," *Physics Today,* November 2004, pp. 36–41.

14. U.S. Government Accountability Office, "Preventing Nuclear Smuggling: DOE Has Made Limited Progress in Installing Radiation Detection Equipment at Highest-Priority Foreign Seaports," GAO-05-375 (March 2005).

15. House Report 108-212: Energy and Water Development Appropriations Bill, 2004 (thomas.loc.gov/cgi-bin/cpquery/?&db_id=cp108&r_n=hr212.108&sel=TOC_288233& [February 3, 2005]).

16. U.S. Government Accountability Office, "Preventing Nuclear Smuggling."

17. Interview remarks to Michael d'Arcy by Joseph C. McDonald, senior chief scientist, Radiological Science and Engineering Group, Pacific Northwest National Laboratory, February 8, 2005.

18. Robert C. Bonner, commissioner, U.S. Customs and Border Protection, remarks at DHS Cargo Security Summit, Georgetown University, December 17, 2004. See also U.S. Customs and Border Protection, *Performance and Annual Report, Fiscal Year 2004.*

19. James Bone, "New York on Guard for 'Dirty Bomb,'" *The Times* (London), July 6, 2002.

20. Interview remarks to Michael d'Arcy by Joseph C. McDonald, February 8, 2005.

21. People have triggered hand-held and fixed radiation detectors in and around New York City after having received medical treatment with radioactive isotopes; see also Charles Graeber, "Building the Nuke Wall," *Wired,* April 2003 (wired.com/wired/archive/11.04/start.html?pg=10 [January 31, 2005]).

22. American National Standards Institute, *ANSI Standard N42.32-35* (New York, 2003); DHS, press release, "U.S. Department of Homeland Security Issues First Radiological and Nuclear Detectors Standards," February 27, 2004 (www.dhs.gov/dhspublic/display?content=3305 [February 3, 2005]); DHS, press release, "Fact Sheet: U.S. Department of Homeland Security Adopted Standards for Radiation and Nuclear Detection Equipment," February 27, 2004 (www.dhs.gov/dhspublic/display?content=3307 [February 3, 2005]).

23. Gabriele Rennie, "Portable Radiation Detector Provides Laboratory-Scale Precision in the Field," *LLNL Science and Technology Review* (September 2003).

24. "Monitoring System Identifies Illicit Nuclear Materials in Transit without False Alarms," *Business Wire*, January 18, 2005.

25. In conformance with the ANSI requirements; e-mail to Michael d'Arcy from Rod Keyser, ORTEC, February 4, 2005.

26. Gabriele Rennie, "Radiation Detection on the Front Lines," *LLNL Science and Technology Review* (September 2004), p. 4; Jenny Hogan, "A Phone to Sniff Out Dirty Bombs," *New Scientist*, December 11, 2004.

27. Based on the blast effect of a 1 megaton nuclear bomb; see National Terror Alert, "Homeland Security: Nuclear Blast and Fallout Information" (www.national-terroralert.com/readyguide/nuclear.htm [March 20, 2005]).

28. Arnie Heller, "Smart Buoys Help Protect Submarine Base," *LLNL Science and Technology Review* (January-February 2004), p. 19.

29. Joseph Callerame, AS&E chief technology officer, quoted in Steven Johnson, "Stopping Loose Nukes," *Wired*, November 2002 (www.wired.com/wired/archive/10.11/nukes_pr.html [January 31, 2005]).

30. Department of Homeland Security Appropriations Act 2006, October 18, 2005 (Public Law 109-90).

31. Remarks of Admiral James Loy, acting secretary for homeland security, February 7, 2005.

32. See Department of Energy, "Radiological/Nuclear Countermeasures Test and Evaluation Complex" (www.nv.doe.gov/nationalsecurity/homelandsecurity/radnuc.htm [December 12, 2005]); Joe Fiorill, "Experts Question U.S. Emphasis on Nuclear Weapons Detection," *Global Security Newswire*, June 8, 2005 (www.nti.org/d_newswire/issues/2005_6_8.html#82E8A0AB [June 8, 2005]).

33. Richard Falkenrath, statement before the Senate Committee on Homeland Security and Governmental Affairs, 109 Cong., 1 sess., April 27, 2005.

34. Interview remarks to Michael d'Arcy by Bruce Clements, associate director of education and training, Institute for Biosecurity, School of Public Health, St. Louis University, June 29, 2005.

35. Some estimates range as high as 16,000 deaths; see the editorial in *Lancet* 356, no. 9245 (December 2, 2000).

36. Katrina Kernodle, "Chemical and Biological Agent Detection Systems—Pilot Programs in Washington, D.C. and Boston Transit," Frances Kernodle Associates (www.fkassociates.com/Chemical%20and%20Biological.html [March 9, 2005]).

37. Interview remarks to Michael d'Arcy by Page Stoutland, deputy division leader for programs, R-Division, Lawrence Livermore National Laboratory, March 4, 2005.

38. Homeland Security Advanced Research Projects Agency (HSARPA) Broad Agency Announcement (BAA) 04-10: Low Vapor Pressure Chemicals Detection Systems (LVPCDS) Program (www.hsarpabaa.com/main/BAA0410_solicitation_notice.htm [March 9, 2005]).

39. Bobbie Johnson, "The Sweet Smell of Security," *Guardian*, January 20, 2005.

40. See, for example, Avir Sensors, Charlottesville, Va., "Platform Technology for Remote Chemical Sensors" (www.avirsensors.com/tech.html [March 9, 2005]).

41. See the National Research Council, "Tracking and Predicting the Atmospheric Dispersion of Hazardous Material Releases" (Washington: National Academies Press, 2003).

42. Interview remarks to Michael d'Arcy by Chris Lins, manager, Southeast Account, Smiths Detection, February 25, 2005.

43. Interview remarks to Michael d'Arcy by Bruce Clements, School of Public Health, St. Louis University, June 29, 2005.

44. John Oxford, "We Can't Afford to Be Caught Napping Again,' *The Times* (London), October 20, 2005.

45. White House, "National Strategy for Pandemic Influenza," November 1, 2005 (http://www.whitehouse.gov/homeland/pandemic-influenza.html [December 12, 2005])

46. Patrick Libbey, executive director of the National Association of County and City Health Officials, quoted by Dee Ann Divis, "BioWar: BioWatch Response Plans Lacking," United Press International, December 8, 2004.

47. Michael P. McLoughlin, program manager, HSARPA, BAA04-18, "Instantaneous Bio-Aerosol Detector Systems (IBADS) Program Overview" (www.hsarpabaa.com/Solicitations/IBADS-Michael-McLoughlin-Briefing.pdf [December 12, 2005]).

48. Homeland Security Advanced Research Projects Agency (HSARPA), Research Announcement 03-01, "Detection Systems for Biological and Chemical Countermeasures (DSBCC)," September 23, 2003 (www.hsarpabaa.com/Solicitations/HSARPA_RA-03-01_Body.pdf [March 9, 2005]).

49. Ann Parker, "Detecting Bioaerosols: When Time Is of the Essence," *LLNL Science and Technology Review* (October 2004) p. 4; Ann Parker, "Rapid Field Detection of Biological Agents," *LLNL Science and Technology Review* (January-February 2002).

50. Bruce Clements and R. Gregory Evans, "The Doctor's Role in Bioterrorism," *Lancet* 364, no. 1 (Supplement) (December 2004): 26–27.

51. Trust for America's Health, "Ready or Not? 2005" (Washington: December 2005).

52. Trust for America's Health, "Ready or Not? 2004" (Washington: December 2004).

53. As suggested by Richard Wilson and others, World Federation of Scientists, International Seminars on Planetary Emergencies, 33rd session, Erice, Sicily, May 4–9, 2005.

54. The Century Foundation, "Breathing Easier? Report of the Century Foundation Working Group on Bioterrorism Preparedness" (New York: December 2004).

55. CDC Public Health Information Network (PHIN): BioSense (www.cdc.gov/phin/component-initiatives/biosense/ [June 29, 2005]).

56. "CDC Emergency Preparedness and Response—Strategic National Stockpile," April 14, 2005 (www.bt.cdc.gov/stockpile/ [March 9, 2005]).

57. Gerald L. Epstein, CSIS, testimony before the Senate Committee on Health, Education, Labor, and Pensions, 109 Cong., 1 sess., February 8, 2005.

58. Department of Homeland Security, *National Response Plan* (December 2004); Elin Gursky, Thomas V. Inglesby, and Tara O'Toole, "Anthrax 2001: Observations on

the Medical and Public Health Response," *Biosecurity and Bioterrorism* 1, no. 2 (2003): 97–110; and Warren Rudman and others, "Our Hair Is on Fire," *Wall Street Journal*, December 16, 2004, p. 16.

59. Trust for America's Health, "Ready or Not? 2005."

60. Kimberly M. Thompson, Robert E. Armstrong, and Donald F. Thompson, "Bayes, Bugs, and Bioterrorists: Lessons Learned from the Anthrax Attacks," National Defense University, April 2005.

61. See testimony of John Deutch, Massachusetts Institute of Technology, before the Senate Committee on Health, Education, Labor, and Pensions, Subcommittee on Bioterrorism and Public Health Preparedness, 109 Cong., 1 sess., May 11, 2005 (www. bavariannordic.com/pdf/marketservice/Deutch_bioterrorism_testimony.pdf [June 8, 2005]).

62. John Mintz and Jody Warrick, "U.S. Unprepared despite Progress, Experts Say," *Washington Post*, November 8, 2004.

63. Trust for America's Health, "Ready or Not? 2004."

64. Trust for America's Health, "Ready or Not? 2005."

65. "Bioterrorism: America Still Unprepared," Democratic Staff of the House Select Committee on Homeland Security, 108 Cong., 2 sess., October 2004.

66. S. Altman and others, "An Open Letter to Elias Zerhouni," *Science* 307, no. 5714 (March 4, 2005), p. 1409.

67. Remarks of Penrose C. (Parney) Albright, assistant secretary for science and technology, DHS, to the Washington Science Policy Alliance, American Association for the Advancement of Science, Washington, March 1, 2005.

68. Ken Alibek, executive director for education at the National Center for Biodefense, George Mason University (and former first deputy chief of the civilian branch of the Soviet Union's offensive biological weapons program), quoted by Chris Schneidmiller in "Universities Prepare New Defenders against Bioterror," *Global Security Newswire*, May 9, 2005 (www.nti.org/d_newswire/issues/2005_5_9.html# E600437C [June 8, 2005]).

69. Michael Barbaro, "Bioshield Too Little for Drug Industry," *Washington Post*, July 26, 2004.

70. Lynne Gilfillan and others, "Taking the Measure of Countermeasures: Leaders' Views on the Nation's Capacity to Develop Biodefense Countermeasures," *Biosecurity and Bioterrorism: Biodefense Strategy, Practice, and Science* 2, no. 4 (2004).

71. Epstein, testimony before the Senate Committee on Health, Education, Labor and Pensions.

72. These are S. 3, Protecting America in the War on Terror Act of 2005; S. 975, Project BioShield II Act of 2005; S. 1437, Bioterror and Pandemic Preparedness Protection Act; S. 1873, Biodefense and Pandemic Vaccine and Drug Development Act of 2005; S. 1880, National Biodefense and Pandemic Preparedness Act of 2005.

73. Peter Shorett, "The Crack in Bioshield's Armor," *GeneWatch* 17 (September-December 2004); "Senate Antiterror Bill Would Raise U.S. Rx Costs $10s of Billions a Year, says Generic Pharmaceutical Association," *Pharma Marketletter*, February 14, 2005.

74. Norman G. Anderson, "Bioterror Focus Should Be on Viruses," *Seattle Post-Intelligencer*, February 27, 2005.

75. Scott Shane, "Bioshield Effort Is Inadequate, a Study Says," *New York Times*, October 15, 2004; and Advisory Panel to Assess Domestic Response Capabilities for Terrorism Involving Weapons of Mass Destruction [Gilmore Commission], *Third Annual Report to the President and the Congress* (2001), pp. 30–31.

76. CDC Smallpox Fact Sheet, "Side Effects of Smallpox Vaccination" (www.bt.cdc.gov/agent/smallpox/vaccination/reactions-vacc-public.asp [October 30, 2005]).

77. New, attenuated smallpox vaccines are becoming available, and the U.S. government is expected to procure them in 2006.

78. "Meeting the Biodefense Challenge: A 'Roadmap' for a National Vaccine Strategy," National Vaccine Strategy Working Group, Chemical and Biological Arms Control Institute (CBACI) (September 2004).

79. Michael Moodie and John J. Callahan, Chemical and Biological Arms Control Institute (CBACI), "Fighting Bioterrorism" (December 2004).

80. Trust for America's Health, "Ready or Not? 2005."

81. U.S. Government Accountability Office, "Nonproliferation: Further Improvements Needed in U.S. Efforts to Counter Threats from Man-Portable Air Defense Systems," GAO-04-519 (May 2004), p. 2.

82. Douglas Jehl and David E. Sanger, "U.S. Expands List of Lost Missiles," *New York Times,* November 6, 2004.

83. Christopher Bolkcom, Bartholomew Elias, and Andrew Feickert, "Homeland Security: Protecting Airliners from Terrorist Missiles" (Washington: Congressional Research Service, February 15, 2005).

84. U.S. Department of State, briefing slides, Fifth International Conference on Export Controls (Budapest, Hungary, September 2003), cited by the U.S. Government Accountability Office, "Missile Protection for Commercial Aircraft," GAO-04-341R (January 2004), p. 11.

85. Bolkcom, Elias, and Feickert, "Homeland Security: Protecting Airliners from Terrorist Missiles."

86. Mark Phelps, "Do SAMs Pose a Real Threat to Civil Aviation?" Aviation International News, January 2003 (www.globalsecurity.org/org/news/2003/0301-sam-threat01.htm [January 13, 2005]).

87. U.S. Government Accountability Office, "Missile Protection for Commercial Aircraft," GAO-04-341R (January 2004), p. 11.

88. As cited by Phelps, "Do SAMs Pose a Real Threat to Civil Aviation?"

89. Paul J. Caffera, "The Air Industry's Worst Nightmare," Salon.com, November 25, 2002; Douglas Barrie and Robert Wall, "Big Headache," *Aviation Week and Space Technology*, August 23, 2004, p. 58.

90. James Chow and others, "Protecting Commercial Aviation against the Shoulder-Fired Missile Threat" (Santa Monica, Calif.: RAND, 2005), p. 9 (www.rand.org/publications/OP/OP106/ [February 11, 2005]).

91. Center for Strategic and International Studies, *Transnational Threats Update* 1,

no. 10 (July 2003) (www.csis.org/media/csis/pubs/ttu_0307.pdf [December 10, 2005]); Phelps, "Do SAMs Pose a Real Threat to Civil Aviation?"; Alan J. Kuperman, "The Stinger Missile and U.S. Intervention in Afghanistan," in *The New American Interventionism: Lessons from Successes and Failures,* edited by Demetrios James Caraley (Columbia University Press, 1999), p. 194.

92. Jehl and Sanger, "U.S. Expands List of Lost Missiles."

93. "The MANPADS Menace: Combating the Threat to Global Aviation from Man-Portable Air Defense Systems," U.S. Department of State fact sheet, September 20, 2005 (www.state.gov/t/pm/rls/fs/53558.htm [October 24, 2005]).

94. "United States and Hungary Agreement on Destruction of Man-Portable Air Defense Systems (MANPADS) Missiles," U.S. Department of State media note, September 30, 2005 (www.state.gov/r/pa/prs/ps/2005/54177.htm [October 24, 2005]).

95. The February 2005 agreement between the United States and Russia to coordinate MANPADS nonproliferation efforts is welcome. See U.S. Department of State information release, "U.S., Russian Agreement on Man-Portable Air Defense Systems/MANPADS" (February 24, 2005) (usinfo.state.gov/eur/Archive/2005/Feb/24-479502.html [June 8, 2005]).

96. Sarah Chankin-Gould and Matt Schroeder, "MANPADS Proliferation," Issue Brief 1 (Federation of American Scientists, January 2004) (fas.org/asmp/campaigns/MANPADS/MANPADS.html [March 29, 2005]).

97. Technical data in this section come from Michal Fiszer and Jerzy Gruszczynski, "On Arrows and Needles," *Journal of Electronic Defense,* December 1, 2002, and Bolkcom, Elias, and Feickert, "Homeland Security: Protecting Airliners from Terrorist Missiles."

98. Chow and others, "Protecting Commercial Aviation against the Shoulder-Fired Missile Threat."

99. Eric Lipton, "U.S. Is Set to Test Missile Defenses Aboard Airliners," *New York Times,* May 29, 2005.

100. Bolkcom, Elias, and Feickert, "Homeland Security: Protecting Airliners from Terrorist Missiles."

101. Bolkcom, Elias, and Feickert, "Homeland Security: Protecting Airliners from Terrorist Missiles."

102. Phelps, "Do SAMs Pose a Real Threat to Civil Aviation?"

103. David Fulghum, "Microwave Weapons Emerge," *Aviation Week and Space Technology,* June 13, 2005, p. 116.

104. Leonard Hill, "El Al to Begin Test of Antimissile System on Aircraft," *ATW Online,* November 25, 2004.

105. Charlotte Adams, "Airliner Missile Defense: At What Cost?" *Aviation Today,* May 1, 2004.

106. Philip Butterworth-Hayes, "Civil Antimissile Systems Take Wing," *Aerospace America,* July 2003.

107. Phelps, "Do SAMs Pose a Real Threat to Civil Aviation?"

108. "Missile Protection for Commercial Aircraft," p. 3.

109. Office of Management and Budget, 2006 Budget Proposal (www.whitehouse.gov/omb/budget/fy2006/dhs.html [February 19, 2005]).

110. Parney Albright, DHS Science and Technology Directorate, quoted by Matthew Brzezinski, "How to Make a Missile Miss," *New York Times,* February 8, 2004.

111. "Missile Protection for Commercial Aircraft," p. 13.

112. Department of Homeland Security Counter-MANPADS Development and Demonstration Solicitation (www.crows.org/ADVOCACY/Legislative/ManPads/MANPADS_Solicitation.pdf [February 19, 2005]).

113. Adams, "Airliner Missile Defense: At What Cost?"

114. Brzezinski, "How to Make a Missile Miss."

115. Chow and others, "Protecting Commercial Aviation against the Shoulder-Fired Missile Threat," pp. 23–27.

116. Michael Sirak and Jonathan Weston, "New U.S. High-Energy Concept Aims to Counter Man-Portable Missile Threat," *Jane's Defence Weekly,* July 30, 2003.

117. "World's First Ray Gun Shoots Down Missile," *Space Daily,* June 7, 2000 (www.spacedaily.com/news/laser-00g.html [January 14, 2005]).

118. Parney Albright, quoted in Harvey Simon, "Laser 'Shield' for Airports Ineffective, DHS Official Says," *Aviation Now,* March 3, 2004.

119. Simon, "Laser 'Shield' for Airports Ineffective."

120. Robert Wall, "Hardening Resolve," *Aviation Week and Space Technology,* August 23, 2004, p. 59.

121. Caffera, "The Air Industry's Worst Nightmare."

122. Chow and others, "Protecting Commercial Aviation against the Shoulder-Fired Missile Threat," p. 18.

9

Conclusion

Michael d'Arcy

There have been intensive and wide-ranging efforts to strengthen the homeland security of the United States since the 9/11 and anthrax attacks of 2001. These have been designed largely to prevent a recurrence of such attacks and therefore have centered on air travel, intelligence sharing, infrastructure protection, stockpiling countermeasures to biological pathogens, and tightening controls on who may enter the country. Though this approach is laudable, as far as it goes, it does not adequately credit the enemies of the United States with the flexibility and ingenuity they possess.

The United States remains highly vulnerable to a range of threats, as do virtually all of its major allies abroad. These include attacks on critical or potentially hazardous infrastructure, especially chemical plants; large scale release of biological pathogens; radiological or nuclear attacks; and surface-to-air missiles. Though action has been taken to screen at the borders and within the country for radioactive materials, the inability to identify specific isotopes of concern is a significant gap in capability, as is the fact that much cargo that enters the United States by sea is not screened for radioactivity at all. Techniques for automated and rapid detection of chemical and biological agents are far inferior, and syndromic surveillance efforts to detect a biological attack are neither standardized nor integrated.

Individual efforts have tackled certain needs but left other, related ones unaddressed; an example is the fact that baggage stored in the hold of an aircraft is screened for explosives, but passengers and commercial cargo generally are not. Coordination among local, state, and federal authorities, both in prevention efforts and response preparation, is lacking, as is coordination between different arms of the federal government. Sadly, that assessment still includes the intelligence agencies. One of the main motivations behind the creation of the Department of Homeland Security was to address the latter shortcoming and, though progress has been made, the necessary process of reorganization is still ongoing. Furthermore, too many different bodies within Congress are responsible for oversight of homeland security, leading to turf wars and inefficiency in scrutiny and governance. On a wider scale, the United States has failed to adapt its homeland security strategy to recognize that close international cooperation is essential.

The U.S. government must undertake a number of structural reforms in order to better carry out its responsibility for homeland security. At the federal level these reforms center on the Department of Homeland Security and the intelligence agencies. The reforms should be accompanied by reorganization of the structure of congressional committees to ensure appropriate, efficient, and transparent oversight of the DHS and intelligence activities. The president and the director of national intelligence (DNI) must clearly delineate the intelligence roles of civilian and military agencies. The DNI must also enhance the sense of community across the agencies. The CIA should remain responsible for foreign, not domestic, intelligence work, and use of the military for covert operations outside the war theater should be avoided. The main focus of FBI operations must continue to be the domestic arena. However, the FBI's modus operandi and crime-solving focus, which are deep seated and do not lend themselves to intelligence gathering, do not offer the best remedy to the severe lack of domestic intelligence that prevailed prior to 9/11. The best course of action would be to establish a domestic intelligence agency, in the mold of Britain's MI5. Short of that, the National Security Service within the FBI, whose creation was announced in June 2005, can become the quasi-separate division needed for gathering domestic intelligence. It should be integrated with the other intelligence agencies.

More coordination is needed between the intelligence and tracking activities of law enforcement agencies in different jurisdictions and at the local, state and federal levels. The current model does not work well enough. Although the FBI runs the joint terrorism task forces (JTTFs) in major cities and is beginning to help state and local police forces more effectively, it is very small compared with police forces, and it has nothing like their presence on the ground. Moreover, it has been slow to change its case-solving ethos. The United States therefore needs to expand its local police intelligence and counterterrorism units. The use of federal funds to recruit an extra 5,000 to 10,000 police officers for this purpose would cost under $1 billion a year. These funds should be allocated on the basis of the threat, and hence they should go predominantly to the largest cities. Two-way information sharing between the federal government and state and local governments must be improved, and the FBI should not be the sole conduit for sharing. More generally, an "information sharing environment" that uses a network approach to facilitate exchange of relevant information between government and public and private sector entities, while respecting privacy, must be implemented.

The divide between the Homeland Security Council (HSC) and the National Security Council (NSC) needs to be addressed. The crossover in personnel between the two bodies and the fact that the National Counterterrorism Center (NCTC) reports to the NSC, not the HSC, means that the division between the two bodies is at best artificial and at worst counterproductive. It does not enhance integration between intelligence agencies or between domestic and foreign efforts. The NSC and HSC should be merged, and some of the staffing burden could be borne by the DHS—that is, certain functions currently performed by the NSC or HSC could be carried out by the DHS rather than the merged body. Recent years have provided numerous examples of flexible modification of NSC processes in partnership with other agencies. The joint role of the NSC and the National Economic Council (NEC) in advising the president on economic issues is but one. The director of the NCTC should be given greater operational authority to ensure interagency coordination.

The link between the intelligence agencies of the United States and those of its foreign partners, though strengthened since 9/11, remains inadequate. There has been progress in sharing airline passenger and shipping data with the European Union, but many other potentially valuable sources of information, such as the European Union's Eurodac database, which tracks asylum seekers, remain denied to the United States. Future information databases should be designed with international cooperation in mind, just as U.S. databases should allow for domestic cooperation. The United States should ensure integration of the intelligence analyzed by different communities in its bilateral foreign relationships, and it should encourage strengthening of the multinational EU bodies, which may lead to better sharing of intelligence between member states and the United States.

A mutual legal assistance and extradition treaty was signed by the United States and the European Union in June 2003. There is still a need, however, for measures on both sides of the Atlantic that allow intelligence information to be admitted as evidence in court and its public disclosure to be prevented. There has been agreement and action on container security, through the container security initiative. The United States and Europe agree on the need to use machine-readable passports and eventually "e-passports" containing biometric information. The development of e-passports is still beset by technological difficulties, and the decision by the United States to use a facial image alone as the biometric in its passports is unwise. The United States should follow the European Union in incorporating fingerprint data; ideally, both also would include iris data. For more reliable domestic identification, federal standards for driving licenses must be mandated.

The security of all foreign airliners (not just those of countries in the European Union) needs to be brought up to U.S. standards, with deployment of air marshals and hardened aircraft doors. The United States has a strong argument for pressing other countries to do more on this type of international cooperation, since its own security directly depends on it. When its partners are developing countries, the United States may need to give technical and financial assistance; the $100 million East Africa counterterrorism initiative (EACTI) is a good example.

Liaison between the United States and the European Union must be streamlined; the number of U.S. agencies involved in international issues has grown in recent years, while the structures of the European Union are even more labyrinthine. Beyond that, the United States must think strategically about its interaction on a Europe-wide, as opposed to bilateral, basis. The authors of this volume believe, with due caveats, that U.S. homeland security would benefit from stronger pan-European institutions such as Europol and Eurojust; hence the United States should encourage the development of those bodies. Moreover, alongside the efforts to establish a consensus on the urgency of the terrorist threat, there should be broad negotiation between the European Union and the United States to establish general rules, consistent with European and American practice, for sensitive types of cooperation that respect civil liberties.

The role of the U.S. military in homeland security generally should be supportive rather than dominant, but its ability to mobilize large numbers in a short space of time can sometimes be important in dealing with a terrorist threat or attack. Its robust communications networks could also be of general use in the wake of a catastrophic attack, and its technical development efforts (through DARPA, for example) can contribute to the broader homeland security mission. The National Guard and other elements in the U.S. military reserve should not, in general, be given a much larger role in homeland security, but there is a case for greater involvement of the reserve component in certain niche activities such as cleanup or the distribution of medications after an attack with a weapon of mass effect. Some of the authors believe that there is no reason to rule out using active-duty forces in such circumstances. The creation of small, dedicated units for this purpose might entail an initial outlay of $1 billion and annual operating costs of several hundred million dollars (if the units involved 5,000 to 10,000 people). Better planning to ensure the rapid availability of existing military forces is also required, as the Hurricane Katrina experience revealed.

With respect to border security, U.S. government efforts have gone a considerable way, but shortcomings remain. The US-VISIT program requires most of those who enter the United States to submit fingerprints and a digital photograph that can be compared to the DHS IDENT database and the record of visa holders. However, the current schedule for phasing in the program means that it will not be fully operational for several years; small entry points in particular are lagging behind. The time frame should be reduced, and implementation of exit tracking of visa holders, currently being tested, should be expedited. This is important to efforts to catch those who would plan or execute attacks by overstaying their visa.

The visa waiver program represents a substantial loophole in U.S security, and although the now-universal use of machine-readable passports has improved matters, biometric e-passports are required for reasonable control over who gains access to the United States. These efforts depend, of course, on having a reliable list of people who ought to be denied entry; consolidation of those lists is progressing and should be completed as soon as possible. In particular, IDENT and the FBI's IAFIS database, which uses ten fingerprints for identification, must be fully integrated, as should domestic and foreign terrorist watch lists.

The Patriot Act increased the number of patrol agents at the U.S.-Canadian border to 1,000, but more are needed. There must be random patrols, their number must be increased, and better equipment must be provided for surveillance and mobility. The traffic of people across the Mexican border is much greater and therefore more worrisome. The Secure Border Initiative, and the announcement that 1,700 extra CBP Border Patrol agents are to be assigned to the Southwest border in 2006, are therefore welcome developments.[1] It is important that both Canada and Mexico themselves develop their border security so that the potential threat to the United States is reduced. The United States should move to a regime in which all people who cross the border, including those in cars, are individually screened.

Screening of airline passengers for explosives, initially in a targeted manner, should be implemented though explosive trace detectors and, when feasible, penetrating imaging. A national trace detector network would cost in the region of $250 million. A comprehensive means of either screening cargo carried on airplanes or hardening aircraft cargo holds also is needed. The threat to aircraft from surface-to-air missiles is real, but the technology to counter them is not yet ready for deployment. The United States and other governments must make preparations to minimize the economic and political consequences of a successful missile attack on an aircraft. To prevent plane-based suicide attacks, there should be greater screening of private aircraft pilots.

Concerning container trade, over the period 2001–04 the number of cargo inspectors grew by 40 percent and the number of inspections by 60 percent. However, only 6 percent of seaborne cargo containers are inspected, and that rate is inadequate. A realistic target for inspections, coupled with those of the CSI and C-TPAT, is 10 to 15 percent. That would not necessitate excessive expenditures on reconfiguring ports and would increase the chances that all containers that posed a substantial risk would be inspected. Further security could be added by the installation of tamper-proof seals and RFID or, better, GPS tracking boxes on cargo containers to ensure their integrity in transit. To prevent the possibility of oil tankers being used as vehicles for nuclear bombs, weapons of mass effect, or other dangerous materials, they should be required to undergo the same system of registration, tracking, and safety inspection as container shippers.

State and local governments have an important role to play in attack prevention as well as in consequence management. Although their role as first responders has been recognized, prevention efforts outside of New York City have been inadequate, and funds have been used in an uncoordinated, inefficient, and parochial way that reflects neither risks nor good practice. Prevention particularly involves the police, and in the larger cities they should develop their own counterterrorism units, coordinated by the NCTC. The equipping of first responders must be managed in a prudent and targeted manner. For example, a major city could purchase several dozen mobile interoperable communications systems, at a cost of $1 million each, to facilitate communication between different first responders. The current national spending of $5 billion a year on first responders is, the authors believe, adequate, if further improvements are made in how the funds are spent.

Since 9/11, the private sector generally has done little to protect itself. That must change. The role of the government should not be to impose onerous security standards everywhere, but to act as a catalyst: the trick is to develop just enough regulation to create incentives for the private sector to adopt effective protective measures. Generally, the optimal approach is to enforce safety standards and to make use of the nation's insurance system in order to harness the power of the market to provide incentives for adopting good practices and for innovation to reduce the cost. Although take-up of terrorism insurance coverage has expanded markedly, it is still insufficient; the system of incentives will work properly only with universal take-up. Hence terrorism coverage should be mandatory on all commercial policies above some minimum threshold, such as several million dollars. Not all insurance companies will support this idea, since it is difficult, given the limited number of terrorist attacks in the United States, to assess their statistical probability and hence the risks from terrorism, and since the losses could be quite great in the event of a successful attack. Therefore the government will have to play the role of financial backstop. Under the Terrorism Risk Insurance Revision Act, passed in December 2005, the provisions of the original Terrorism Risk Insurance Act have largely been extended until December 31, 2007. The amount of losses that would trigger the federal backstop, and the insurance companies' deductibles, have rightly been increased to recognize that the private sector must bear greater responsibility for the burden of insurance. The eventual aim must be a situation where the industry can operate without any federal backstop or, at most, with only extreme, catastrophic losses covered by the government, which would charge for this service.

There are various steps that should be taken by specific sectors to improve security against terrorism, spurred by the mechanisms described above and, when necessary, government legislation. Chemical and nuclear plants are possible targets for low-tech attacks that would have huge consequences. The U.S. chemical industry still has no legal framework to guide its security measures (which so far it has taken voluntarily with only limited commitment), and passage of a bill to rectify this, including periodic safety assessments and commonsense solutions, should be a priority. The threat posed by individual plants should be dealt with in a hierarchical manner, and moves should be made in consultation with the private sector to use less dangerous chemicals as alternatives where possible. Sales of dangerous chemicals should be monitored and regulated, and their transportation should be more closely guarded so that they are routed away from cities. Nuclear power plants are now relatively well protected, but the areas where low-grade waste is stored often are not. That increases the likelihood of a radiological attack, and so the level of security must be improved.

Appropriate safeguards often can be expensive to incorporate into existing structures but relatively cheap to build into new structures, and they frequently offer benefits besides helping counterterrorism efforts. Large buildings should be fitted, for example, with air filtration and circulation systems that would minimize the permeation of chemical or biological agents. Other steps can be taken to protect buildings against bombs and infrastructure attacks, and such steps should be reflected in new building codes. These would include using elevators that descend to the nearest floor in the event of a power outage, siting important buildings back from roadways, using shatterproof glass in lower floors, and controlling access to sites. These standards need not be applied to all buildings immediately; again, the goals are to protect against catastrophic attack, to maximize measures that provide dual-purpose benefits, and to let the hidden hand of the market do as much of the work as possible.

Technology can make a powerful contribution to many facets of the effort to increase the level of homeland security, and the government has an important role to play in ensuring that it is developed as quickly as possible and appropriately deployed. The DHS Science and Technology Directorate is well-funded, and bodies such as DARPA and HSARPA are enlisting academic and private sector expertise to develop technologies for the near, medium, and long term. Should HSARPA prove to operate successfully, its relatively small funding should be increased. The Safety Act makes a sensible compromise by providing liability protection for new technologies deployed in response to a terrorist attack, but the special case of vaccines administered in advance of an attack, for which comprehensive testing may be impossible, should be addressed legislatively to provide a similar level of protection. The nation's current abilities to develop vaccines, antibiotics, and antiviral drugs to combat a biological attack (or a flu pandemic) are inadequate; either the private sector should be more fully enlisted in this effort or the government should develop an autonomous R&D capability.

In this book the authors suggest how the United States can maximize the effectiveness of the enormous efforts that it is making to increase its homeland security, focusing on those tasks that would yield maximum benefit per dollar spent in terms of countering catastrophic threats. We believe that our proposals learn from the experience of the years since September 11, 2001, and could be implemented readily in the current circumstances, without undue additional expenditures or organizational upheaval. Present U.S.

homeland security programs do leave a number of vulnerabilities unaddressed. The United States must find a happy medium between an excessive sense of urgency and demand for high expenditures on one hand and the growing national trend toward complacency on the other.

Note

1. Department of Homeland Security, press release, "Secure Border Initiative (SBI) Update," December 8, 2005 (www.dhs.gov/dhspublic/interapp/press_release/press_release_0805.xml [December 13, 2005]).

APPENDIX

Figure A-1. *Doses of Inhalation Anthrax Antibiotics Stockpiled*

Millions

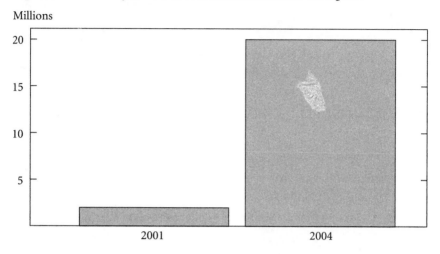

Source: For 2001, see "Secretary Thompson Testifies on HHS Readiness and Role of Vaccine Research and Development," Department of Health and Human Services, October 23, 2001 (www.hhs.gov/news/press/2001pres/20011023.html [February 2, 2005]). For 2004, see "HHS Fact Sheet: Biodefense Preparedness: Record of Accomplishment," Department of Health and Human Services, April 28, 2004 (www.hhs.gov/news/press/2004pres/20040428.html [February 2, 2005]).

Figure A-2. *Doses of Smallpox Vaccine Stockpiled*

Millions

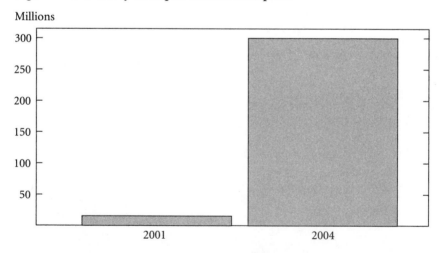

Source: "HHS Fact Sheet: Biodefense Preparedness: Record of Accomplishment," Department of Health and Human Services, April 28, 2004 (www.hhs.gov/news/press/2004pres/20040428.html [February 2, 2005]).

Figure A-3. *Number of U.S. Border Patrol Agents*[a]

Number

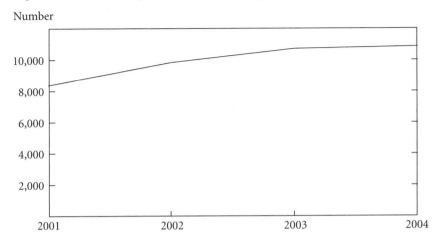

Source: For 2001, see Michael A. Pearson, executive associate commissioner for field opera-tions, U.S. Immigration and Naturalization Service, testimony before the Permanent Investiga-tions Subcommittee of the Senate Government Affairs Committee, 107 Cong., 1 sess., November 13, 2001. For 2002, see Matthew Purdy, "Looking over the Northern Bor-der, and over Their Shoulders," *New York Times,* November 24, 2002. Numbers for 2003 and 2004 were provided by U.S. Customs and Border Protection, Public Affairs Office, February 10, 2005.

a. Numbers are for the end of each year.

Figure A-4. *Number of First Responders Trained*

Number

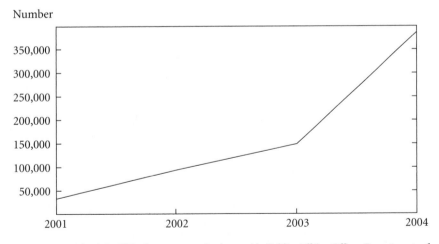

Source: Michael E. O'Hanlon, communications with Public Affairs Office, Department of Homeland Security, February 7, 2005.

Figure A-5. *Percentage of Shipping Containers Inspected*[a]

Percent

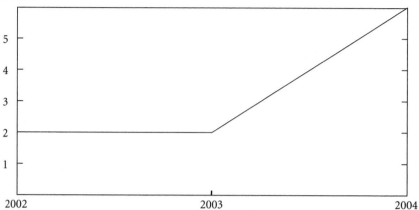

Source: For 2002, see Bill Miller, "Customs Chief Seeks Checks Overseas of U.S.-Bound Cargo," *Washington Post,* January 18, 2002. For 2003, see Verena Dobnik, "On the Nation's Water, a Daunting New War against Terror for the Coast Guard," Associated Press, March 28, 2003. For 2004, see Clark Kent Ervin, former inspector general, Department of Homeland Security, "Mission: Difficult, but not Impossible," *New York Times,* December 27, 2004.

a. Percentage of total arriving at U.S. ports.

Figure A-6. *Number of Foreign Students Enrolled in U.S. Institutions of Higher Education*[a]

Number

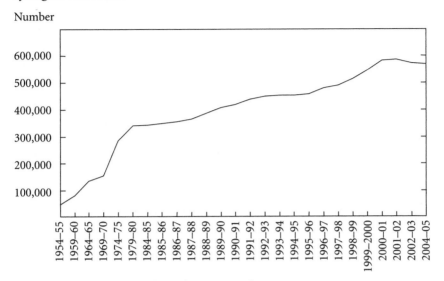

Source: (http://opendoors.iienetwork.org/?p=49931).

a. According to the best data available, the annual change in the number of foreign students enrolled in U.S. institutions of higher education in 2003–04 declined for the first time since 1954. The number of international students enrolled as a percentage of the total student body peaked in 2002–03, constituting 4.6 percent of students.

Table A-1. *Homeland Security Budget Authority, by Agency*

Millions of dollars

Agency	2005 enacted[a]	2006 enacted[a]	2007 request
Department of Agriculture	595.9	563.0	650.3
Department of Commerce	166.7	181.1	217.8
Department of Defense[b]	17,187.9	16,440.4	16,697.8
Department of Education	23.9	27.5	25.8
Department of Energy	1,562.0	1,705.2	1,699.6
Department of Health and Human Services	4,229.4	4,229.2	4,563.3
Department of Homeland Security	24,549.1	25,675.9	27,777.0
Department of Housing and Urban Development	2.0	1.9	1.9
Department of the Interior	65.0	55.6	55.4
Department of Justice	2,766.9	2,991.5	3,279.8
Department of Labor	56.1	48.3	58.7
Department of State	824.1	1,107.9	1,212.5
Department of Transportation	219.3	181.0	206.0
Department of the Treasury	101.5	115.8	133.4
Department of Veterans Affairs	249.4	308.8	313.4
Corps of Engineers	89.0	72.0	43.0
Environmental Protection Agency	106.3	129.3	183.3
Executive Office of the President	29.5	20.8	24.6
General Services Administration	65.2	98.6	95.9
National Aeronautics and Space Administration	220.5	212.6	203.7
National Science Foundation	342.2	344.2	387.4
Office of Personnel and Management	3.0	2.7	2.8
Social Security Administration	154.7	176.8	183.8
District of Columbia	15.0	13.5	9.0
Federal Communications Commission	1.8	2.3	5.4
Intelligence Community Management Account	72.4	56.0	55.0
National Archives and Records Administration	17.1	18.2	18.1
Nuclear Regulatory Commission	59.2	79.3	70.3
Postal Service	503.0	0	0
Securities and Exchange Commission	5.0	5.0	5.0
Smithsonian Institution	75.0	83.7	80.4
United States Holocaust Memorial Museum	8.0	7.8	7.8
Corporation for National and Community Service	17.0	20.4	14.9
Total Homeland Security budget authority	**54,383.0**	**55,046.0**	**58,282.9**
Less national defense (DoD)	−17,187.9	−16,440.4	−16,697.8
Non-defense Homeland Security budget authority, excluding BioShield	**37,195.1**	**38,605.7**	**41,585.1**
Less fee-funded Homeland Security programs	−3,444.1	−4,130.0	−6,022.0
Less mandatory Homeland Security programs	−2,193.6	−2,232.0	−2,454.1

Agency	2005 enacted[a]	2006 enacted[a]	2007 request
Net non-defense discretionary Homeland Security			
budget authority, excluding BioShield	31,557.4	32,243.7	33,109.0
Including BioShield	2,508.0	0	0
Net non-defense discretionary Homeland Security			
budget authority, including BioShield	34,065.4	32,243.7	33,109.0
Obligations limitations: Department of Transportation	78.2	121.0	99.7

Source: Office of Management and Budget, *United States Government Budget: Fiscal Year 2007, Analytical Perspectives*, February, 2006, Table 3.1, p. 20. Available at www.whitehouse.gov/omb/budget/fy2007/pdf/spec.pdf (February 2006).

a. Totals for 2005 and 2006 include supplemental appropriations.

b. The revisions to the Department of Defense (DoD) homeland security funding estimates also better reflect actual spending by the department. Previously, the DoD homeland security funding estimates were derived from an annual report issued by the DoD comptroller's office that identified funding spent on combating terrorism activities. Now, DoD has been able to identify discrete, homeland security–related projects, programs, and activities within the budget accounts of the various service branches. As a result, the funding estimates are more precise and integrated with the DoD budget. DoD re-estimate: 2005, +7,541; 2006, +7,992. Coast Guard re-estimate: 2005, _940; 2006, _790. Office of Management and Budget, *United States Government Budget: Fiscal Year 2007, Analytical Perspectives*, February 2006, pp. 19–20.

Table A-2. *Homeland Security Funding, by Budget Function*

Millions of dollars

Agency	2005 enacted[a]	2006 enacted[b]	2007 request
National defense	20,581	20,771	20,430
International affairs	824	1,107	1,213
General social science and technology	619	616	655
Energy	102	124	125
Natural resources and the environment	288	285	316
Agriculture	578	541	611
Commerce and Housing Credit	649	160	193
Transportation	8,109	8,433	9,632
Community and Regional Development	2,759	2,201	2,722
Education, Training, Employment, and Social Services	164	168	163
Health	4,276	4,347	4,626
Medicare	8	12	14
Income Security	9	11	17
Social Security	151	173	179
Veterans Benefits and Services	250	310	314
Administration of Justice	14,241	14,784	16,210
General Government	778	819	862
Total, Homeland Security budget authority	**54,386**	**54,862**	**58,282**
Less national defense (DoD)	−17,186	−16,441	−16,699
Net discretionary, Homeland Security budget authority, excluding BioShield	**37,200**	**38,421**	**41,583**
Less Fee-Funded Homeland Security Programs	3,444	−4,127	−6,019
Less Mandatory Homeland Security Programs	2,194	−2,232	−2,455
Net discretionary, Homeland Security budget authority	**31,562**	**32,062**	**33,109**
Plus BioShield	2,508	0	0
Net discretionary, Homeland Security budget authority, including BioShield	**34,070**	**32,062**	**33,109**

Source: Office of Management and Budget, *Budget of the United States Government: Fiscal Year 2007, Analytical Perspectives,* Table 3.13, p. 33. Available at www.whitehouse.gov/omb/budget/fy2007/pdf/spec.pdf (February 2006).

a. FY 2005 enacted estimates include supplemental appropriations.

b. FY 2006 estimates exclude supplemental appropriations.

Table A-3. *Department of Homeland Security Spending and Credit Activity*

Millions of dollars

Agency	2005 actual	2006 estimate	2007 estimate
Spending			
Gross discretionary budget authority			
Departmental management and operations	541	791	958
Office of the Inspector General	82	82	96
Citizenship and Immigration Services	158	114	182
United States Secret Service	1,175	1,200	1,265
Customs and Border Protection	5,325	5,898	6,580
Immigration and Customs Enforcement	2,987	3,630	4,444
Transportation Security Administration	5,719	5,870	6,223
Coast Guard	6,324	6,812	7,117
Preparedness	3,984	4,032	3,420
Federal Emergency Management Agency	3,084	2,731	3,093
Science and Technology	1,110	1,467	1,002
Domestic Nuclear Detection Office (non-add)	—	315	—
Domestic Nuclear Detection Office	—	—	536
Information Analysis and Infrastructure Protection	887	—	—
United States Visitor and Immigrant Status Indicator Technology	340	337	399
Federal Law Enforcement Training Center	222	279	244
All other	10	4	4
Total gross	31,948	33,247	35,563
Less fee-funded activities	−2,519	−2,621	−4,631
Total discretionary budget authority (net)	29,429	30,626	30,932
Memorandum: Budget Authority from Enacted Supplementals	67,145	−23,078	—
Total discretionary outlays	38,358	43,846	42,765
Mandatory outlays			
Flood Insurance Fund			
Existing law	1,314	17,556	165
Legislative proposal	—	5,040	560
Citizenship and Immigration Services			
Existing law	1,479	1,749	1,777
Legislative proposal	—	—	25
All other			
Existing law	−2,793	3,592	−1,708
Legislative proposal	—	—	−31
Total mandatory outlays	944	22,907	788
Total outlays	39,302	66,753	43,553
Credit activity			
Direct loan disbursements			
Disaster assistance	—	692	355
Total direct loan disbursement	—	692	355

Source: Office of Management and Budget, *Budget of the United States Government, Fiscal Year 2007*, p 144. Available at www.whitehouse.gov/omb/budget/fy2007/budget.html (February 2006).

INDEX

Air travel security: air cargo screening, 6, 106, 142–43; air marshalls, 55–56, 105–06; baggage screening, 140, 142; explosives screening, 139–43; firearms, defense against, 139–40; foreign carriers of U.S. citizens, 6, 55–56, 104, 105–06; missile defense, 115–16, 155, 170–76; 9/11, changes following, 3; no-fly lists, 62–63; passenger screening, 6, 35, 139–43; physical searches, 140; PNR data requirements, 29, 61–63; for private aircraft, 6, 105; reforms necessary, 6, 98, 104–06, 187, 189; syndromic surveillance, 165–66; TIA system, 35. *See also* Cargo container security, *under* Technology development

Al Qaeda, 4–6, 86, 170, 171–72

American National Standards Institute (ANSI), 159

America's Shield Initiative, 102

Anthrax stockpiles, 194*f*

Antibiotics, 3, 166–69, 191, 194*f*

Antidote treatment nerve agent auto-injector (ATNAA), 163

Antiviral drug development, 164, 166, 168–69, 191

Aviation and Transportation Security Act, 61, 140

Bhopal chemical disaster, 158

Bioagent autonomous networked detectors (BAND), 164–65

Biological attack: countermeasures, 7, 13, 133–34, 146, 163–69, 194*f*; material oversight rules, 3; prevention, 6–7, 82; response strategy, 118, 162, 165

Biometric identification, 98, 135–39. *See also* passports

BioSense program, 165

Bioshield Bill, 133

BioWatch program, 164

Bonner, Robert, 60, 158

Border security: air borders, 61–63, 105; assistance to non-Western countries for, 99–100, 103; border control documents, 63–64; changes, post-*9/11*, 3; Coast Guard role, 106–09; costs of improving, 102, 104, 105, 108, 109; EU cooperation in securing, 60–65; exit tracking for, 98; foreign students and, 99, 197*f*; funding improvements to, 103; land borders, 97, 100–04; people, identifying and monitoring for, 50, 63–64, 97–100, 134–39; at ports of entry, 101, 106–09; reforms necessary, 98–99, 101–03, 108, 188–89; Schengen system for, 28, 65; spotlighting function of, 96–97, 101; terrorist watch lists, 86, 97–98 . *See also* Air travel security; Cargo container security; Customs and Border Protection (CBP); Passports; Transportation security; Visa waver program (VWP)
Borrell, Josep, 68
Buses. *See* Public transportation; transportation security
Bush, G. W. administration: CIA authority over HUMINT, 22; domestic intelligence collection measures, 18; East Africa counterterrorism initiative, 100; intelligence sharing efforts, 18; on international cooperation, 27; ISE implementation, 33; National Strategy for Pandemic Influenza, 164; organizational response to *9/11*, 25; TTIC established, 18

Canada, 101–02, 114, 115, 138
CanPass program, 138
CAPPS II passenger screening program, 35

Cargo container security: commercial cargo on passenger jets, 105; container security devices (CSDs), 146; container security initiative (CSI), 10, 60–61; EU participation in, 51, 60–61, 196*f*; inspections for, 106–09, 196*f*; international cooperation on, 10, 51, 146–47, 158; known-shipper program, 105, 143; radioactive material detection, 157–59; reforms necessary, 144–45, 189; screening methods, 144–48; technology development, 146, 147; tracking technology, 108, 146–48
Catastrophic attacks: reducing overall risk of, 75, 78; Reserves role, 117–18; response responsibility issues, 88; ripple effects of, 6. *See also* First responder community; Infrastructure protection; Weapons of mass effect (WME)
Centers for Disease Control and Prevention (CDC), 164, 165
Chechen rebels, 172
Chemical attack: Bhopal chemical disaster, 158; countermeasures, 161–63; infrastructure protection, 74, 81, 83, 87; prevention, 139, 146; response strategy, 118, 162–63, 165
Chemical Biological Incident Response Force, 118
Chertoff, Michael, 129
CIA (Central Intelligence Agency): DoD cooperation/tensions, 21; FBI relation, 20; HUMINT manager position, 22, 24; *9/11*, changes following, 3; reforms necessary, 185; roles and responsibilities, 22–25
Ciluffo, Frank, 74
Cities Readiness Initiative (CDC), 167
Civil liberties protections, 33–35

Clinton, Bill (William Jefferson) administration, 30
Club of Berne, 57
Coast Guard, 108–09, 159
Commission on the Intelligence Capabilities of the United States Regarding Weapons of Mass Destruction. *See* Robb-Silberman Commission
Connect-the-dots problem, 2, 28, 55, 66
Container security initiative (CSI), 10, 60–61, 106, 158
Corzine, Jon, 83
Counterterrorism Security Group, 30
Cruise missiles, 13, 115–16
Customs and Border Protection (CBP), 61, 106–07, 147, 158, 195f. *See also* Border security
Customs-Trade Partnership against Terrorism (C-TPAT), 61, 106–07, 147

Defense Advanced Research Projects Agency (DARPA), 130–31
Defense Intelligence Agency, 21
Defense Science Board, 23
Defense Threat Reduction Agency, 160
Department of Defense (DoD): communications networks, 116; creation of, 7; DNI authority and, 18–19, 24–25; FBI/CIA cooperation/tensions, 21; FEMA cooperation, 9–10; Goldwater-Nichols reorganization, 7, 38; improvement recommendations, 187–88; intelligence gathering strategy, 22–25; response mobilization ability, 9–10, 115, 117; role of, 22–25, 114–15, 187–88; technology development efforts, 116 . *See also agencies of*
Department of Energy (DoE), 158, 160–61

Department of Health and Human Services (DHHS), 169
Department of Homeland Security (DHS): accomplishments, 2; air cargo screening plan, 143; container cargo tracking plan, 147–48; creation of, 7; directorate, 18, 79, 169; FEMA disaster response and, 2, 7; known-shipper program, 105, 143; missile defense standards, 174; radiation detector standards, 159; reforms necessary, 185–86; roles and responsibilities, 25
Department of Homeland Security Appropriations Act, 160
Department of Homeland Security Appropriations Bill (*2006*), 200–01f
Directed infrared countermeasure technique (DIRCM), 174
Directorate of Intelligence, 32
Director of national intelligence (DNI): intelligence dissemination role, 34; intelligence reform role, 24–25, 38–39, 185; military intelligence, authority over, 18–19, 24–25; NCTC-relation, 30–31
Dirty bombs, 84, 157
Domestic intelligence activities, pre-*9/11*, 17–18, 27
Domestic Nuclear Detection Office (DNDO), 157–58, 160

East Africa counterterrorism initiative (EACTI), 100
Education, foreign students, 97, 99, 197f
Entry requirements. *See* Foreign entrants to U.S.
E-passports, 134–38, 187–88 . *See also* Passports
Eurodac, 65

Eurojust, 56–57

European arrest warrant implementation, 67–68

European Border Agency, 56–57

European Council and Commission, 28, 54, 56, 60–63, 67–68

European Court of Justice, 62–63

European Parliament, 54, 62–63, 68

European Union: air travel safety measures, 140; counterterrorism capabilities and policies, 28, 52–53, 55, 56–57; counterterrorism coordinator, 54; Data Protection Directive, 61; e-passport requirements, 137–38; as source of terrorist activity, 50 . *See also* Homeland security, EU cooperation with

Europol, 56–57, 68

Explosive detection system (EDS), 140, 142, 143

Explosive trace detection (ETD), 140

Falkenrath, Richard, 4, 79, 83

FBI (Federal Bureau of Investigation): CIA relation, 20; DoD liaison, 21; domestic intelligence activities of, 37; Europol liaison, 57; field intelligence groups (FIGs), 32; information sharing by, 31–33, 37; limitations of, 32–33; local law enforcement coordination, 122–23; National Security Branch, 32; *9/11*, changes following, 3; NYPD overseas liaison program, 20–21; reform efforts, 31–33; reforms necessary, 122–23, 185–86; State Department liaison, 20

FEMA (Federal Emergency Management Agency), 2, 7, 9–10

Firearms, defense against, 140–41

First responder community: consequence management role, 120–21,
156; counterterrorism resources, 119–20, 123–24; funding, 120–22, 123; homeland security reserve corps, 117; local law enforcement agencies role, 119–20, 122–24, 186, 189; mobilization ability of, 117; numbers trained, 195*f*; prevention function, 119, 122–24; reforms necessary, 120–21, 186, 189; resource allocation to, 121–22; response responsibility issues, 88; response strategy, 120–21, 162–63; role of, 113–28

Food and Drug Administration (FDA), 168

Foreign entrants to U.S.: fingerprint requirements, 136–37; passport requirements, 18; students, 97, 99, 197*f*; visa waver program, 50, 63–64, 98, 134–35

Framework of Standards to Secure and Facilitate Global Trade, 51

France: counterterrorism policies, 52; homeland security cooperation, 53, 55–56; terrorism insurance requirements, 79

German, Mike, 122

Germany-U.S. cooperation, 53, 58, 68

Goldwater-Nichols Act, 7, 38

Goss, Porter, 5

Government, federal: motivations for infrastructure protection, 74–76, 78; role in technology development, 130–34, 168–69

Government, state and local: integration into federal efforts, 2; protection efforts, 2; reforms necessary, 189; response preparedness, 156, 167, 169. *See also* First responder community

Greenspan, Alan, 80

Hazardous ordnance engagement
    toolkit (HORNET), 174–75
Health Insurance Portability and
    Accountability Act (HIPAA), 165–66
Homeland security: actors in, 113; bud-
    get authority, 198f, 199f; Congress in
    increasing and reorganizing, 7;
    Europeanization of, 66; legislation
    for, 119; reforms necessary, 6–7, 31,
    184–92
Homeland security, EU cooperation
    with: border security, 51, 60–64,
    196f; Europol and Eurojust role,
    56–57; extradition treaty, 58–59, 68;
    information sharing, 28–29, 55–57,
    61–62, 64–65, 68; judicial coopera-
    tion, 59; MLATs, 58–59; PNR
    requirements, 29, 61–63, 68; reforms
    necessary, 56–57, 65–69, 187;
    response to U.S. agenda, 48, 51–57;
    trade relationship role, 50; VWP, 50,
    63–64, 98, 134–35
Homeland security, international coop-
    eration: air safety measures, 55–56,
    98, 105–06; border security, 100–04;
    cargo container security, 10, 60–61,
    106, 146–47, 158, 196f; challenges,
    49–51; EU role in, 51, 61; future of,
    64–69; goals, 49; outside the EU
    framework, 51–56; passport security,
    98, 103, 134–35; port security,
    106–09; post-9/11, 48; reforms
    necessary, 48, 186–87; trade relation-
    ship role, 49–50 . See also specific
    countries
Homeland Security Act, 134
Homeland Security Advanced Research
    Projects Agency (HSARPA), 130–33,
    139, 159, 160, 162
Homeland Security Council (HSC), 19,
    25–27, 186
Homeland security reserve corps, 117

House Permanent Select Committee on
    Intelligence, 18, 39–40
House Select Committee on Homeland
    Security, 87
Human Intelligence Directorate, 21–22,
    24
Human intelligence strategy
    (HUMINT), 22, 23, 24
Hurricane Katrina, 7, 9
Hustinx, Peter, 65

IAFIS system, 103
IDENT database, 98, 103
Information network security, 3, 34
Information sharing: foreign coopera-
    tion, 27–29, 55–57, 61–62, 64–65, 68;
    9/11, changes following, 3; privacy
    issues, 29, 34–35, 61–62, 64; reform
    recommendations, 33–37 . See also
    Intelligence reform
Information sharing environment
    (ISE), 33–37
Infrastructure protection: dams/levees,
    88; incentives for, 76–78, 80, 190–91;
    negative externality resulting from
    inadequate, 74–76; 9/11, changes fol-
    lowing, 3; private market investment
    in, 74; public health, 165–68. See also
    Catastrophic attacks
Infrastructure protection in private
    industry: building entry checks, 83,
    143; for buses, boats, barges, 76–77,
    84–86, 106, 161; chemical and
    nuclear industries, 74; chemical
    industry, 81, 83, 86, 87; costs, retrofit
    vs. new systems, 82, 89, 105;
    employee training for, 85; energy
    infrastructure, 88–89; explosives
    protection, 82; food industry, 86–88;
    funding for, 84–85, 87; insurance as
    mechanism for, 78–87; keys to
    improving, 73–74; motivations for

government intervention, 74–76, 78; nuclear materials, 81; public structures, large, 89; skyscrapers, 89; for trains and trucks, 76–77, 84–86, 106, 161; truck bombs defenses, 82–83; water systems, 87–88 . *See also* Air travel security

Instantaneous bio-aerosol detector systems (IBADS), 165

Insurance, anti-terrorism, 78–87

Intelligence community, 3, 37–40

Intelligence reform: civil liberties concerns, 33–35; culture of community for, 37–39; DNI-NCTC relation, 30–31; DNI role in, 18–19, 24–25, 34, 38–39; FBI efforts, 31–33; foreign cooperation in, 27–29, 65, 186–87; HUMINT role, 22, 23, 24; military-civilian intelligence functions, 22–25; NCTC-NSC relation, 30–31; overview, 185–92; privacy concerns, 33–35; roles and responsibilities clarifications, 20–24, 30–31, 36; state and local government as resource in, 35–37

Intelligence reform, improvements recommended: congressional oversight enhanced, 39–40; diplomatic strategy development, 29–30; FBI domestic security operations, 31–33; HSC-NSC merge, 25–27; information sharing, 27–29, 33–37; personnel strategies, 37–39; roles and responsibilities clarified, 20–25; training component, 37

Intelligence Reform and Terrorism Prevention Act, 3, 18, 24, 28, 30, 33–39, 142

Intelligence sharing. *See* information sharing

International Civil Aviation Organization (ICAO), 135, 136

International Standardization Organization (ISO), 135, 148

Interpol, 64

Iraq war, 5

Jackson, Michael, 139

Joint Intelligence Committee, UK, 27

Joint Intelligence Community Council, 19, 25

Joint Military Intelligence Program, 19

Joint Situation Centre, EU, 28

Joint terrorism task force (JTTF), 31–32, 36

Known-shipper program, 105, 143

London bombings (*2005*), 68, 84

Loy, James, 107

Madrid bombing (*2004*), 28, 54, 55, 57, 68, 84

MANPADS (man-portable air defense system), 155, 170–76

Markle task force report, 33, 35, 38

Medical countermeasures for catastrophic attacks, 7, 13, 133–34, 164, 166–69, 191, 194*f*

Megaports initiative, 158

Mexico, 101, 102–04

Military intelligence, 22–25

Missile defense, 115–16, 155, 170–76

Motassadeq, Mouunir al-, 59

Moussouai, Zacarias, 53, 68

Mueller, Robert, 31

National Clandestine Service (NCS), 22, 24–25

National Counterterrorism Center (NCTC), 18–19, 27, 30–31, 37, 186

National Economic Council (NEC), 186

National Guard, 113, 115–19, 166–67, 188

National Institute of Standards and Technology (NIST), 136, 137
National Institutes of Health (NIH), 167
National Intelligence Program, 19
National Intelligence University system, 38
National Response Plan, 156, 166
National Security Agency (NSA), 18
National Security Branch (NSB), 32
National Security Council (NSC), 19, 25–27, 186
National Security Service, 185
National Strategy for Homeland Security, 47
National Strategy for Pandemic Influenza, 164
NATO, 66
New York City Police Department (NYPD), 20–21, 65
9/11, changes following, 3
9/11 Commission report recommendations: Congress create intelligence committee(s), 39–40; culture of sharing, need for, 33; DNI director established, 18–19; DoD responsibility for paramilitary operations, 23; hardened cargo holds installed, 143; NCTC established, 18
9/11 terrorist attack, Mounir al-Montassadequ trial, 59
North American Aerospace Defense Command (NORAD), 114, 115
Northcom, 88–89, 113, 114–16
Northrop-Grumman, 174–75
Nuclear attack, 3, 74, 156–61
Nunn-Lugar-Domenici legislation, 119

Office of Homeland Security (OHS), 25
Office of Intelligence and Analysis, 37
Office of Screening Coordination and Operations (SCO), 138–39

Oklahoma City bombing, 119
ORCON (reduced originator control), 34, 36

Passenger name record (PNR), 29, 61–63, 68
Passports: with biometric identifiers, 63–64, 86, 98–99, 134–39; Patriot Act requirements for, 18; vulnerabilities, 134
Patriot Act. *See* USA PATRIOT Act (*2001*)
People, identifying and monitoring, 50, 63–64, 97–100, 134–39
Personal radiation detectors (PRD), 158–59
Pope, William, 51
Ports of entry. *See* border security
Privacy issues: European Union, 29, 61–62, 64; information sharing, 29, 61–62, 64; millimeter wave technology, 142; passports with biometric identifiers, 64, 135–36, 138; RFID cargo container tags, 147; syndromic surveillance, 165–66
Private industry: biosecurity research and development, 168; financial assistance expectations, 75–76; missile defense systems, 174–75; reforms necessary, 190–91; technology development with government funding, 131, 133; transportation security concerns, 76–77, 84–86, 106, 161 . *See also* Infrastructure protection in private industry
Program for Response Options and Technology Enhancements for Chemical/Biological Terrorism (PROTECT), 162
Project Bioshield, 166, 168
Public transportation, 143–44, 161–62

Quijas, Louis F., 122

Radioisotope identification devices
    (RID), 158
Radiological dispersion device (RDD),
    157
Radiological threats, countermeasures,
    156–61
RAND Corporation report on missile
    defense, 170, 174, 175
Rapid automated biological identifica-
    tion system (RABIS), 165
Red cell exercises, 5
Reduced originator control. *See*
    ORCON (reduced originator con-
    trol)
Reid, Richard, 4, 50
Reserves, 115, 116–19
Ridge, Tom, 5, 47, 137
Robb-Silberman Commission, 21–22,
    24, 32, 38–40
Russia, air safety, 104

Safety Act, 133, 168
Schengen border information system,
    28, 65
Science and Technology Directorate,
    131, 132
SCO. *See* Office of Screening
    Coordination and Operations (SCO)
SCUD missiles, 115–16
Seafarers' Identity Documents
    Convention, 139
Seaports. *See* Border security
Secretary of Defense, 18, 19
Secure Flight database, 99
Senate Select Committee on
    Intelligence, 18, 40
SHARE network, 65
Shipping. *See* Cargo container security;
    transportation security

Shoe-bomber, the, 4
SIGINT agencies, 27
Smallpox stockpiles, 194*f*
Sniffer dogs, 143, 145
South Carolina chlorine gas leak (*2005*),
    86
Stinger missiles, 171
Strategic National Stockpile (SNS), 166,
    169
Strategic Support Branch (DoD),
    22–23
Student exchange visitor information
    (SEVIS) system, 97
Support Anti-Terrorism by Fostering
    Effective Technologies Act, 133, 168
Surface-to-air missiles (SAMs), 12–13,
    155
Syndromic surveillance, 165–66

Taliban, 172
Technology development: air travel
    safety, 140–42; biosecurity, 168–69;
    cargo container security smart
    boxes, 146, 147; chemical sensors,
    162; costs of, 131, 132, 140, 141, 142,
    158–59, 160, 162, 163, 164–65,
    173–75; e-passports, 134–36;
    explosives defenses, 141–42; federal
    role, 130–34; fingerprint scanners,
    137; funding for, 130–33, 139, 159,
    160, 162, 168, 173, 174; human test-
    ing for, 133–34, 191; introduction,
    129–30; liability protection provi-
    sions, 133–34, 168; for missile
    defense, 173–75; people, secure
    identification of, 134–39; private
    sector and, 131, 133, 174–75;
    radioactive material detection,
    158–59; reforms necessary, 132–34,
    137, 191; surveillance systems,
    139–40; threat anticipation efforts,

133; WME countermeasures, 156, 158–60, 162–65, 168–69, 173–75

Tenet, George, 5

Terrorism, defenses against: connect-the-dots problem, 2, 28, 55, 66; European Union, 28, 52–53, 55–57, 67–68; funding, 186; global, 4–5; post-*9/11*, 1–7, 13–14; vulnerabilities, 4, 6, 8–13, 184–86 . *See also* Infrastructure protection

Terrorism insurance, 78–87

Terrorism Risk Insurance Act (TRIA), 80, 190

Terrorism Risk Insurance Revision Act (TRIRA), 80, 190

Terrorism risk models, 79

Terrorist attacks: attempts post-*9/11*, 4; London bombings (*2005*), 68, 84; Madrid bombing (*2004*), 28, 54, 55, 57, 68, 84; Tokyo subway attack (*1995*), 161

Terrorist identities database (TID), 98

Terrorist Screening Center, 103

Terrorist screening database (TSDB), 98

Terrorist Threat Integration Center (TTIC), 18, 30

Terrorist watch lists, 5, 97–99, 136–37

Thompson, Tommy, 87

TIPOFF list, 98

Tokyo subway attack (1995), 161

Total/Terrorism Information Awareness program (TIA), 35

Townsend, Frances, 26

Trains. *See* Public transportation; transportation security

Transportation security: costs of, 140, 141, 142, 145, 146, 159; explosives and, 139–44, 145–46; firearms, defense against, 140–41; people, secure identification for, 134–39;

private industry, 76–77, 84–86, 106, 161; reforms necessary, 140, 142–45, 148; time considerations, 139–40, 145, 158, 159; worker identification credentials, 139. *See also* Border security; Cargo container security; *specific types of transportation*

Transportation Security Act (*2001*), 28

Transportation Security Administration (TSA), 2, 141

Transportation worker identification credential (TWIC) initiative, 139

Truck bombs, 82–83

Trust for America's Health, 165

United Kingdom, 52, 55–56

USA PATRIOT Act (*2001*), 18, 63

U.S.-Europol agreement (*2002*), 68

USS *Cole* bombing, 108

U.S.-VISIT program, 98, 136–37

Vaccines, 7, 13, 133–34, 164, 166–69, 191, 194*f*

Vehicle and cargo inspection system (VACIS), 106, 107

Visas Mantis program, 99

Visa waver program (VWP), 50, 63–64, 98, 134–35

Weapons of mass destruction (WMD), 118, 155

Weapons of mass effect (WME): economic damages from, 157, 170; medical countermeasures for, 7, 13, 133–34, 164, 166–69, 191, 194*f*; psychological damages from, 157, 170; response improvements recommended, 162–69; technology for defense against, 156, 158–60, 162–65, 168–69, 173–75

133; WME countermeasures, 156, 158–60, 162–65, 168–69, 173–75

Tenet, George, 5

Terrorism, defenses against: connect-the-dots problem, 2, 28, 55, 66; European Union, 28, 52–53, 55–57, 67–68; funding, 186; global, 4–5; post-*9/11*, 1–7, 13–14; vulnerabilities, 4, 6, 8–13, 184–86 . *See also* Infrastructure protection

Terrorism insurance, 78–87

Terrorism Risk Insurance Act (TRIA), 80, 190

Terrorism Risk Insurance Revision Act (TRIRA), 80, 190

Terrorism risk models, 79

Terrorist attacks: attempts post-*9/11*, 4; London bombings (*2005*), 68, 84; Madrid bombing (*2004*), 28, 54, 55, 57, 68, 84; Tokyo subway attack (*1995*), 161

Terrorist identities database (TID), 98

Terrorist Screening Center, 103

Terrorist screening database (TSDB), 98

Terrorist Threat Integration Center (TTIC), 18, 30

Terrorist watch lists, 5, 97–99, 136–37

Thompson, Tommy, 87

TIPOFF list, 98

Tokyo subway attack (1995), 161

Total/Terrorism Information Awareness program (TIA), 35

Townsend, Frances, 26

Trains. *See* Public transportation; transportation security

Transportation security: costs of, 140, 141, 142, 145, 146, 159; explosives and, 139–44, 145–46; firearms, defense against, 140–41; people, secure identification for, 134–39;

private industry, 76–77, 84–86, 106, 161; reforms necessary, 140, 142–45, 148; time considerations, 139–40, 145, 158, 159; worker identification credentials, 139. *See also* Border security; Cargo container security; *specific types of transportation*

Transportation Security Act (*2001*), 28

Transportation Security Administration (TSA), 2, 141

Transportation worker identification credential (TWIC) initiative, 139

Truck bombs, 82–83

Trust for America's Health, 165

United Kingdom, 52, 55–56

USA PATRIOT Act (*2001*), 18, 63

U.S.-Europol agreement (*2002*), 68

USS *Cole* bombing, 108

U.S.-VISIT program, 98, 136–37

Vaccines, 7, 13, 133–34, 164, 166–69, 191, 194*f*

Vehicle and cargo inspection system (VACIS), 106, 107

Visas Mantis program, 99

Visa waver program (VWP), 50, 63–64, 98, 134–35

Weapons of mass destruction (WMD), 118, 155

Weapons of mass effect (WME): economic damages from, 157, 170; medical countermeasures for, 7, 13, 133–34, 164, 166–69, 191, 194*f*; psychological damages from, 157, 170; response improvements recommended, 162–69; technology for defense against, 156, 158–60, 162–65, 168–69, 173–75

Weapons of mass effect (WME), types of: biological, 6–7, 82, 118, 146, 162, 163–69, 194f; chemical, 74, 81, 83, 88, 118, 139, 146, 158, 162–63, 165; MANPADS, 155, 170–76; nuclear, 3, 74, 156–61; radiological, 156–61
WMD civil support teams, 118

Worker identification credentials, 138–39
World Customs Organization (WCO), 51, 148
World Shipping Council, 148

Zarate, Juan Carlos, 26